Not Pretty,
But Precious

John Hay

Contents

NOT PRETTY,
BUT PRECIOUS

BY

John Hay

Not Pretty, But Precious.

Mille modi veneris!

Part I.

Mr. Norval: It is now four weeks since your accident. I have made inquiry of your physician whether news or business communications, however important, brought to your attention, would be detrimental to you, cause an accession of feverish symptoms or otherwise harm you. He assures me, On the contrary, he is sure you have not been for years so free from disease of any sort, with the sole exception of the broken bones, as now. This being so, I venture to approach you upon a subject which I doubt not you are quite as willing to have definitely arranged, and at once, as myself. I can say what I mean, and as I mean it, so much better on paper than in conversation--as I have so little self-possession, and am so readily put out in the matter of argument--that I have determined to write to you, thinking thus to be better able to make you understand and appreciate my reasons and motives, since you can read them when and how you choose.

I have been your wife three weeks. The horrible strangeness of these words is quite beyond me to compass; nevertheless, realize it or not, it is a fact. I am your wife--you, my husband. Why I am your wife I wish simply to rehearse here. Not that we do not both know why, but that we may know it in the same way. You, a handsome, cultivated man, whose dictum is considered law in the world of fashion in which you move and reign, with an assured social position, a handsome fortune, and a popularity that would have obtained for you the hand of any beautiful or wealthy woman whom you sought, have deliberately chosen to make me, a poor, plain, brown-faced little school-teacher, your wife. Not because you wanted *me*, not because you thought or cared about *me*, one way or the other, but simply because, in a time of urgent necessity, I was literally the only available woman near you. It chanced, from many points of view and by a chain of circumstances, that I was particularly available. So you married me. The reasons for such a sacrifice of yourself were--you had behaved badly, very badly, to a lady, compromising her name and causing a separation between herself and her husband. Within a few months, her husband having died, both herself and her father had determined to force you to make her reparation by marriage. Going to work very warily, they had taken an opportunity, after a very luxuriant and fast opera-supper, when you were excited by your surroundings and flushed by the wine you had been drinking, your head very light, your judgment very heavy, to draw from you a promise of marriage at the expiration of the year of mourning for her husband. As soon as you became aware of what you had done, you ignominiously fled, and after a Western tour were about to sail for Europe when this unfortunate accident overtook you. Your narrow escape from death, upon having been thrown from the carriage of a distinguished gentleman while driving with him behind a pair of celebrated racers, gave such publicity to your adventure that your *amorata* was at once aware of your whereabouts. The fear of this had taken possession of you as soon as you were able to think of anything, and the dread that she would follow and marry you while you lay helpless was made a certainty by this telegram from an intimate friend in New York, received the sixth day of your illness:

"It's all up with you, old fellow. The R. has heard you're fast with a broken leg, and she starts on Monday for Boston. Have the clergy ready, for it's marriage."

Then in your bitter need you remembered having talked with me in this hotel-parlor the very day of your accident. I had been a school-friend of your dead sister, and for her sake, on the rare occasions of your seeing me, you have always been polite and kindly patronized me. Now, lying helpless and unable to extricate yourself from your dilemma, you recalled the evident pleasure upon my foolish, tell-tale face at seeing you, the delight I had betrayed in the attention you had shown me, such as finding a seat at dinner for myself and my old lady friend, although some elegant and fashionable girls were waiting with ill-suppressed eagerness for your escort. Remembering all this, knowing as you did that I was poor, wearing out my life in teaching, in your sore need you suddenly thought, "I wonder if the girl wouldn't marry me? She'd make a good nurse, could look after my traps, and, though she is as ugly as sin and a nobody, wouldn't be the deuced disgrace to a fellow this Rollins woman will be. At all events, she'll save me from that fate if she takes up with my offer. It's a choice of evils, and this would be the least; and I'll try it." This, in plain, unadorned speech, was what you thought. Then you sent for me, began very pathetically to talk of your desolate state, your family all dead, and so on; that it had been sadly brought home to you how alone you were while lying sick, hour after hour, in this great hotel, with only your valet to attend to you and take an interest in your well-being; and that, day after day, as you lay thinking of your fate, my face had come before you, recalling tender memories of your lost and dearly-loved sister. Then you had remembered that as girl and boy we had been lovers, and really cared very much for each other. As you got this far toward your ***grande denouement***, something in my face, I suppose, made you realize that if you were to compass your ends with me it must be by honesty only. Then you blurted it all out--in, as I could not help thinking as I listened, as school-boyish and abashed a way as if you had--well, as if you had not been a consummate man of the world, rather noted for your ***aplomb***.

It came across me (as I heard you in dumb amazement, with crimson face and trembling frame) that even the best polish of years' laying on will crack somewhere under very hard pressure. Well, you were honest and told me all, never pretending, as you had at first essayed to do, that it was out of any lingering regard for myself as your sister's friend that you sought me now, but simply on account of my availability. Had there been some bright young beauty with wealth and station at hand, no thought of me would ever have entered your mind: all this I understood at once from your half confessions--all this, I was glad to find, you had at least enough honor to let me know, although you risked what to you in your actual situation was very perilous--a refusal.

I asked until the next day to consider the matter--whether it would be better to take service with you, exchange for my boarding, clothing and incidental expenses the daily care of your comfort and pleasure, or earn my bread in the old wearing way. And the second day after that we were married. That is all. I believe that to be a simple statement of the facts in your case: I am right, am I not?

The day after our marriage your lady-love and her paternal ancestor came. At my own suggestion and with your eager consent I received them, and the result you know.

Now for my own reasons for this strange marriage. You are aware that my father was a professor of mathematics in various schools and colleges of the city where he lived, teaching in the school, among others, in which your sister and myself were pupils. I believe you know that when a young man he had eloped with and married one of his scholars, the daughter of a rich and proud family, who discarded her. For years she was a stranger to them, until her husband had won a name and handsome fortune for himself: then she was taken into favor again, her husband's distinction in the scientific world being supposed to add lustre to the family name. Alas for us! it was a favor that has cost us dear. I was their only child. When my sweet, pretty mother lay dying she left to me, her sixteen-year-old child, my dreamy, unworldly father as a legacy. "Take care of him: he knows no guile, and your uncles will wrong him if they can," she said. And they did, or one of them. Ere the bitter agony of my mother's death had enabled him to return to his duties, it was discovered that one of her brothers had forged his name and literally stripped him of everything.

Of course, then he went to work again to earn our daily bread--not with his old love or ability, but in an inert, feeble way that was pitiful to see. I think from the day my mother was buried he was dying. Some people, you know, die hard--some part with life lightly, as if it was a faded robe they shook off to don a brighter one. Others--my father was one, and I am like him--see one by one their trusts, their hopes, their loves die: then with a deathly throe sunder themselves from life. But pardon my digression.

When I was twenty my father died. Since then, spite of expressions of disapproval and offers of support from my mother's family, I have maintained myself by teaching in the schools where my father had been known, preferring to do without assistance so long as I had health. One of my uncles desired to take me into his family, and thus wipe out the wrong done my father by his brother, and my aunts proffered me an income out of their private means. I mention this to do them every justice, but I think even a man of fashion like yourself will acknowledge the impossibility of my accepting, while I could avoid it, a life of dependence. I could not accept favors from those who had treated my dear parents unkindly; so I have e'en gone my own way for these last ten years, and led a not unhappy life, if a busy and rather wearing one.

My gay cousins, all of whom you know well--the Wilber girls, Leta and Jennie, pretty little Lou Barton, and another set of Wilbers whom I think you do not know so well, who are married now--my gay cousins, then, most of them beauties, all of them rich and fashionable, are somewhat ashamed of me, and have let me feel it in every petty way that we women know so well how to find. I am ugly and poor, my earning my own living is a spot upon their gentility, and I have unfortunately, and quite against my will, more than once given them cause for serious annoyance and apprehension. Then, one of our uncles, who is a bachelor and very rich, has insisted that I am never to be slighted--always to be invited to everything in the shape of a party given by the family. If it lay with me, of course I would never accept these invitations, but I have had it explained to me over and over again that my not doing so is visited upon the party-givers in one way or another by our masterful uncle Rufus. So, occasionally, very much against my inclination, I leave my little third-story room, with its cozy fire and humble adornments, and sit in the corner of their great rooms, a "looker-on in Vienna" in every sense.

I have many kind friends: it would be strange if in all these years I had not found some who did not care for outward advantages. I have dreamed my sweet love-dream, and it is over, and the roses have grown above my buried hopes.

Since then I have let one idea fill my life to the exclusion of everything else, putting away from me all desires and thoughts of other needs; and that too has left me. I call it an "idea" for lack of a better name. I had put away all thought of marriage with my bright youth, but took into my heart instead what I deemed would serve as well--a friendship for another woman. For ten years we knew no separate life--I thought no separate hopes. She had loved, been on the eve of marriage, her lover had died: that was her heart's history, and henceforth the idea of love had fallen out of both our lives--not the idea only, but the possibility of love. I thought so--she *said* so.

I trusted her and loved her with a perfect love. I wound my hopes about her: I gave up all my life to her as if she had been my lover. I never cared to form other friendships. I deprived myself of all possibilities of making other ties of any sort, and with the first opportunity she whistled me down the wind, and cared no more for me than if she had never professed to love me. She had been my one bright thing--she was sweet and winsome--the one golden gleam in my sombre life. My future was bound up in her so completely that when she severed the fine, close cords (brittle, yet so strong) which had bound us together for years, she cut into my heart--nay more, wrested from me all my sweet trusts and faiths. If she is false, who else in all God's earth is true? I pity myself very much. You, of course, will not see why her marrying should make a difference if we loved, and will call me selfish. Not so, not so! She might have married as soon as it pleased her, and I should have been glad. It would have made a difference, of course: she must in some sort have been parted from me, but that I could have borne if it made her happy. But from her acceptance of her lover--about whom we will say nothing, save that he was the sort of man she had always held in abhorrence--she has coolly ignored my right to any part or lot in her fate. She had told me (or I, poor fool! thought so) every hope and fear of her life: now she told me what she chose, and was astonished that I expected more--hurt that I seemed changed and did not find my friendship flourish on crumbs after being nourished for years from full loaves--was quite unhappy that I cared so little for the minor concerns of her life, when, good lack! I did not know what I might or might not ask and not be snubbed; for once she told me there were things due to the man one is going to marry (at that time she had not got to the extent of saying whom one loves) that could not be spoken of to me. Of course she had only to mention the fact to me to make it perfectly plain, and henceforth he and his doings, his belongings and himself, all of them of the tamest sort at best, were a sealed book to me. And again she quenched a feeble effort of mine to get back to my old place, by telling me such topics she could discuss only with her sister, "her shadow sister" she prettily called her. So I am desolate!

Knowing this, you may understand in some degree what could induce a little waif like me to accept such an offer as yours. I think no one in all God's earth is more desolate than I. In my heart I bear always that unforgotten love in my life. I have only a barren waste to show. It is as if I had started from a lovely, radiant garden in the fair morning of my life, in which I had left the bright, sweet rose of my love, and walking along a narrow, dark path, had clasped hands with, and drawn my light and warmth from, a figure walking close beside me; and though from all

sides as I walked forms had come to me, offering me fair fruits and sweet flowers,
I declined them all without ever a word of thanks, being so content with my one
companion. And suddenly, when all my youth, all my prospects of other things,
had gone, this idealized one had withdrawn its hand-clasp, and turning on me a
face I did not know, faded into darkness, leaving me nothing but my broken hopes,
a wreath of withered flowers,

"Tangled down in chains about my feet."

You do not of course realize how the old French *emigre* blood in my veins, inherited from my father, makes this a very vital matter to me. We cling to our hopes
very tenaciously while they abide--then we are distraught. We loved, my father
and I, very few, but those with a clinging oneness that is wellnigh pain: he loved
my mother and myself--that was all. Likewise I had my two: they having failed
me, my life is a blank. I have heard of empty-hearted people: I know now what the
phrase means. I am empty-hearted: I have not one hope, one particle of faith, one
real, honest desire, except to "drie my weir," as the Scotch say, doing my duty as
best I may, as it comes to me. But I have a woman's hatred of pity: my cousins have
long accorded me a contemptuous pity for being an old maid. I laughed their pity to
scorn while I had Esther Hooper. What more did I need? We could enact over again
the sweet old life of the Ladies of Llangollen.

We had planned our lives a thousand times. Poor we both were, yet we would
put something away every year for our old age, and work cheerily on until we could
work no more, then creep to our nest like a couple of old kittens, and cuddle down
by our warm, pleasant fire--together, and therefore content. Well, you see it was
not to be: she had grown affrighted, I suppose, at the thought of all that weary life
with only me, and has married a man who outrages all her delicate instincts and
traditions of an accordant husband. But why speak of him? He supports her, and she
has escaped the obloquy of old-maidism. She has married a maintenance. She says
she loves him, so of course she does.

For myself, my health, which has always been very rugged, has failed me utterly this last year; but as my bread depends upon my ability to endure daily and
constant fatigue, I have forced myself to endeavor to get up the amount of strength
required for my winter's work by the present expedition, planned for me by a
friend. Bah! what do I talk of friendship for? An old lady who was once a teacher

in the school from which my father had married my mother, and who, I think, had cared with more than friendship for him, has in these last few years fallen heir to a small property--not a very great deal, but enough to enable her to live in comfort, and exercise her kindly heart in deeds of charity occasionally. She has chosen for years to occupy rooms beneath my own, and has always been a sort of mother to me. Most of the pretty things that have fallen into my life, and most of its pleasures, have come to me through her. She has many troublesome faults, as we all have, but she is old, and I have always had Esther to talk them over and laugh them off with, so have borne them easily. This year, because she saw I was dying, she took me with her to the mountains of Vermont, and I have got a new lease of life, and new capacities for suffering as well.

On our way back she was suddenly attacked with the illness which detained us at this Boston hotel. Here your accident laid you up, and the rest came as I have told.

You have married me to rid yourself of a union with a woman you detest, being utterly indifferent to me. I have married you because I cannot bring myself to go back to that old teaching-life, now so cold and gray. I think I can earn my board in taking care of your belongings, and the having saved you from a dreadful fate must compensate to you for the little of my presence you will for the future be compelled to endure. It need not be much or long continued if we start with a fair comprehension of each other.

This brings me to the reason of all this long history. I have always looked upon marriage without love as nothing more or less than legalized vice. I think you, who are so intrinsically a man of the world, will have imbibed the (so-called) sensible and popular views upon such subjects, and will at once coincide with me that in such a union as ours--a literal ***mariage de convenance*** on both sides--my ideas are not unwise. Since upon you will henceforth depend my maintenance (as I of course understand that a wife who worked for her own support would be a disgrace to you: indeed, I doubt whether the having married a girl who has already done so is not a cause of shame), I ask that now, when Mrs. Keller is about to leave me, and my arrangements as your wife must be finally made--when, in fact, her giving up her room necessitates my coming to yours, her leaving compelling me either to go with her, or come, as of course I must, to you--we may have a definite understanding as to our future relations.

You have been kind enough to approve of the little I have been able to do for you since our marriage--to say to Mrs. Keller you did not know what it was to be taken care of in sickness; and to myself you have more than once laughingly spoken of a wife as a good institution, adding, that had you known how comfortable it was to have some one about you to think of and care for you, you would have invested in the article before; and so on. I am glad of this: I am pleased that my society has not proved repugnant to you; for since it has been no annoyance in its first trial, I think we can manage that it shall not be so in the future. I would ask, as an especial piece of mercy to "your handmaiden," that you will grant her some favors at the outset of our somewhat tangled fate. Please let me be your sister. It is for your well-being the world should know me as your wife, and, the Lord helping me, I will be a willing, faithful helpmeet to you, caring most for your comfort and happiness, spending and being spent in your service; never demanding or desiring your attention, except so much as is due me in outward seeming; interfering with none of your pleasures or pursuits, or thrusting my needs or feelings never before you. I have no expectation of winning your love: it has been an understood thing from the first--that is something neither expects from the other--therefore any show of caressing fondness upon your part would be quite out of keeping with our position. I have watched with some amusement, and a little pain that you should imagine it requisite, your attempts at petting me during these last two weeks. Poor, helpless man! it was a little hard to have to pretend an interest and tenderness you did not feel. Will you let this cease, with every other demonstration of affection, in our private relations?

For the rest, claiming nothing from you, giving you nothing but the services for which you render me a full equivalent, I grant you, as far as I have a right to do so, the largest liberty of action. We are only jealous of those we love: therefore all women will be as free to you as they have hitherto been or their will accords, save that you have debarred yourself for a time from offering any one of them marriage. I hope to be so little trouble to you, and so serviceable to you in many ways, that you shall realize to the full that if an unloving union could be so much more comfortable than a bachelor's life, a life passed with a loving and beloved wife would be bliss indeed, and so when my life has ended you will not be sorry that I stopped in your path a few years. For I shall not trouble you very long. I am a poor little perfumeless flower, having no sweetness or beauty with which to charm the eye or senses, only fit to grow among the kitchen herbs--rue and thyme, and such old-fashioned things. But I need a great deal of sunshine, spite of my plainness, to keep life in me. And now that all the heat and passion of love, all the sunny hopes and glow of friendship, have left me, I shall just fade and fade until some day you will find the poor little weed has dropped to earth for ever.

I am but two years younger than yourself, and women, especially women with a great sorrow, age cruelly fast. I look and feel older than I am--you wear your years like a crown, and appear younger than you are. I have made my little venture on life's ocean--made and failed: my barque, freighted with a few cherished hopes, has been wrecked, and though I have reached a rock to which I can cling for a time, yet I am terribly hurt, the waves have buffeted me cruelly, and in a little while I shall let go my hold and float out--out into the ocean of eternity. Ah! there is comfort after all: life *is* hard, but afterward there is peace and rest!

I am nearly through this long tirade. Pardon its length: it is my first, and shall be my last, heart-outpouring to you; and if it make you comprehend me, I shall not have written or you have read in vain.

Your income will not support the establishment your position in society would require if we went to housekeeping; besides, you would feel as if you must then be more stationary, more in your own home, than is at present your custom, therefore in a degree in bondage. And a hotel-life is very expensive and very cheerless. You have kindly said you intended dividing your income with me, giving me half. At first I was indignant at the idea, but now I think I see that it will be in every way the best. One of my cousins has been occupying a very elegantly-appointed suite of rooms on Twenty-fourth street. Harry writes me he is going very suddenly to Europe. His rooms will of course be vacant: he talks of renting them furnished. I have thought, if you would not object to it, we might take them off his hands. I have calculated that the part of your means you intend for me will meet all our expenses of every sort if you permit me to have the arranging, of our daily affairs. I will pay the rent and meet all the expenses of our living out of this sum, leaving you your reserved funds to meet your ordinary requirements and pleasures. By this arrangement, you see, I shall get my living free, and I am sure shall have a surplus over and above our expenses, as I am a good manager and used to making the most of everything.

There is one sacrifice which, do we enter into this arrangement, I must ask of you--that when we return to New York you give up your valet. For more than one reason: I cannot have a spy upon the mode of life we are to lead. I am foolishly sensitive of the position of a neglected wife, and I feel assured your gentlemanly instincts will prevent your ever offering any observable slight to the woman who bears your name. Besides, in the apartments I propose our taking there will be no room for a man-servant, and one of the maids connected with the house will be all the assistant I shall require. When you are away on your frequent excursions to all parts of the world it will be very easy to provide yourself a servant. Will you try for a few weeks how well I can supply, or have the place supplied, of this man, whom you intend in any case to dismiss? This is all. Next week, the doctor thinks, you may be moved to a lounge, and perhaps the week after be able to travel, or at farthest the week following.

I acknowledge to the womanish feeling of being exultant at the idea of the envy I shall awaken in the breasts of your adoring circle of lady friends--my lady cousins among them--in having, spite of my unattractiveness, secured the husband they have long striven by every wile to win. Ah! they little know, and I trust never may, why I, without seeking, have ensnared their *rara avis* to be my legal bondsman. Rather a contradiction in terms!

The pretty fiction of our sudden marriage being a renewal of an old love-affair is more of an untruth than I am used to letting pass, and yet has enough truth in it to make it reality, since you were the hero of my girlish dreams. So we will let the explanation thus worded, which you have written to my uncles and stated verbally to Mrs. Keller, stand; also, that the undue haste was caused by your pressing need of me during your accident. I think, indeed, from my cousin Harry's letter yesterday, and one from Shelton last week, they have taken the idea that we have been spending the summer together, and that you were following me home when you were stayed in your mad career by a broken leg.

I am done; are you not thankful? There have been some things in this letter very hard to say, which, if I were braver or knew you better, I should have liked to be more outspoken about. But enough has, I think, been said to make you appreci-

ate my earnest desires and my reasons for them. I am most truly,
 PERCY.

And he, prone upon his back this warm September day, read this long epistle from his new wife, then laid it down and closing his eyes murmured softly, "What a strange little puss it is!" Lying in the dim light her hand had created for him, he thought of his own troubles and hers, just as she had stated them. The blood would flush up to his brow as her cool ignoring of his surpassing attractions, to which all other women accorded their full meed of praise, rose up before him. He of whom it had been said if he beckoned with his finger women left their duties, gave up their very life to do his pleasure!--he to have the girl he had honored by making his wife, a little brown woman, plain and almost *passe* (he was man enough not to care for her poverty), show she cared no more for his love than he did for hers I--was as indifferent to him as he to her! Indifference from a woman was a new experience to him, and annoyed him.

Yet her quaint, frank letter touched him. What did she mean by dying soon and letting him be free again? Poor little midge! was she dying of a broken heart because a treacherous woman had fooled her out of a part of her life? Poor little robin! she was his wife now, and he could heal the worst heartache in any woman's breast. He had tried that thing before, and succeeded, even if he broke the heart afterward. Die, indeed! Not if he knew it: even Death should not have a little woman he meant to be good to.

And as he remembered all her faithfulness to him during these weary weeks of pain, he thought, "By Jove! beauty's not all, for no woman, had her face been like that of Phryne of Thebes, or her charms as entrancing as the bewitching Dudu's, could have been more lovely in her kindness to me. How brave and strong she has been! What a faithful little soul it is! Always ready, day and night, to do just what I want done and in the way I want it, never knocking things about or fidgeting round, but just ready-handed, neat and bright. God knows, a handsome woman wouldn't have risked the spoiling her beauty by all these weary, sleepless nights, especially for a man she did not love." And then to think she was actually willing to work and slave for him, and support him out of her share of the booty, and let him fool away his own on other women! "Wonder what the little dame means to buy her own fine things with, for even robins must get clothing? I'll ask her that. Bless the little woman's soul! she makes me think of her so much that I believe I'm half in love with her. Um!" and he stopped: "I'm getting sentimental and poetic, I swear! But if it were in me to love anything that was not beautiful, I believe I could love this little girl, who has come into my life so strangely. She owns up to having loved, and is done with all the stale farce. Some fools," and he felt very indignant, "slighted her because she had no beauty, though, upon my soul, now I think of it, I'm not so certain about that. There's a something in her face takes a man's breath--something that one would rather die than lose if he once loved it, and which once loved would be better than any beauty. What's that Spenser says?--

'A sweet, attractive kind of grace,...   The lineaments of gospel books,'

That's just it: it's a look that makes one think about one's prayers, if one only knew them. But whether the man slighted her or not, he missed it--confound him!--in losing such a love. I'll make her tell me his name. And as for being my sister, that's all nonsense, of course, as she's my wife." Then more thoughtfully, "Well, maybe not: a household where there is no love is cruel--I knew that in my early home--and children are a beastly trouble, and as expensive as a man's wines. She's a brick, this wife of mine, and as sensible as steel. I'll put myself in her hands for better or for worse, I vow I will!

"The jolly way she manged that Rollins affair was proof poz of her ability. Her cool assumption of wifely dignity--her actually bringing them up to see me without announcing their coming to me, and never letting them have one bout at me, was beyond anything! It's like a dip in the sea to recall it all. Her breezy voice coming in before them was all the warning I had: 'Oh certainly, you can come up and look at him, but not talk to him: he's nervous and feverish, and I cannot permit even such old friends as you doubtless are to say anything to him. You know, of course, the doctor thought he needed constant attention, and caused us to hurry our marriage in a most Gretna-Green style; but I could not nurse him unless we were married. And it did not matter so much, after all, since we had loved'--and she hesitated with the prettiest affectation of having said something she ought not--'we had cared for each other since we were quite children. Ross's sister Bell was my school-friend.' Then she brought them straight to the bed, and stooping down gave me the only kiss with which she has honored me--her show kiss, I call it--saying, 'My darling' (how soft she said it, too, with a little trilling cadence upon the sweet old word!)--'My darling, you are not to speak, or even look, save this once: now I must cover up my dearie's eyes;' and she laid her cool hand over my eyes and held it there while they stayed. 'These are some kind New York friends, Mr. Rollins and his good wife'--and a faint pressure on my face emphasized the joke--'who are come to see you. I cannot understand all they mean, except that you have been behaving badly, making these good people's daughter believe you meant to marry her, when of course you were only going to marry your little, ugly Percy. Oh, my bad boy, what shall I ever do with you? Oh the hearts you have broken while you have been waiting for me! Ah! dear, bad boy!'--and, as if overcome with tenderness, she laid her cheek down on mine. I clasped my arms about her--the first and last time I've had a chance, by George!--but she sprang away with a laugh: 'No, you shall not be petted for being bad. Why, Ross, these dear people came to take you and marry you to their beautiful daughter, for I know she's a beauty, since her mother is still so handsome.'

"Oh, it was gorgeous, to see the Rollins standing there in all her Cleopatra-like splendor, utterly upset and put down by my little brown berry! And the impossibility of correcting such a mistake without putting herself in an absurd position actually stopped the Rollins speech, and--Lord help me!--I thought that mouth could only be closed by bon-bons and a man's kisses--any man's, *par exemple*. And her poor old catspaw of a *pater* stood helpless before my little hurricane--a very reed shaken by the wind. Then my sea-breeze spoke again: 'But the doctor will shed vials of wrath upon me for letting you see strangers.' (It must have cut the Rollins sore to be called a stranger to me!) 'But these kind friends could not realize your being ill, so I was fain to let them see my Apollo in his box; but we will go now if you please;' and she positively ushered them out in wordless dismay, bidding them good-bye at once, and seeing them no more. I thought she would have rushed back to laugh the scene over with me, but that shows how little I know her. When, in the course of an hour, she did come, it was with such an utter ignoring of having done a smart thing, waving aside my admiration of her *finesse*, that I was taken aback. She said sadly, 'I am unused to falsehood, and *finesse* of any sort is distasteful to me. I quenched this woman this time, but, in spite of her bad, hard face, I pity her very much. You, and such men as you, have, I suppose, made her what she is, God help her!' So by this good little girl's management I am rid of my troubles. I declare I'll do just what she wishes, and be thankful my follies have worked me no more harm."

Then he began to wish she'd come in, and to feel aggrieved and neglected because she did not come--to feel an eager desire to see her and talk the matter of the letter over with her. But he had read it through again twice ere she appeared, and then, to his dismay, equipped for a journey, and saying, in the most matter-of-fact, nonchalant manner possible, "Ross, Mrs. Keller has come to say good-bye. I am going with her to Newport, where she makes the only perilous part of the trip--the, to her, dreadful change from cars to boat. So I shall be away all night, of course."

Then Mrs. Keller came forward with--"I hope you don't mind my taking her off, Mr. Norval?"

"But I do mind it deucedly, madam," he said. "Why, Percy, I don't like your traveling alone this way at all. Why can't James go with Mrs. Keller?"

"Not for the world, Ross, thank you. I'm used to taking care of myself, and of Mrs. Keller too, for that matter. I'm not much of a traveler, because I have not had much of a chance--none, indeed, except what she's given me--but somehow I always manage to come out right. You are very kind to offer to spare James, but he's your necessity. I have told him about the medicines, and how to loosen the bandages at night. So I expect to find you better than usual when I get back. He knows your ways so much better than I, and I sha'n't be here to interfere;" and she went about arranging little matters as she spoke, and not looking at him.

But Mrs. Keller saw the look of annoyance upon his face, and said, "But, Percy, Mr. Norval dislikes your going, and you're bound to stay."

"Oh, nonsense, Mrs. Keller! Of course he don't care particularly, as I am going to be away but one night, and he's got to spend all my life with me;" and her face saddened, he thought. "I'm sure to come back to-morrow: my cousin Shelton says, 'Percy always manages to be at hand when she's wanted.' Am I to write to Harry that we will take the rooms? I must do it at once, or he may let some one have them;" and she came and stood beside him.

He answered, sullenly, "Do just as you like about it: it's no concern of mine."

"Of course I shall do nothing of the kind. If you had liked the idea, been very much pleased with it, it would have been different. I only threw out the suggestion as a mere suggestion. But we will think of it no more." All this in her quick, bright way, without a shade of annoyance visible, and she began talking of something else as if the matter was settled: "The hotel-keeper will put a sofa-bed into your dressing-room for me to-morrow, so I shall be quite out of the way when your callers are here. I have told them about bringing my trunk in there from Mrs. Keller's room: James will attend to it all for me. So, as long as you are a 'prisoner of hope' in here, I'll reign supreme in the dressing-room. Now say 'Good-bye,' Mrs. Keller: James will put you in the coach while I finish my adieux."

"But, Percy, you mistake," he said, quite humbly, when her old friend was gone: "you do talk a fellow down so confoundedly," with a laugh. "I like your idea about the rooms most heartily: indeed, I like all your ideas, all your letter, except where you are so deucedly severe upon me; but even that is true, and I like it when you tell me of it. I think your management the best in everything, and I expect to be as happy as a king, or rather a good subject, with my little queen to rule over me and keep me in order in our new domain."

She clasped her hands in a quick, passionate sort of way at his words, as if they gave her a pang. He saw that, but her calm face and voice made him half doubt if it meant anything. "Are you quite sure, or are you only saying it because you think I have a wish to go there? I thought you did not seem to like it just now, and indeed I do not care: I shall be quite content with whatever you arrange when you are well."

"No, Percy: write and say we will take the rooms from the time he leaves them. I"--with a half-abashed laugh--"I was only cross because you are going away. I shall miss you sorely, dear, and I'm sorry you're going and are so glad to go--that's all."

Her face turned crimson to the very temples, and she said, "I'm sorry I made my arrangements without consulting you: I will not do so in future. I did not think you would care one way or the other."

"You've been so good to me, little one, and I'm so unused to being cared for except as a society ornament, that I think I shall never be able to get along without you again."

Her eyes filled with tears which she would not let fall, and she said, "You are very kind to say so: I will be more careful in future. But I must go now." He waited in quite an eager expectancy to see if she would kiss him. "Take good care of yourself, and be sure I shall come by the first train;" and she started to leave the bedside.

He caught her dress and drew her toward him, holding her hands: "Is that all, Percy? Is there nothing else?"

"I think not, Ross," she said, doubtingly, but coloring painfully.

"Kiss me good-bye, Percy." She held down her face instantly, and when he had kissed her, drew herself away without a word; but he clasped his arm about her: "You have not kissed me after all, my darling."

"My kisses are nothing worth now, Ross: their sweetness died out years ago. Yours are good enough for both;" and she laughed and left him.

He was bitterly chagrined: it seemed a little thing to make him feel so mortified. That she should leave him willingly, that doing so she should refuse to grant him so small a favor, when almost all other women--her own pretty cousins among them--had denied nothing he chose to ask, it was incomprehensible!

"By Jove! I never cared so much for a little thing in my life as her leaving me and not caring to kiss me. I swear, I'm a perfect baby about her! Little, truthful, honest soul! I believe she could make another creature of me if she cared enough for me to try. There is something restful in truth and honest purity, after all: one feels safe, and grounded on a sure place. It's good to have a little fairy lying close in one's bosom; and I vow I'll have my little brownie there yet, though I have to go as suitor on a regular courting expedition to my own wife before I win her heart. Curse this old lover of hers, who bars her heart against me! And curse my own past follies, which make a good woman fear to trust me! Marriage is a sell generally, even when a vast amount of so-called love is brought to the sacrificial altar; so perhaps I shall not make a bad thing of it if I win my wife's heart after she knows me *au fond*, instead of in the glamour of gas-light flirtations. Poor little heart! What a pitiful story it is! How quaintly she writes her pathetic, desolate history! What a ready pen the little woman holds!" and he took out her letter again. "I declare, the child has better attractions than beauty--a lovely, faithful soul."

But though he was tender of her in his thoughts, he was a hard master that night: everything went wrong, nothing pleased or contented him, and the sullen, much-tried servant at last announced that with the morning he would leave his master to his own devices.

"Go, and be damned to you!" was the savage reply; and the man took him at his word, decamping, after making a few necessary arrangements, as soon after breakfast as he could.

"And I have been as good to that fellow the year he has lived with me as I could," thought Ross Norval as hour after hour he lay alone wanting everything--water, the papers, a handkerchief. There was nothing he did not want, and he could reach nothing but those nauseous medicines. "Service cannot be bought: in very truth, love and patience must be a free gift. However, now even love and patience seem to have fled from me. I want my wife--I want her awfully."

Percy, with her sad little heart lying as heavy as a plummet in her breast, was just as bright and useful and entertaining to her cranky old friend as if life was a boon instead of a bane to her. You know from her letter how bitter life was to her; and I think if you have ever known sorrow and a great disappointment, you will comprehend how it was possible for her, with the fear of God before her, and a desire to be His faithful child, to make this match for herself. Anything was better than the dull stagnation into which she had fallen: she had felt this year, unless some great change came to her to take her out of this weary groove in which she was set, she must go melancholy mad. She had laid out a hundred schemes, all of them, she knew, impracticable; and now, in a strange, providential way, this chance to change every thought and action of her whole life had come to her. Do you wonder much she accepted it? I think it was not strange.

That night after his offer (the night she had asked for in which to decide, although she said to herself, with a bitter little shrug as she made the request, "A woman who hesitates is lost"), as she lay awake pondering the whole matter, she thought: "It can't be worse than it is, and it won't be very long either way, I think. I can be faithful to him, make and mend, dig and delve, if needs be, for his benefit, in return for the honor he does me in giving me his name and protection. I shall expect nothing, literally nothing, from him that wives usually demand. I, who have borne for years with the caprice of school-girls, can surely bear the humors of one man, especially when his name shields me from other sorts of ills. I have rather plumed myself these last few months upon having learned the depth of meaning and force of truth there is in that expression from **Sartor Resartus** I used to think so wicked: 'Say to happiness, I can do without you--in self-renunciation life begins,' I can try it now. I need not be a spaniel or fawn upon my lord, and yet I can obey and honor, if he will let me, this man to whom I shall vow myself for life. For life! Can I endure it all the years I may have to live an unloved wife--so near and yet so far from him to whom I am bound? Will it not be a death in life? Will it be better than this dead, cold monotony I now bear? Better or worse? Ah, there's the rub! I can never hope to win his faithful, abiding love. Even did use make me acceptable to him, I could not trust its continuance. And yet who knows whether, if I try to keep a pure life and an honest purpose to walk before him worthily every day, I may not win from him at last a sort of respect and friendship that will be next to love? I will some time let him know of the friends my literary efforts have brought me. I know he will be proud of the judgment that scholarly men, whose opinions he honors, have placed upon the heirloom of intellectual ability that has been my sole dower from my dear father and his learned ancestors. And when I am Ross Norval's wife I will reveal myself to these letter-friends of my inner life, and, meeting them no longer in the spirit only, let them see eye to eye their hidden sister, their 'nebulous child,' as they have half playfully, half angrily, called me. A husband's hand shall rive the rock in which their crystal has been for years embedded.

"Oh, Ross, I shall be glad to come to my inheritance through you; to gather my band of chosen ones into my actual, as I have long held them in my inner, life; to know those at last whom my unprotected woman's state has hitherto forbidden me to know. And if I take him, if I give myself to him, I shall at last have the desire of my life. Ah, Ross! you will never know that your boyish flattering, which meant nothing to you, and should have meant nothing to me, did really mean so much that it simply broke my heart, leaving me at sixteen so utterly incapable of loving any man but yourself that since then no hand has ever touched the seal which closed the fountain of love and passion in my heart for ever. Ah! I wonder what penalty there is for those who carelessly destroy our hopes and blot out all possibilities of love from us? What would you say, Ross Norval, if you knew that the last kiss I ever gave to any man was given you that cold, dark day they buried my father? You came with a note from Bell--she was dying, she said; after to-day no one but her family would be admitted to her: would I come and say good-bye to her, even from my father's grave? I went with you, and stayed an hour with her. Then you brought me, more dead than alive, back to my desolate home, and taking me in your arms carried me from the carriage to my bed. As you laid me down you said, 'My sister's little friend, I am glad to have seen you once again. Bell tells me all these years I have been absent you have been pleasant friends to each other. You are dear and sweet because she loved you. I shall never see you again perhaps, for when she dies I shall have no ties here and shall go elsewhere. Kiss me good-bye,' and I did.

"For a year after that I was alone: then Esther Hooper came, and I was not wretched. I have had my share of lovers and friends--what girl has not?--have had rare treats of music, of books and paintings, and shared their pleasant harmonies with an appreciative soul; and I have been very contented.

"But now I am desolate again, and out of the darkness you have come and beckoned me to follow you and stand near you all the rest of my life. It will be happiness enough, as much as is good for me, to live with you, even if I am nothing to you, for, oh, I love you very faithfully!"

And so, you know, they were married, with only the doctor and Mrs. Keller to witness the ceremony; and at once, with her little decided way, the sort of certainty that years of self-dependence give, she became his nurse, attending to him as persistently and indefatigably as if the sole purpose for which she had been born was that. From the first service she rendered him--bathing his head and face through an intense August day with iced water delicately perfumed, arranging the curtains so that the air, when there was a breeze, blew freely to him, though the glare of the sun was gone, and his room in dim, soothing shadow--she seemed a blessing to him. Some hours after she came with her bright, quick ways, arranging his disordered room, bringing order out of chaos on his dressing-table, never peeping into things, and yet getting them into beautiful order, and, wonderful to relate, keeping them so: the air seemed to grow cooler, his medicine less bitter, the time shorter, and his broken leg and weary back to ache less acutely.

One day she said in a shy way, "Mr. Norval, if you will let James lay out your things, I will see what mending they need, and will sit here and do them, so you sha'n't spend so many hours alone. Mrs. Keller has made some friends in the house, and they kindly sit with her so much that she does not need me."

"But, Percy, what's the use of James having a hand in it? Here are my keys," with a laugh as he handed them to her: "you know they are a part of the worldly goods with which I did thee endow; and the keys always belong to the female department by right, don't they?"

She took them with a vivid blush. "Shall I look over your trunks and bureau, then?" she asked.

"Certainly, while I go to sleep and dream what a jolly thing it is to have you here." Then, pretending to sleep, he watched her with careful hands examine his belongings, with a contemptuous little smile at this piece of bungling mending or an anxious frown over that frayed place. Then how neatly she folded and laid back all the good, and seated herself with a pile before her and began to sew! When he opened his eyes she handed him the keys.

"No, Percy, keep them: I make all right and title to them over to you," he said.

From that day he seemed to feel delight in her companionship, reading to her hour after hour while she sewed, always choosing some poetical or light bit of reading--"To suit my capacity," she thought.

So they had gone on week after week--with the single exception of the Rollins episode--without any change. He was a rare favorite in society, and every day received a host of calls from gentlemen, baskets of fruits and flowers from ladies. Always, when a card was sent up, she would gather all her womanish "traps" together and go to Mrs. Keller--this, too, in spite of his earnest invitation to her to remain.

"No: you can have a pleasanter call with no ladies present, and Mrs. Keller needs me. I'll be back in time for your medicine."

Once or twice some one, more intimate or free than usual, would run up unannounced and catch her there. Her acceptation of the situation was, he thought, perfect. Without a shadow of embarrassment she acknowledged the introduction, "My wife," did the honors of the occasion, said a few words regarding his state, and with some such words as "I will be back in an hour or so, Ross," would leave the room.

Thus he was utterly unaware of what her abilities were. Whether she was capable of holding a conversation, or could hold her own in society, he could not opine; and it annoyed him keenly, for he was, like most society-men, very punctilious regarding the manners of the particular woman who belonged to him. That she was, in fact, an elegant conversationalist, quick and brilliant at repartee, a fine linguist and an intelligent thinker for a woman, he did not dream.

Nevertheless, the mere having her about him day after day, with her dainty little ways, grew to be a pleasure to him: the making her grave little face, with its haunting look of sorrow, break into smiles, the light come into her soft gray eyes, became a real delight to him. Then the color flushed over her cheek at his lightest word, and he found a real interest in watching it glow and fade from her pale face.

"She's the sort of **brune** that colors well," he thought. "Old Sir John's fancy of--

'Her cheek was like a Cathrine pear,   The side that's next the sun'--

suits her exactly. And her hair, with the glint of gold in the chestnut hue, would be a glory in a beautiful woman. Every motion of her heart shows in her face. She'd never make a woman of the world: she cannot hide her feelings, but lets one read them like an open book." Which was all he knew about it, since, spite of her treacherous color, those years of hard duty had trained her into the most perfect self-control on all needful and great occasions and matters.

How he missed her light step! how he had wanted her all these two days! for, though it was scarcely past noon, and she had gone late the day before, he was sure it was that--"And seems like six, by George!" But, as he lay feverish and famished for a drink, a very ill-used man, she opened the door, and the air seemed lightened of its troubles at once.

Part II.

"Shall we go to Niagara for our wedding-trip?" Mr. Norval asked when the doctor had taken his last fee, pronouncing his patient cured.

"Unless you care particularly about it, I would rather go straight to New York. I have canceled all my school-engagements by letter, having taken a new service"--and she bowed to him--"and Mrs. Keller promised to see to my little rooms and their belongings; but I should like to see Harry before he sails."

"Want to make him promise to be a good boy while he's away?" said he with a smile.

"Something like it," she answered, laughingly. "But Harry's not a bad fellow, at all."

"Well, then, let's start for home to-morrow;" and they made their arrangements to that effect, though he was disappointed, for in an unwonted moment of confidence she had told him of the pictures of travel to be taken, the glories to be first seen together, never apart, both in Europe and America, that had been among the happiest dreams and made up a large part of the talks between herself and her lost friend, Esther Hooper. He felt that her indifference to seeing the glories of Niagara and the sublimities of the White Mountains was caused by his companionship not being her heart's choice (which was all he knew about it!), and the idea gave him angry pain and a passionate desire to win her in spite of all.

As they stood the next morning ready equipped for their journey, he put his arm around her, saying, "I've been very happy, little wife, here with you. Are you glad you happened to be here that August day, and that I saw you?"

"I have had no cause to regret it," she said quietly.

"But you are not glad," he said, taking his arm away.

"As glad, Ross, as I can be for anything--more glad than I am for most things."

He looked at her with a sigh. "My father--and I am like him--loved only once." Her words came constantly into his mind. "I came too late," he thought; and it seemed to him this little plain woman, looking wan and pale in the early morning light, was better worth winning than any other earthly thing he had ever known. He had left her side, and was standing looking with a frown out of the window as they awaited the summons to breakfast. After a while she came and stood beside him, leaning her head against his arm. He turned slightly toward her, but took no further notice of the action. She stayed so for a while, then said, softly stealing her hand in his as it lay upon the window-ledge, "Dear Ross, I *am* glad: I am happier than I ever dreamed it possible for me to be. I would not undo the deed we have done so long as you are content. I like being with you dearly, and I like to think that so long as I live I shall be your wife--your little girl to whom you are so very tender and good."

"My Preciosa"--and he drew her into his arms--"so long as we both shall live, you mean. I want no life without you now." Then turning her, face up, he scanned it hastily: "You are so white, my pet, so deathly pale! Are you ill, my Percy?"

"No, no," she said quickly. "I think I need my breakfast: I have been up a couple of hours, and I did not sleep very much all night."

"My poor little girl; when I get you safely home in those famous rooms of ours, perhaps you'll get some rest. But you talk in this strange way of dying: just now you did, and once before in your letter. What makes you do it? Is there anything the matter of which you have not told me?"

"Nothing--only my life seemed ended, Ross, as if all my places were filled and I was no more needed, so that I had got in the way of hoping for death as a boon which God would send me soon."

"But you do not now?--you don't want to die and leave me desolate?"

"No, dear! indeed, no! though I don't think you'd care really." He clasped her in a closer embrace and kissed her reproachfully. "Well, yes, just at first, perhaps. Yet so long as you want me, I want to stay and be your willing, working wife. I've got a new reason and aim now: I have you, dear old Ross."

"Oh, Percy, I *do* care. God knows even the thought of it gives me a bitter agony, I know you cannot trust me yet, because I married you so carelessly, and because you think I can't be true to one woman with my battered old heart. But that's because you judge me by what my long, unloved life has made me. No good woman ever made me love her before. I never knew how beautiful a pure life was, my darling, until I knew it through watching yours. When I think of all you have saved me from, which would have caused my undying gratitude had I learned to hate you--as if I ever could!" and he paused to kiss her--"when I think of all the new and better hopes you have awakened in my heart, I feel--God knows I do--as if He had sent my angel, and let her drag me out of a hell into which I was plunged, and year after year sinking deeper. Stay with me, dear: I will be true. I never cared for any woman in the way--in the deep, absorbing way--I do for you. I wish you would believe me."

"I do, Ross--you are so good to me, so good! Oh, Ross, Ross!" and she held up her face to his, "you are so good to me!" She clung to him one moment, then suddenly, as soon as she could trust her voice, said gayly, "But it's breakfast-time, and your wife is so unromantically hungry;" and with a sigh that nothing more ever came of their talks he took her down.

When they reached New York the next afternoon, they drove at once to the rooms they had engaged. Percy's cousin, Harry Barton, was there to welcome them, having come round from his hotel for the purpose.

"Why, Norval," said he--they were old acquaintances--"you've won our bone of contention, after all. I wonder what we shall do, now that Percy's safely landed out of our reach? You're a brave man to dare our rage."

"Don't, Harry!" said Percy, putting her hand on his arm.

"I won't, dear, if you say not;" and he covered her hand with his own. "I always did do your lightest bidding, little girl, didn't I?"

"Yes, you're a dear old cousin. Ross knows how much I appreciate your kindness to me always. Why, I gave up what he calls my 'bridal tour,' partly because I wanted to come back and say 'good-bye' to you."

His face flushed crimson at her words, and, all his careless, fashionable manner gone, he said, "Did you, Percy? You always were good."

"That, and because--because I shall be so sorry if you join this African expedition."

"Don't ask me not to, Percy--don't ask me to stay now you have broken my hope for ever. I shall go to the dogs, dear, if I stay here now."

"I don't want you to, Harry. Only your mother is so delicate and getting old, and she loves you beyond all the rest of the world, though you think she don't because she has been cruel to me. It will break her heart if you join this dangerous enterprise. Stay in Europe, go to Heidelberg and finish the course you so foolishly broke up. They'll blame me, Harry, for all the evil that comes to you."

"Well, I'll think about it, dear." Then to Ross; "Does she kiss you, Norval?"

"Well, I can't say she does," said that gentleman, who had been a surprised listener to their talk, and it annoyed him to have to confess she did not.

"Nor let you kiss her, either?"

"Well, yes," with a laugh. "She can't very well help that, you know."

"Don't you believe it: if she didn't want you to, you'd never kiss her, I know. Why, we three cousins, Sheldon, Mac and I, have tried every way to get her to kiss us for years, and never succeeded. You're a lucky dog!"

"He's my husband, Harry;" and she laid her head down on Ross's arm.

"Don't, Percy!" said her cousin with a quick motion of his hand: "I'll be gone soon;" then hurriedly and gayly: "Let me do the honors of your new domains. And, Norval, I have a great favor to ask of you. My little cousin's *amour propre* won't be touched, or herself involved now she's a married woman, by taking an honest gift from me, and all brides take bridal gifts, you know. I want you to let me give her all the traps I've left in the rooms. It isn't much grace to ask, old fellow, seeing you're to have her always and I not at all."

"Why, certainly, Barton, I have no objections if she has none."

"Percy, you've never let me give you anything all these years, you proud little soul, nor any of the rest of us: you've come scot-free from all our endeavors to snare you through all your hard-working life. You won't go quite empty-handed to your husband's arms, just to plague me, will you?"

"No, indeed! I'm delighted to have all your pretty things. I saw them once, you know, when you gave your mother her birth-night party;" and they began their round of inspection. "But, Harry, you've refurnished the whole suite!"

"You didn't think I was going to make you and Norval (I can't call you Cousin Ross yet, old fellow--I hate you too bad, you know) cast your lines among my smoke-and-wine-scented traps, did you?"

As she saw how exquisitely he had chosen everything, how delicately he had regarded every one of her tastes in his selection, and thought how little reason he had to be good to her, she turned quickly and put her arms about him. With a shuddering sob he held his own out as if to clasp her, saying, "May I, Ross?" The answering nod was scarcely given ere he had gathered her to his breast, murmuring, "Percy! Percy! my lost darling!"

As he held her thus, she said softly, "Promise me, Harry--dear old Hal--promise me this!"

"Anything, everything, Percy," he said.

"That you will give up Africa and go to Heidelberg."

"I will, I will, since you wish it."

She drew his face down and kissed him on his mouth, two long, sweet kisses, saying, "Good-bye, and God bless you, cousin!"

He stood like a blind man as she gently drew herself from his embrace, then wringing Ross's hand in a grasp that made him wince, he strode out of the house without a word.

Percy, going to where her husband sat, said humbly, "I was so sorry for him, I could not help it. You do not care--very much?"

"Harry Barton loved you and wanted to marry you?"

"Yes, Ross. I've been very unhappy about it for years, he's wasted his life so, and angered his family. Indeed, it was not my fault: I never gave him reason."

"Yet you married me without a pretence of love, and he's richer and handsomer and a better man than I, every way? I don't understand it, child."

"Yes, I married you, knowing you did not love me." His arms almost crushed her at that truth. "He may be richer: he is no better, I think, and"--holding his face between her hands with a quizzical survey for an instant--"it's barefaced scandal to assert that he is as handsome, by one half. Poor, handsome Ross, to think that all your manifold charms should have purchased you only ugly little me!" and she laughed a merry, mocking laugh at his protesting hug. "It's true, though--it's the very climax of opposites, a perfection of contrasts." Then, her light manner gone, she added: "You are very, very good to me, Ross. He would never have been so patient of my old griefs and lost loves. I told you my masculine cousins were always crying for the grapes that hung out of their reach, you know." Then suddenly growing grave: "Oh, Ross, it was not my fault: I could not help it. I think the boys got to pitying me because they thought my life was hard, and because their sisters treated me very cruelly sometimes. Then my uncles very foolishly ordained that I should teach their sons their Latin and help them with their studies. So out of school-hours my time was mostly spent with one or the other, or all of them. Sheldon Wilber and I are of the same age, and having been my father's constant companion, I was better up in all his studies than he was himself; so I used to do his college lessons with him, until he got to thinking, as he used to say, I was his very breath. Then afterward I gave the other two the benefit of what we had studied, got them out of scrapes, and indeed, being with them so much, kept them out. Don't let's talk about them any more, Ross: I have 'fessed' all now."

"Not all, my sweet: you have not told me who it is that has shut your heart from us all."

"Don't, Ross!" and she shrank away from him as if he had struck her a blow.

"Ah, well, my wife, keep your secret: I'll not touch your sacred past. I'll try to learn to be content with my little sister, thankful I have so much."

"Oh, Ross, my good, kind Ross!" and she clasped her arms around his neck in passionate, longing regret, "if I might tell you all--if I might!"

"Tell me nothing, dear, you would rather keep. I am infinitely content to even have you thus, and know you love me somewhat. Yes, I know, sweet," he said with a sad smile as she kissed his hand in passionate regret--"the very best you can, with all the heart you have. I know, I know!"

Quite late in the evening, Sheldon Wilber came. After sitting an hour or so, talking gayly, he rose to go. When they were standing he said, "Percy, I had just left the Flemmings before I came in here."

"Had you? I hope they are all well, especially Miss Lizzie, who is so pretty."

"They're all well enough. She--Miss Lizzie the pretty--is going to be married."

"To be married!--to whom?" she asked.

"To my honorable self: don't you congratulate her?"--with a bitter laugh. "I asked her to-night if she'd have me, and she said 'Yes.'"

"I am so glad, Sheldon--so very glad!" and she held out her hand.

"Are you? It's more than anyone else is but my mother. Well, no--I suppose the Flemmings are, to get another daughter off their hands, and she to have a safe man to pay her bills. And of course all our cousins and sisters will be glad to have another house to dance the German in; so it is rather a jubilee occasion, taking it all in all."

"Oh, Sheldon, how hard and bitter you are! She loves you, I know, and the rest think you will be happier with a good wife to care for."

"Yes, the wife I cared for would have made me supremely happy, but *vive la bagatelle!* I want to know when I am to tie this knot?"

"Whenever she wishes, of course," she answered.

"By the Lord, no! If she gets me, she's got to take me when *I* choose."

Percy went up to him and put her hands in his: "She'll be a good wife, and, dear Sheldon, you'll be a good husband to her."

He looked at her curiously, then answered, "I'll try: I'll begin by letting her set the hanging--no, I mean the wedding--day. Norval, I know you'll be good to our little girl--better, likely as not, than the rest of us would have been had we got possession of her. Only remember, old fellow, the shadows must never come to her through you, or some of us will make a shadow of you. Would you mind my coming around sometimes to see the little woman? If you'll let me come and spend an evening now and then with you both, it will keep me from getting utterly down-hearted, and maybe will make me a better husband to the future Mrs. Sheldon Wilber. I'll never come without sending word to know if I may." And the poor fellow took himself away.

"How they love you, dear! It's strange you took me, and I thought I was conferring a favor on you! I'm ashamed to remember it now, but it was so."

"Yes, I know"--and she laughed--"but it's not strange, Ross. Any woman would have chosen you: I have always heard of your successes with women. And you know it was take or lose when you gave me my chance. I had but one choice; it was not likely you would drop your handkerchief before me a second time; so I took you quick, before some other woman caught you."

She kept a light, gay tone thus far, standing the other side of the grate from him, but when he came near as if to draw her toward him, she said hurriedly, "These boys have been too much for me, and tried me terribly. If you will not care, Ross, I think I'll say 'Good-night,' though it's early. Don't stay in, if you would like to go to your club or anywhere, because it is our first evening. You see, I am going to desert you first. It's part of the compact, you know, that I am never to be in your way."

"Oh, Percy," he said, in a very boyishly aggrieved tone, "I don't want to go anywhere where you are not."

"You will soon get tired of that, Ross. But I'm glad you don't want to go to-night: I doubt your being quite able to walk much in the evening. Yet I feel as if I must say 'Good-night' and get myself in the dark. Why? I'm unstrung. The newness of my life with you, the traveling, this coming home with you to a place where I am to know either joy or woe, and all this talk with Harry and Sheldon, have been almost more than I could bear;" and her lip quivered. "It's all I have been able to do this last hour to keep from crying, and I do hate to cry before people." The long-suppressed emotion of all these weeks had broken bounds and she shook with sobs, while every nerve seemed quivering, and all she said was, "Ross, Ross! please forgive me! I am so sorry to be so foolish!" And though he strove by every tender method to comfort and soothe her, it was in vain; and at length, really frightened, he carried her to the little room she had appropriated for herself, and as tenderly as a mother, though as shyly as a girl, put his poor little done-out wife in her bed, too weak to resist his kind services, indeed, scarcely noticing them.

The next day, when he returned from what he and his friends, by an agreeable fiction, called an "office," where he generally spent as many hours as served to give him a flavor of business and a figurative title as a businessman--where were to be found the best cigars and choicest wines, and generally a pleasant circle of good fellows congregated--he found Percy with the most charming little dinner awaiting him; the table exquisite in the finest, whitest napery, gleaming with silver, sparkling in glass, and every dish cooked and served in quite Parisian style, and the little lady herself in the brightest toilette, with such a matronly air that he could hardly realize the scene of the last night's misery.

"Tears all gone, Ross, tragedy played out, and the little woman who keeps house for you is herself again, and has been as busy as a nailer. Are nailers busier than other men, I wonder? All your boxes came. Such bliss as it was to us poor women to feast our eyes upon all that heritage of linen and silver, and china and glass! Your mother must have been a famous manager, Ross, to leave you such a store. I'm so glad we've got that old place on the Harlem stored with all this beautiful array. Do you know, Ross, I think I've discovered my especial calling to-day? It's housekeeping, and I elect myself to go some time to that lovely old mansion and expend myself in hospitality. I'll invite you to come and visit me."

Flying about the room, then making him seat himself in the cozy chair which was placed for him at the table--"the side that's next the fire," she said--rattling gayly on of all her day's employment, she caught the look upon his face and came to his side. "What were you thinking of, Ross?" she asked, anxiously.

"What a little tornado you were, for the first thing, and how I liked seeing you busy among our household gods; also and moreover, that you had not given me a chance to say a word; and worst of all, that you had never given me my kiss of welcome, my rightful perquisite." Instantly she held up her face. "Ah, pet, you are always submissive; but never aggressive: still, this is sweet. And I was wondering what had become of the weeping willow I left."

"Wasn't I a silly goose, Ross?" she said, a little breathlessly.

"Well, no, dear: you were very nervous and worn-out."

"I hate nervous, fidgety women so: they're detestable with their whims."

"I did not find you so, but I'm glad you're over it, all the same."

"And so am I. You could not make me cry like that again, Ross, if you were to pinch me."

"But I did not make you cry."

"Yes you did, though. In truth, I was unstrung, and you were so kind and unlike what any one had ever been to me before, so different from what I had expected when we were married "--and her lips quivered--"that it touched me to the quick."

"Why, darling, did you think I was going to be a brute to you?"

"I thought you would be nothing to me, one way or the other--simply forget me, and be utterly indifferent so long as I kept your clothes made and mended, and did not bother you about my wants or tastes or opinions."

A flush came over his face at the truth of her words. It would have been just so had he found her what he expected her to be; but he said, "I don't think any one could treat you like that, little girl." Then, while they ate their dinner, he told her of his day's doings and of his determination for the future: "I have a good opening--no man better. I mean to attend to my practice hereafter, make a name and fortune for my sweetheart, and in a few years we'll go to Europe and see the sights. Ah, Percy, such a vista, such a new life, such a bright future, as I see opening before me! But, first of all, I am going shopping with you, young lady, to-morrow. I have ordered a carriage at eleven, and we'll buy all those pretty fixings you women doat on. Do you know, little bride, I think all my vanity is going to take the form of having you more prettily dressed than your cousins, mine ancient flames when I was a bad boy?"

"Oh, Ross," with a little laugh, "you can't do it: you can't make a rival specimen out of your bad bargain. Nothing will make me a beauty."

"Don't, Percy! I do like beauty. I have run after and made a fool of myself for years over pretty women, but I like your face, just as it is, better than any other woman's face I ever knew. If I could change you any way, I would not do it. Your face is beautiful to me, though I know it is not a pretty one: you are like sunlight to me." His voice shook, and he strained her slight form to him with a clasp that was positive pain. "I said I would not change you, but I would if I might put that old love out of your heart for ever. Why, in those far-off years when we were childish friends, did I not know my truest life lay in winning you? It is strange! I have never failed to gain the love I wanted until now, when I want the only one that would complete my life. Dear Percy, love me all you can. If there are things in me--and I know there are many--which turn you from me, tell me of them and I will change them if I can."

"Oh, Ross, don't, don't! I am not worthy of such words."

"Oh, little Preciosa, I am glad to have even a little of your heart: the half of your love has come to be more to me than the love of all the world besides."

Do you think it was not agony for her to hear such words as these and make no response to them, fearing lest with assurance should come satiety? And yet the knowledge of his growing love was very sweet to her, and worth the agony.

They settled down in their new home, and were purposely "out" to all callers during the next month--then returned the cards that had been left for them. As they grew accustomed to their new life, she thought to see his pleasure and interest in it wane as the novelty wore away, but it was not so. That love of home which is, after all, the truest test of a really manly nature, seemed to grow upon him. It was always so bright and cheery by their cozy fire, the glare of public rooms, the noise and glitter of theatres and concert-rooms, struck him with a feeling akin to disgust, after the soft, subdued light of his home, and his wife's merry, breezy voice. He sang and played for her, never giving a thought to her having any musical ability, since she never touched the instrument. He read to her hour after hour, having at last discovered her taste and ability to understand the kind of books he relished, perfectly content if she would favor him by sitting near enough to him to let him pull down that wealth of "tresses brown," a glossy cloud about her.

Of course this Arcadian life could not continue in the very heart of Sodom. Society was not going to lose Ross Norval if he *had* made a fool of himself and married a little nobody. So callers flowed in upon them, and Ross, having in boyish glee arrayed himself in purple and fine linen, took her in state to see his friends.

Of course her cousins and their friends hated her: she had won their *bonne louche*, and the crimson of her plainness and poverty, of the having to "have Percy always around to please Uncle Rufus," was pink to the enormity of her being Ross Norval's wife. And "why he married her," and "of course he's dead tired of her by this time," were their politest surmises.

One morning they paid a cousinly visit--a triple call. "And, by Jove!" thought Ross as he watched her haughty little face and *nonchalant* manner, "she's no milk-and-water nature, though she's always so sweet-tempered with me. She's got all the temper a true nature ought to have."

"To think of your ever getting married, Percy, and to Mr. Norval, of all men!" said Miss Leta Wilber. "Why, we thought him engaged to the beauty and belle of last winter, Miss Agnes Lorton."

"Well, yes, Leta, old girls like you and I are rather off the cards: we don't expect to catch the prizes generally--we leave that for these younger ones, like Jennie and Lucille," said Percy, coolly.

"A Roland for your Oliver, Leta!" laughed Jennie Wayne. "I never venture to break a lance with Percy: she always has an arrow in reserve to pierce you with. I suppose you've found that out, Mr. Norval?"

"Found what out? I fear I don't follow you, Miss Jennie," said he.

"That she's very able to take her own part, this little cousin of ours," said she, her beautiful face scarlet at his manner.

"Is she, though? Well, I like that amazingly, do you know?"

"Like ill-tempered people?" said Miss Leta, snappishly. "Is it possible?"

"Ill-tempered people?" with a wellbred stare. (Is there such a thing?) "No, indeed! Why, birdie"--and he leaned over, and, taking her hand, raised it to his lips--"to think of any one calling you ill-tempered!"

"You silly boy!" laughed she. "I'll take my hand if you please, and don't you believe but what you've married a termagant."

The girls said afterward, in recounting the scene, it was simply disgusting. Leta vowed, "The little baggage must be a witch and throw spells over people. Look what fools she's made of our boys for years, and Ross Norval, with all his splendid endowments, is just as bad."

"And he did use to admire your form, Leta," said Jennie, maliciously. "I've seen him waltz you until it was hard to tell which face that long blonde moustache belonged to."

"Ditto, cousin, and worse, if gossips speak the truth. But don't let's say ugly things to each other. We both hoped to win him once, and we have both lost him. The little wretch will watch him like a hawk, and never let him come near a body."

"Oh dear!" said her sister Laura, "if I only knew I was to do a German with him to-night, I'd be happy: he holds one better than any man I know; and if Percy will let him dance with a body occasionally, I'd as leave she should have him as the rest of you."

"Unless he'd chosen yourself, Laura, I suppose?"

"Well, yes, that would have made a difference, even to my laziness, especially if she'd have made dear old Harry stay at home by marrying him."

That's the way they talked, yet in a couple of weeks after each house had sent her an invitation to a large party--"for you and Mr. Norval, dear Percy"--and the invitation-cards stated the fact.

"It's my Viking they want," laughed she: "they take his mouse in for the sake of securing him. He's such a credit to the family!"

"Well, it's your Viking they won't get," said he.

"Now, Ross, don't be a bother, dear, and complicate matters. They will say--and be glad of the chance--that it's my fault. You've such a passion for dancing, they will say I prevented your coming. And besides, as I dance so little, you'll ask them as much as ever?"

"How do you know I am so fond of it, Percy?"

"I've watched you too many years not to know that. You forget that, though a flower unnoticed and unseen--a very wall-flower in fact--I have been a looker-on in Vienna. I might have made a point of that, Ross, if I'd thought in time, and 'hung i' the walls of Venice, a sightly flower.' You were the bright particular star, or sun, in whose light all the fairest flowers disported themselves. Why, I could tell you every woman--that is, of your own set--you've been what Jennie calls 'bad about,' for years." He held up his hand deprecatingly: she laughed gayly. "Never fear. I don't intend to name them: I have not time to go over such a thing of shreds and patches. Ah! the hopes I've watched you raise to heaven and then dash to earth!"

"Oh, Percy, I don't wonder that you are afraid to trust me now: I am paying the penalty of my years of folly."

"That's nonsense, Ross. I don't believe in fashionable women's hearts. You were too good for them, and they led you on always," she said, almost passionately.

"That's my good darling trying to excuse her sinner. But how was it you never danced at any of those parties? Harry and Mac are both good dancers, and Sheldon's the best waltzer I ever saw. How is it you never danced with them?"

"With them, indeed! Why, that would have been an aggravation past enduring to my rich relations. Sheldon had actually the insolence to tell his sister Leta that I was the best waltzer in society. Think of the prize you've got, young man!"

"I do always, sweetheart," he said, answering her gay tone with a grave one. "Did you waltz much with Sheldon and the others?"

"I never waltzed with any of them in my life. Why, Ross, I never let them speak to me at parties, except by turns to take me out to supper and home."

"But how have you managed to keep up your waltzing then?"

"Oh, Mr. Vanity, men are not all. Esther and I waltzed constantly: then I used to help Lucille, who is my favorite cousin, 'along in her paces;' and the children at our school-parties doat on me as a partner. Would you like to know who was the last man, and indeed almost the only one, I ever went round a room with?" and her face turned crimson, though she laughed.

"Indeed I should--curse him!" he said under his breath.

"Your honorable self, at Madame's school-party;" and she sprang away from his outstretched hands with a mocking laugh.

The day of the party she wrote a few little violet-perfumed notes, and sent them off. This is a specimen:

"DEAR DOCTOR: You have so often wanted to know your 'nebulous child,' and been indignant that she hid her face from you behind her veil of clouds, you will be pleased to know that the sunshine has dispelled the clouds, and made her at last able to meet the starry train of which you are the sun. Will you greet Ross Norval's bride at the Wilber party to-night as the child you have trained and been so good to in the past, and who, ever honoring you, is still your loving child for the future? If you'll ask me prettily to-night, I'll sing the foolish words I made for the sweet, tripping Languedoc air you sent me last year. I am, now and ever,

"MIRA CANAM."

In consequence of these notes, when Ross led his wife into the room, arrayed in a crimson cloud of his choosing, which made even her brown face a picture, all her bronze hair, her husband's glory, floating round her far below her waist, confined lightly here and there by diamond clusters, which sparkled like stars amidst its creped luxuriance--"Daring to dress in the very height of the fashion," said Leta, "and all those diamonds on her--his mother's, of course;" and of course they were-- the consequence, I say, was, that first one distinguished man and then another met her with a warm greeting--"deucedly warm," thought the jealous fellow, who was so uncertain of her yet, and wanted all of her--and were introduced to "my husband." Taking for granted that "my husband" was glad to get her off his hands, they took possession of her, to his infinite disgust.

These were the men with whom she could talk, whose minds struck diamond flashes from her own, whose thoughts she had followed for years, and who looked upon her as their peer, and deferred to her opinion on many things. And she, knowing Ross was her amazed listener, was stirred to do her best before him--glad her triumph over her relatives should be in his presence and brought to her through his means. It may not have been a lovely thing in her to desire or enjoy a victory, but ah! it is so natural, and my little heroine had had hard lines meted out to her for years. Besides, no woman is free, you know, from vanity: only men are that.

She stood near the door of the dancing-room. Ross came to her after every dance, but it was always, "Not me yet, Ross--Leta, or Jennie," or whoever stood nearest her. Even the girl to whom report had given him (with reason) the year before was, at her open entreaty, which he could not evade, his partner; but half the time he stood beside her, forgetful of the dance in listening to the conversation in which she bore so large a part.

A lull in the music after supper announced the suspension of dancing hostilities for a time, that due strength might be gathered for the last waltz, and then the German. The time was occupied by a very weak tenor, who came to an ignominious end in the middle of "Spirito Gentil." Miss Jennie Barton and her cousin Laura gave a sweet duo, in rather a tearing style, Jennie being a fast young lady everyhow; another lady sang a Scottish ballad as if it had been manipulated by Verdi; then one of the gentlemen said, "Mr. Norval, I hope you will lay your commands on your wife to sing for us."

"I hope that will not be needed," he said, bowing (thinking with a pang, "They all know her better than I do"). "I am sure she will do equally well if we all beg the favor of her."

"She has promised me to sing," said Dr. B----, "my pretty Languedoc air, which she has--"

"Now that's enough, you foolish old doctor!" and she went to the piano. "Foolish old doctor!" He was the great gun of the scientific world: the people about looked aghast at such impertinence, but the "great gun" only laughed and said, "I am mute if you command."

How her hands trembled as she began! This was her last and greatest card: by it she had always felt she must hold him to her for ever, or lose her husband's love in time. She had never touched the piano before him or sung a note, but much of her leisure since their return to New York had been taken up, when he was out, in keeping herself in practice against the time when she should have a chance to play for him and sing to him. She played the sweet air, with its Mozart-like, mournful cadences, entirely through ere she felt nerved enough to begin. Then she sang in such a voice as made the most indifferent pause--a voice that was like purple velvet for richness, as sweet as the breath of an heliotrope to which the sun had just said adieu, as clear as the notes of an English skylark--this little song:

"See, love! the rosy radiance gleams
Athwart the sunset sky:
List, love! and hear the bird's sweet notes
In lingering cadence die.
Clasp, love, thy clinging hands in mine,
And, holding fast by me,
Trust, love! I will be true, my dove,
Be ever true to thee--
So true, sweetheart, I'll be,
Sweetheart, to thee!

"Come, love! I waiting pine so long,
And weary watch for thee:
Dear love! amidst my darkest night
Thy star-like face I see.
Heart's love! ah, come thou close to me:
I'll shelter thee from harms,
From every foe or secret woe,
Close clasped within my arms:
Lie safe from all alarms,

Sweetheart, with me."

While they listened to her, those careless men and women, they thought they began to understand why this little, plain girl had won Ross Norval. While everybody praised her, he stood utterly silent, too moved for words she saw, and refusing to sing again, she went up to him as the band began to play. "My waltz, Ross," she said. He put his arm around her with a loving gesture that made those about them smile, and whirled her off.

"He's the hardest hit man I've seen for years," said one.

"And that such a thing should come to pass, as Ross Norval in love with his own wife, is beyond belief--after making love to everybody else's!"

"That's it! He was always the darling of fortune: the choicest fruit always dropped his side the wall."

But Ross, as he held her in that "tight hold" which was so much admired by his partners, said only, "Percy! Percy! I do not know you at all. How cruel you are to me! Everybody knows you and your gifts but me."

When the German had commenced he came to her and whispered, "Do you care for it?"

"The German, Ross? Indeed no: I am tired too, and was just coming to ask you if I might let old Mr. L---- take me home: he says it will be no trouble."

"And you would not have asked me to take you?" he said, reproachfully.

"Take you away from the German, Ross! Such an unheard-of thing as that! You must think me very selfish. Indeed; I am not where your pleasure is concerned: I only want you to enjoy yourself."

"Then, for Charity's sake, let's go home," he said.

"With all my heart if you really wish it!" and she started; then pausing: "Are you going because you think I want to go? I do not indeed: I will stay gladly."

"I am going because I want to--because I am dead tired, and long, with a perfect passion, for our cozy room, the dim firelight, and my darling toasting her pretty slippers."

"You dear, foolish Ross!" and she was gone like the wind. On their way out, Sheldon Wilber met them in the hall, and, handing her something, said, "To-night, little girl: if you have ever doubted, doubt no more. And remember, a trusting heart is a priceless one;" and he was gone.

When they were home and comfortable, Ross said, "My wife, it was cruel to let me learn your wonderful gifts through strangers: it has hurt me cruelly."

"Oh, Ross, don't say so! Hurt you! I hurt you, my love, my love! I had hoped no pang of the lightest sort would ever reach you through me, and now I've grieved you sorely! It's all due to my morbid fancies, dear. I could not ask to sing to you lest you should not like my singing: I think I should have gone mad if you had not liked my voice, Ross I have so hoped it would be pleasant to your ear! Do you like it, Ross? Is my voice sweet to you?" and she held his face between her hands and looked eagerly and steadfastly into his eyes.

"The sweetest thing I ever heard. It thrills my blood yet, that love-song you sang."

She gave a little cooing laugh: "That is *your* love-song, dear--your very own." Then she said, gravely, "I must tell you *all* about myself now, Ross, so you shall never be able to reproach me with having given you pain. No matter, dear: it was, true," she said in answer to his caressing protest, "and I feel the hurt through you. I am your wife. The reason those gentlemen are so fond of me is because--Wait;" and she slid from his embrace and brought a pile of books: "this and this are mine; these two I translated from the German, others from the old Provencal tongue, with which my father made me familiar." Then she told him how lovingly she did this work, how kind scholarly men had been to her, and how eagerly they had sought to know her otherwise than by letter--"Until, to-night, I bade them find Ross Norval's wife, and know the little girl who, shielded by his name, feared nothing any more."

"Percy," he said, quite humbly, "you must bear with me, dear. I lose all hope of winning you when I learn these things of you."

"But you are not sorry, Ross? I will not write any more if you dislike literary women."

But he stopped her: "Dislike it! I am proud as a king of all your endowments. But, sweetheart, you said a word just now that is worth all else that you have told me--a word, I know, you said only half meaning it. Oh, my little girl, will there ever come a time when, meaning it and out of a full heart, you will say, My love! my love!"

She held him tight a long, long moment, then with one lingering love-kiss on his lips--her very first--she said faintly, putting him away from her, "Ross, not now--wait, my dearest. Sheldon gave me this to give to you to-night;" and she held out a little worn letter, then buried her face upon his breast and tremblingly waited while he read it. It ran thus:

"Sheldon, my cousin, it can never be: give up all hope for ever. I kill it now, because it is best you should know the truth. I almost give up my life, my cousin, when I make my heritage of woe known to you. You will pity me, Sheldon, when you realize what agony the confession you thus wring from me gives my heart. But if it cures your passion it is not borne in vain. I love with an undying love, a faith that knows no change, an endurance that years of neglect have not weakened, that years of cruelty could never change, a man who would laugh to scorn my very name. I love--and have loved since I was sixteen years old, until now--Ross Norval. Keep my secret.

"PERCY HASTINGS."

It was dated four years back.
"Ross, Ross! you know it now! Oh, my love! my love!"

*   *   *   *   *

I will attempt no painting of the effect that confession had upon him. But after a long, long time she whispered, "I will sing the last verse of your song, dear, which only you shall ever hear." And lying on his breast, she sang--

"Dear love I thy face above me gleaming
A sunset radiance gives:
Ah, love! thy tones' sweet cadence dying
Sings in my heart and lives.
Clasped, love, close to thy heart, thy birdling

Foldeth her wings in peace--
Trusts, love! feeling nor cold nor shadow,
Finding at last her ease,
From fear a safe release,
Heart's love, with thee."

MARGRET FIELD.

The Victims of Dreams.

My friend Bessie Haines had no mother, but her father was such a very large man that I remember thinking, when I was quite a child, that a kind Providence had intended to make up her loss in that way. She and I did not live in the same city, but managed to keep up a lively friendship through the medium of correspondence and half-yearly visits.

I was a complete orphan, and my uncle, with whom I lived, was her father's attached friend. She had a very happy home, and I was glad to enjoy it with her, particularly when my uncle accompanied me, for then her father and he became absorbed in each other, and left us to our own devices--not very evil ones, but too childish and trifling to claim the sympathy of such very grave men as they were.

We had both become tall, womanly girls, but Uncle Pennyman and Mr. Haines called us children, and treated us as such; and Bessie was just writing to me about her father's telling her she must begin to think of serious things, when my uncle remarked to me that the time was approaching when I should prepare myself to assume the duties and responsibilities of a rational female. Just as if we had waited to be told this, when in fact Bessie and I had been consulting about our bonnets and dresses in the most grave and mature manner for years past, and arranging our future on plans that for variety and agreeability could not have been surpassed had we been brought up on the **Arabian Nights** and Moore's **Poems**, instead of Baxter's **Saint's Rest** and Pollok's **Course of Time**.

"There are several questions of vital importance that have been growing daily stronger in my mind," said my uncle Pennyman. "My friend Thomas Haines has a gift in clearing points and expounding meanings; so that I feel it to be for my mind's edifying and my soul's profit to go to him for counsel."

I was delighted to hear this. I wanted to see Bessie, and I blessed the bond that united these good brothers in Israel and drew us together so often. Mr. Haines was good at texts, and my uncle was wonderfully expert at dreams. Mr. Haines was a great dreamer, and my uncle constantly stumbled over passages needing elucidation. So we lived in harmonious intercourse, and Bessie and I talked of all our plans and delights while they got themselves entangled in obscurities with a commentary under each arm.

It would have appeared, from Mr. Haines' dreams, that Bessie's mother had been a most fussy and bothering lady, though I was told by the housekeeper, who knew her well, that she was the mildest and most timid of little wives while living.

According to these visions, she was constantly troubled in her spiritual state on the greatest variety of small subjects; and my expert uncle, in expounding her communications, was always able to draw from them strong religious lessons, and to administer much strengthening comfort to his friend the dreamer.

"I was hoping papa would soon have a vision," said Bessie when we were settled together all comfortably, and she had told me how glad she was to see me again. "Mrs. Tanner said last week that she was sure he was going to have another, because the spire which he felt he was directed in his last dream to put on the little chapel was all complete, and the missionary outfit which he had believed himself called upon to provide was ready and gone to the South Seas, and he naturally looked for more work. When he said last week, 'Bessie, I have sent for Brother Pennyman concerning a visitation in the night,' I was so glad, for, Winnie dear--would you believe it?--I have been dreaming too, and I want you to tell me if I have read my dream aright."

Now, this was the most wonderful thing that Bessie Haines could have told me--the most startling and least to be expected altogether; for if ever there was a wide-awake girl, it was she.

I suppose my perfectly frank stare said as much, for she blushed a little, and continued with a very suspicious flutter, which I had learnt, in the case of young engaged persons I knew, to look on as a bad symptom:

"I do not mean dreaming with my eyes shut, you know, but having deep, serious thoughts, unlike the gay fancies that have held me captive all my life."

"Dress trimmings and poetry?" I suggested.

"Yes, yes--all the useless, perishable fancies of thoughtless youth," she replied.

This sounded more like an Essay on Vanity than Bessie Haines, and I really was astonished, and had nothing to say for a little while, during which she, being full of her subject, went on:

"I can scarcely trace the beginning of the--the awakening, shall I call it?"

"You called it a dream before."

"Yes, dear Winnie, but it is so hard to know how to classify new emotions, and this is such a peculiar one that it seems nameless. You know papa feels bound, ever since that water-dream he had, to go down to the Mariners' Chapel on Sunday afternoon, and I used to read solemn poetry when it was too warm or too cold to go with him. Well, about two months ago it was fearfully warm, and papa had come home a fortnight earlier from the shore, on account of a suspicion he had that he had dreamed something and had forgotten it as soon as he awoke. This indistinct warning made him think we had better go home at all events, and home we came the first week in September, to the roasting, dusty city. But I did not then know that I was perhaps drawn back for a purpose; and oh, dear Winnie, there may be something in papa's visions, after all."

"He has had a good many of them," I said.

"So he has," assented Bessie; "and I was inclined to be impatient at this one, since it brought me home in the heat, and the house seemed so lonely, because Mrs. Tanner was still in the country with her married daughter."

"She having received no spectral warning," I hinted.

"Oh dear! no. Mrs. Tanner never dreams: she's opposed to it. Well, the first Sunday was so warm that I took up *Solemn Thoughts in Verse* instead of the Mariners'; and after I had read eight pages, it really seemed as if I had better have tried the heat out of doors, it was getting so gloomy within. So I got up and dressed, meaning to walk out and meet papa, and return with him. I don't know whether it was the *Solemn Thoughts* that confused me, or whether I was not paying attention, but I actually lost my way by turning at the wrong corner, and so came down Barton street toward a little chapel that I had often noticed before. Two dreadfully red-faced and short-haired little boys were at the entrance by the small iron gate. They had disagreed about something, I suppose, just as I came up, and they instantly began to fight, with the wickedest determination visible in their freckled little faces.

At first, they kicked at each other, and growled out some awful words without the least sense, but with a great deal of profanity in them, and then they laid down their little books and tracts, and apparently tried to pull each other's head off. Of course it made me quite wretched to see them hurt each other in that shocking way, and so I interfered and tried to reconcile them, but the naughty little souls must have had a certain amount of kicking and scratching on hand to dispose of, for they united in bestowing it all on me the moment I came between them.

"I was just trying to save my dress and lace sacque from their boots and claws, when a reverend gentleman appeared at the door, and the bad boys became sneaking cowards at sight of him. I picked up their little tracts, while he tried to apologize for them; and it was so sad, Winnie, to think that those dear children had not profited by their lessons: one was called 'Love One Another,' and the other, 'Be Meek and Lowly.'

"While we were talking a lady joined us, and I went into the school at their invitation.

"Winnie, do you know anything practical about Sunday-school?"

"I went to one, and was for years in the class of an elderly maiden lady who urged us all to learn Scripture and hymns. I was so expert and high in favor that I could repeat forty verses at a time as glibly as a parrot."

"But I don't quite mean that sort of thing," said Bessie. "I mean a real, earnest teaching-place, where children are gathered in and told all about Christ's love and mercy--where they are softened and won to better thoughts and kinder actions, and their poor little minds filled with shining truth, instead of street dirt and abuse."

"I never thought about it before, but such an institution could not help being a popular one, and a very useful one too," I confessed.

"Oh, I am so glad, so very glad, that you approve, dear, for I am engaged in that work; and I did not want to write it to you, for somehow it seemed so strange for such a thoughtless, silly girl as I have been to attempt such a serious thing."

"As teaching in a Sunday-school?"

"Yes, in a sort of mission school for little scholars of the lower classes. Miss Mary Pepper and I have at this time nearly two hundred boys and girls of all ages, and some of them are very interesting and lovable, while others are--"

"Like the two gladiators who introduced you to the scene?"

"Yes. I am afraid there are quite a number of that kind; but, Winnie, you must like Miss Mary Pepper. Oh, she is one of the most excellent women I ever knew, so truly, so nobly, so devotedly good. You cannot imagine what a comfort it is to me to be with her--to feel that I am under her influence, and may learn from her to be a little like her."

"Miss Mary Pepper?" I repeated: "then she is a young lady?"

"No--not young: indeed, she is rather elderly."

"An old maid," I remarked, coldly. "She is pretty and sweet, though faded, I suppose."

"Why, no--not to look at: her nature is beautiful, but her manner and figure are rather--rather unprepossessing at first."

"A stiff, hard, straight-laced old maid," I said, contemptuously. "Well, really, I cannot see the fascination--"

Bessie's face flushed painfully: "I confess that dear Miss Pepper's person is not so beautiful as her nature, but, Winnie, it is the cause of doing good and trying to be good that draws us together so closely; and of course I do not love her as I love you, my dear, precious first friend."

These last words were full of balm, for of course it was the sting of jealousy that had made my heart resent the venerable Pepper's powerful influence over my dear Bessie. Being once assured that it was a second-rate power, and that I still held my supremacy, I entered into the Sunday-school question like a second Raikes, and volunteered to help, and try to learn the way to the young hearts that beat under the pugilistic exterior of the juveniles of Canon lane, where the mission chapel was.

Then, having become one on this serious subject, we began to wonder what Mr. Haines' dream might portend this time, and prepare our minds for the verse from the prophecies over which dear Uncle Pennyman had made his latest stumble.

"Mrs. Tanner thinks it was something about a journey, and she is quite out of sorts on the subject: for, as she says, the house can't be shut up without worriment, and as to staying in it alone she really has not got the nerve."

"I do not think that Uncle Pennyman will interpret it that way, because he cannot go too, as he is at present very deep in the minor prophets, and has fallen out of humor with all the commentaries."

"I am so glad!" said Bessie, placidly--"so glad, I mean, that we need not go: I think every one must find his life-work at home."

I stared a little at this, because I knew that only a few months before Bessie Haines had wanted very much to find style and fashion abroad; but I remembered the Sunday-school, and tried to be as serious and convinced as I could; and to that end I talked a good deal of church interests, and the prophecies, and *Light in Obscurity*, a new work which had utterly confused me at the first chapter, but which I had read through to Uncle Pennyman one warm July day when he stayed at home to keep Tom's birth-day.

That reminds me: I have not mentioned Tom, but as he was away at college, and Bessie never seemed to like to talk of him--I'm sure I can't see why--it is quite natural that he slipped out of my memory.

He was a ward of Uncle Pennyman, who called him his son, and indeed had adopted him formally.

How two such opposite people ever came to love each other as they did, I never can explain. It was not a natural, commonplace affection: it was a strong, deep, earnest love, as firm in the hearts of both as the life that caused their throbbings.

Tom was wild and full of frolic: if there is a graver word than gravity, it should be used to describe Uncle Pennyman's demeanor. Tom was quick and restless by nature, but his good sense and determination to make a niche for himself in life, and fill it respectably, had toned down his exuberant spirits into active energy; while Uncle Penny man's naturally slow tendencies had become aggravated by the ponderous character of his pursuits and tastes: all hurry was obnoxious to him, and he firmly believed that haste was another name for sin. Yet the solemn, slow old man loved the busy, merry young one, and neither saw any fault or failing in the other.

There was no earthly relationship between Thomas Gray Pennyman and me, and yet I was always spoken of as his sister by my dear, worrying old uncle. Tom did not seem to like it, and I knew I did not.

People often said to me, "What a splendid brother you have, Miss Pennyman but what a pity that all these handsome brothers have to be given up to stronger ties!"

How utterly silly! I never had any patience with such nonsense.

There was not much comfort in talking to Bessie about him. I'm sure I do not know why, but I suppose she saw that I avoided the subject; so I was really quite surprised when she said to me, laughing and looking a little mischievous--

"Mr. Tom is to join us by and by, your uncle says. I hope we may be able to make it pleasant for him. I believe he likes Mrs. Tanner: he used to like her buns when he was a boy, and I hope he has not forgotten the fancy."

Tom coming to visit the Haines! Such a thing had never happened before, and must mean something now. I began to feel quite uneasy, though I really could not have explained why.

We never had much of my uncle's or Mr. Haines' society except in the evening: they spent the day going about together and worrying texts of Scripture with other good old men, before whom Mr. Haines liked to show off uncle's Bible knowledge. They took some pious excursions in company, and had a solemnly festive time, I have no doubt, for they always came in looking perfectly satisfied with the result of their day.

It generally took some time to hear the dream and find its proper interpretation. While it was pending the expounder generally gave out his puzzling verses, and then both pondered a good while before they arrived at their conclusions and made them known.

Both the dream and the text must have been of an unusually difficult nature this time, for a whole week went by without either transpiring; and although Bessie and I watched for some allusions to them in our morning and evening family worship, at which the two good men officiated alternately, yet not a hint could we gain until one night at the end of the week it seemed from Uncle Pennyman's prayer that the matter in some wise referred to Bessie, since Divine guidance was sought under many rhetorical forms for the welfare, future and temporal, of "the young handmaiden, the daughter of thy servant, who would fain know thy will concerning her."

"Bessie," said I that night, when we got up stairs, "I think I have found out what your father's last dream was: I solemnly believe that he means to send you out as a missionary."

Now I thought I had said something calculated to make Bessie turn pale and gasp, but I could scarcely believe it when I looked up, expecting to find her almost fainting, and saw her pensively, but by no means alarmedly, shaking her head.

"I am not devoted enough, Winnie, love," she remarked. "I have not the grand self-abnegating spirit necessary for such a work. No; mine is a home field."

If I had not known about the young warriors of Canon lane, I should have thought her demented: as it was, I could scarcely wait for the next day, which was Sunday, to be introduced to the scene which had already produced such a marked change in her character and tastes.

It transpired during breakfast that Uncle Pennyman's peace had been disturbed by a verse in the book of Nahum, that talked about the lions and lionesses, and their whelps and prey, in what appeared to him a mysterious manner. Mr. Haines, who was a dear, good man, elaborated it so that we all felt as if we had made a visit to the Zoological Gardens, and afterward been carried into Babylonish captivity. My uncle followed his words with a brightening face, and when they grew particularly mixed and long-syllabled, he would exclaim softly,

"It is a great gift! a great gift!" and seem really overcome with the magnitude of his friend's powers.

I never saw any harm in Uncle Pennyman's texts: they never worried any one but himself; though I must confess that verse about Ephraim being a cake not turned affected us a little. But that was because he had the ague, and Mr. Haines was attending some kind of convention; and what with the chills, and that unexplained cake of Ephraim's, we were kept a little uncomfortable for a time.

But Mr. Haines' visions were perplexing: no one could tell where their signification might point; and this sending for Tom (of course he would never have thought of coming if he had not been sent for) made me quite uneasy.

I began to fear that this would be the first time I had ever gone to see Bessie without enjoying the visit; and as we walked along to Canon Lane Chapel together, her manner was so absent and fluttered that I really did not know what to do.

"It is a delightful and meritorious thing to be pious, no doubt," I said to myself, "but it has not improved the manner of my dear Bessie: on the contrary, I should say it has entirely shaken her nerves, and given her palpitation of the heart."

When we reached the chapel we found quite a number and variety of youths already collected around the door, and when we went into a large and airy room, well lighted and filled with seats, a goodly selection awaited us there.

A lady stood on a small platform with a bell in her hand: she had a large, bony figure, and a long, bony face, and turned her eyes toward us without changing their

expression into any beam of recognition, as she used her voice without any soften-
ing tone or tender cadence whatever:

"Miss Haines, good-afternoon. Mary Bryan, where's your brother? John Mott,
you have dropped your tract. Miss Pennyman, glad to see you. Sarah Harper, give
your sister a seat."

Bessie had pushed me on her attention between the monotonous sentences she
jerked out at her scholars, and she gave me five words just like the rest, and dropped
me off again.

Bessie seemed to become calmer after she had looked around the room once in
a hasty, fluttered way, and placing a chair for me, she threw herself energetically
into her philanthropic work.

I never knew before what a serious thing it was to be a Sunday-school teacher,
or how varied the requirements for such duty were. Thirst seemed to be a prevail-
ing agony among the scholars, and it seized its victims as an epidemic does--without
warning. They would just reach their seats and drop into them listlessly, or gain
them by energetic contest with some previous intruder, and after an empty stare
around them would be taken with a sudden pang, expressed in writhing, shaking
the right hand wildly and gasping, "Teacher, I want a drink! I want a drink!"

Then they were subject to a terrible vacillation on the subject of their hats:
they would almost consign them to the care of a monitor appointed to hang them
on the pegs made and provided, when a sense of their preciousness would suddenly
present itself to their minds, and they would rescue them wildly, and throw themselves on the defensive while they sat upon or otherwise protected the contested
article of dress.

There were six windows with broad sills in the room, and every child seemed
beset with a passionate desire to leave its seat and lodge itself in a surreptitious manner on one of these perches, as if they had been posts of honor.

Whether bits of bright tin, glass bottle-stoppers, ends of twine, broken sticks
and marbles were accessions to biblical instruction, or were only so considered
by the pupils themselves, did not transpire, but poor Bessie seemed to find them
stumbling-blocks in her path, and Miss Pepper had no sooner confiscated one lot
than another appeared in circulation and broke the story of Joseph's coat into a
parenthetical narrative:

"Israel loved Joseph so much that as a particular proof of his parental regard (James Moore, stop putting that stick in your brother's eye) he prepared a variegated garment known as a 'coat of many colors.' (John Mink, take that marble out of your throat, or you'll swallow it.) The bestowal of this beautiful gift (Mary Dunn, put your ticket away, and, Sally Harris, let her hair alone) awakened feelings akin to envy and bitterness in (Jane Sloper must not borrow her cousin's bonnet in Sunday-school) the bosoms of his perverted brethren. (Hugh Fraley will leave those strings at home, and, William Grove, stop climbing over the bench.) Alas! what sorrow can evil and disobedient sons, too little conscious (Dicky Taylor, bring that insect to me) of the sacrifices and prayerful struggles of their venerable parents (no, Henry, not another drink), call down upon their already care-burdened minds!"

Of course I felt sure that Miss Pepper was in earnest and meant to do good, but I suspected that she had not what my uncle called "a gift" with children, and I saw how much harder it made it for Bessie, who really was a natural teacher, and who contrived to rule with a steady but gracious firmness, and to win with a sweet simplicity that explained itself to the minds of little ones.

I wondered not a little at her infatuation on the Pepper question when I saw how contrary their ways and influence were. There were plenty of nice, interesting little girls among the two hundred, and some very well-behaved boys too; but Bessie set herself to win the unruly, and it was a lesson to thoughtless me to see her do it. One terrible little soul, with a thin, wiry body and tight-cropped head, fell into a conflict with a square-set, hard-faced boy, and they rolled under the seats together just as Miss Pepper had succeeded in raising the ill-used Joseph out of the pit with words of three syllables. Bessie went to the rescue, and separated and inverted the combatants, only the soles of whose boots had been visible a moment before. She sat down with them, and although I could not hear her words, I saw that they were slowly smoothing the angry creases of both the thin and the square face.

"Then let him stop a-callin' me 'Skinny,'" was the last outbreak of the injured lean one, and his antagonist confessed--

"I won't say nothin' to you no more if you stop grinning 'Flathead' at me."

Before Miss Pepper had succeeded in describing the paraphernalia of Eastern travel and the approach of the Ishmaelites, the two were induced to shake hands silently across their gentle mediatrix, whose face suddenly grew radiant with the sweetest blush I ever saw as the door opened and a new feature was added to the scene.

I do not mean to detract from the good impulses or high motives of my dear girl when I say that this was the key that opened the subject to me, and made it bright and plain. It wore the form of a truly good and good-looking young gentleman, who had just enough of the clergyman in his appearance to show that he honored his holy calling above all things. He gave Bessie a glance that set my heart at rest--for I naturally felt anxious that the blush and brightness and other signs should not be thrown away on an unappreciative object--and then he went right into his work. Oh dear! what a difference! One could not imagine, without seeing for one's self, what a beautiful sympathy could do with material that a hard, dry purpose could only irritate. Of course he bowed to me, and met Miss Pepper like an old friend, and then he began, and in beginning caught every single wandering mind, and held it with that mysterious fascination which individualizes, and convinces each one that he is the particular soul addressed.

He had been spending the hour of his absence from us in the chamber of a little fellow, one of our number, who had been terribly hurt by the machinery of a factory in which he worked. He took every one of us there with him, awakening our liveliest interest, and making us anxious to be helpful to every suffering fellow-creature. Some of us had to cry a little at the kind remembrances the poor crushed child sent us, and we felt quite self-reproachful that we had not thought more of him, and been quieter and more orderly in every way. Then, without any dry, hard preaching, he planted that lesson, left it to take root without digging it up again with personal exhortation, and told us something else. Surely no one could have better divined just what we wanted to know, and just how we would have liked it related. Love first of all; then cheerfulness, simplicity, and a strong, earnest enthusiasm that made attention compulsory and the attraction irresistible.

I do not believe I ever felt better satisfied in my life than when he closed and the orderly dismission began: then he turned to Bessie, and I saw that my friend had found the mission of heart-and soul-work, and was being drawn heavenward by the hand she loved. Such a timid tenderness as pervaded his every look and word! such a sweet consciousness as lighted hers! I laughed at my folly about Tom, and felt that I should be delighted to see him at Haines', and introduce him to the dear, good clergyman whom Bessie had the good sense to appreciate.

The Rev. Charles Pepper was the nephew of Miss Mary. I soon changed my prejudiced opinion of that lady into a clearer view of her merits. She was the Paul that planted: being a woman of wealth and strong religious bias, she had built the mission chapel, gathered together the children and taught them, while her good nephew added the superintendence of the school to his church duties in a different quarter.

"Bessie, does your father know--?" I began as we went homeward together.

She interrupted me: "About Miss Pepper? Oh yes, indeed! She called to ask his permission for me to teach them, and has been at our house twice since.

"You know I don't mean her at all," I said, laughing. "I mean her nephew, Bessie Haines."

But Bessie faltered: she had not the courage to speak freely, since it was evident they had not spoken so to each other yet. She knew she loved and was beloved, but could not force the delicate secret into words, since it was yet unavowed between them.

"All I am afraid of, Bess," said I, determined to make her practical, for she was as ethereal as if she and her love meant to live in the clouds all their days--"all I am afraid of is, that your father's vision may threaten your peace; for, rely on it, Bess, it is about you and you alone, or why should uncle keep praying for you as a 'young damsel,' and 'handmaiden,' and 'female pilgrim,' and all that?"

Bessie seemed troubled, but she could not be brought to confidence until the minister had opened his heart to her. I saw that, and though I had never had a warning dream in my life, I felt it was my mission to help her.

The Rev. Charles and I had had a little, a very little, talk, but I saw that Bessie had named me to him--that pleased me; that he was very desirous of gaining my good-will--that pleased me too. So I had happened to say that I admired church architecture, particularly Gothic: some one had said that his church belonged to that style, and he immediately, offered to take us to examine it. I asked him to call for us next day, and he delightedly promised that he would.

I told Bessie, and the ungrateful creature was alarmed and nervous, and gave way to all sorts of nonsense; but I consoled her and admired him in a way that seemed to give her satisfaction. The next morning I made a startling discovery.

I went into the little bookroom that opened out of the great old-fashioned back parlor, where uncle and Mr. Haines sat every morning with Scott and Clarke and Cruden open before them: I went in very quietly, and didn't make much noise when there. Mr. Haines was talking in a slow, set way, and I could hear the scratching of a pen over stiff paper.

"Would you mention my reasons for recording this, my dear Daniel?" he said to Uncle Pennyman.

"I have set them down at the commencement," said my uncle, who was acting as scribe. "I have said that, your mind being clear and your feelings at ease, you retired to your couch on the night of the 28th of October; that the form of your dear wife seemed waiting for you, since you became conscious of her presence immediately after your sinking asleep; and so on."

"Yes," said Mr. Haines, witty a deep sigh: "it is a great thing, no doubt, to be so guided in the visions of the night, and I have many times considered myself greatly favored by the knowledge of the ministry of my dear wife's blessed spirit; but, friend Daniel, if she had been a little more explicit in this instance it would have been a great comfort to me. Follow me now, friend Daniel. You have got it down to where she spoke. Well, she raised her hand and seemed to point to the couch of Dorcas Elizabeth" (that was what Bess had been baptized, and was called by her father on solemn occasions)--"my thoughts had been dwelling on the child, and her increasing age and future duties--and she said, 'Marry her wisely to Thomas,' and repeated the words three times."

I heard the scratching pen and Mr. Haines' depressed, uncertain sigh, and my own heart sank heavily. There was no Thomas to marry her to but our Tom, and such a thing was simply preposterous and wicked. I could not, I would not, bear even to think of it.

Oh, good Mrs. Haines, departed so long ago! why should you come back troubling us about such, things? and, above all, why could you not as well have said Charles as Thomas?

"I have that set down," said Uncle Pennyman. Mr. Haines sighed again in that anxious, uncertain way of his:

"During the first day after the visitation, Daniel, I could not recall whether my wife's appearance said, 'To Thomas, marry her wisely,' or as we now put it down;

but since you have set it clearly before me, and your son will so soon be here, I feel that I am justified in having it stated in that way, and that Providence is guiding me."

Oh how my heart rose against Uncle Pennyman as I listened! He was the one to blame for such a shameful, foolish notion stealing into Mr. Haines' head! Left to himself, any name would have suited him equally well, and here was Tom's thrust in without any earthly reason. It was really dreadful! I could scarcely stand on my feet when I remembered how Tom loved his adopted father, and with what unselfish devotion he always spoke of him. "If he's told that it will be a family blessing, he never will have the heart to deny them and grieve Uncle Pennyman. Poor Tom! he is so shockingly unselfish himself that he would rather enjoy a sacrifice than otherwise, I suppose." So ran my thoughts, and I grew desperate. Desperation awakens courage. Tom would be there in the evening, and if anything could be done it had to be done at once.

I slipped out silently as I came: no one heard me. I did not mean that they should do so, for, to confess the truth, I was listening on purpose. I dressed to go out with Mr. Pepper; so did Bessie, though I must say she was very nervous and uncertain about it. "You know papa does not know him in--in the character of a friend of mine," she said, hesitatingly. "Miss Pepper introduced him, and that is all."

"But that is no reason why it should be all," I said to myself, and paid no attention to her little bashful fussiness.

When he arrived, I saw in his eyes that he meant to take advantage of the opportunity I was making for him, and so I boldly carried out my plan. We started, and had gone a block or two when I discovered that they were becoming unaware of my existence and completely absorbed in each other. "Poor dears!" I thought, "let them have a still better chance." So I stopped in the most natural way possible at a window where trimmings were displayed, and began to stare at some ribbon. "The very shade!" I said: "I would not miss it for anything. Pray go on slowly, and I'll join you presently. Keep on till you reach the church--I know the way. And be sure you stay till I come. No, you shall not come in: I insist that you go right on, and do not bother. I have a sort of pride in making bargains, and they never can be made in company, you know." I laughed and wouldn't listen to their waiting, and managed it so well that they went away as unsuspecting and tender as two lambs. I waited till they were out of sight, and then I started straight for home.

I was in high glee till Mrs. Tanner came up stairs.

"There are great preparations making for Mr. Tom," said she with a portentous face. "Mr. Haines has given more orders about his reception than I ever knew him to issue before; and, what seems strange, he actually insists on my calling him Mr. Thomas, when I never can get my tongue round anything but Mr. Tom, in the world."

Both seemed threatening--the preparations and the name; and when Mrs. Tanner asked where Miss Bessie was, and heard that she had gone out, she shook her head and said that she was afraid her pa wouldn't like it. This convinced me that she too had guessed the nature of the vision, and made me more than ever anxious to save poor Bessie and Tom from mutual unhappiness. The first effort was made, and I must consider the next step. I felt nearly sure that by this time the two dear Sunday-school workers had become personal in their conversation, and taking up my position on the broad sofa in the quiet, shady back parlor, I set myself to thinking out the plan. It was a great, solidly-furnished old room, staid and handsome like the rest of the house, and meant for comfort in every particular. Over the mantelpiece, and directly opposite to me, was a life-size picture of Mrs. Haines, a very young lady with a mild shyness of expression and a great deal of flaxen hair. She had died when Bessie was a baby, and was altogether a more childlike and undecided person than her daughter. The wonder therefore was that she should have become so dictatorial in the visions of the night, and undertaken to control the family affairs after so many years, never having meddled with them while there was a living opportunity.

I was just thinking how useless it would be to appeal to Uncle Pennyman without--without saying something about Tom (and that under the circumstances could not be thought of: it made me burn all over merely to have it in my mind for a moment), when I became drowsy, and had not time to question the feeling until I was sound asleep.

A murmur of voices roused me, or perhaps I was going to wake at any rate, for they were singularly low, and the speakers quite unconscious of my presence. I looked up, and in the faint light coming between the bowed shutters and lace curtains I saw the Rev. Charles and Bessie directly under the portrait of Mrs. Haines.

He had thrown his arm around her, and, although she struggled just a little in the embrace, held her to his heart.

"Oh, I cannot believe it," she was saying: "it is like a dream. And Winnie too!-- to forget all about dear Winnie just because I am so happy. It is selfish and unkind, dear, I am afraid."

He told her I was too good, too lovable to quarrel with their bliss, and held her to his heart while he looked up to the flaxed-haired, baby-faced mother for a blessing with quite a glow of feeling on his face and real tears in his eyes.

There was something in mine I suppose, for when I looked too I could scarcely believe them: the portrait seemed to show a different face entirely. The blue eyes bent down on those upturned to meet them with a look I had never beheld in them before, and the delicate little pink mouth seemed to tremble with a blessing.

"Am I dreaming?" I almost asked it aloud, and the question and the sound of Uncle Pennyman's voice in the book-room gave me a new idea. Softly I slipped from my place and out at the open door, leaving the absorbed ones to themselves, and joined my uncle and Mr. Haines where they were preparing for another conflict with the commentators.

"I have had a dream," I said solemnly.

"A dream!" repeated they.

"Yes, and it was so lifelike that I must tell it to you, for I am convinced it is no common warning, but one full of meaning and truth."

They gazed at me blankly, and I went on, fearing to stop an instant lest I should lose my courage:

"I was lying on the sofa opposite Mrs. Haines' portrait--"

"The very place where I lay when last I dreamed," murmured her husband.

"And I saw Bessie and a gentleman hand in hand beneath it, looking up into the sweet face for a blessing; and oh such a heavenly smile lighted it while the beautiful lips seemed to murmur, 'She will marry wisely, dear Thomas!'"

Mr. Haines was so shaken by my words that my heart misgave me. He covered his face with his hands. "She used to call me dear Thomas," he said, and the tears ran through his fingers.

"Then the name was *yours*" said Uncle Pennyman with weighty consideration. "You remember I said it was capable of a double application: those things are wonderful, and interpret each other. Winnie, my dear girl, could you distinguish this person's face?"

Before I could answer, Mrs. Tanner at the door said, "Here's Mr. Tom, bless his heart! I never can learn to call him anything else."

Tom was *so* glad to see me! Yes, I may as well tell it, for it told itself: dear Tom never seemed so glad before.

"Was it his face, Winnie?" whispered Mr. Haines.

If ever *No* was said with energy and decision, it was in my reply. The parlor door opened just as we were about to go in all together, shaking hands and making kind speeches over Tom, and Bessie and the Rev. Charles appeared in the act of taking leave of each other.

"That's the face!" I cried dramatically; and then I really and truly did faint--stone dead, as Mrs. Tanner said afterward--for I was not used to telling lies, and even white ones were exciting things to tell, and scarcely justified themselves to my conscience by the magnitude of the good they were to do.

When I came to myself, Bessie was hanging over me with all the love she had left from Mr. Charles, I suppose; and I heard Mr. Haines and Uncle Pennyman talking with Tom, and trying to explain to him the remarkable nature of the vision that had overcome me. I sat up, and tried to laugh and declare that it was nothing at all, though my heart kept throbbing.

"You have all had dreams," said Tom: "you have yet to hear mine. Uncle, I dreamed that Winnie and I loved each other, and that I asked you for her and you said yes."

"No, Thomas," said Uncle Pennyman gravely, but with a kind of breaking about his mouth: "your eyes were open when you had that vision, and you must not jest with serious subjects. But it is well you mentioned it, dear boy, and it is well our child Winnie received such a remarkable direction, since it throws light on friend Haines' visitation, and apparently the happiness of that excellent young minister and our dear Bessie here."

"The young man has just expressed himself in corroboration of the vision," said Mr. Haines, much affected.

Bessie threw her arms round her father, then round me, and then she ran away. Mr. Haines and Uncle Pennyman went out to their commentaries, Mrs. Tanner to see to her buns: Tom and I were alone.

"What is this about, Winnie darling?" he said.

"Tom," said I, "we are all the victims of dreams."

MARGARET HOSMER.

The Cold Hand.

There is a rocky hill in what was till recently the town of Dorchester, looking out over Boston Bay. It takes its name from the stiff black savins with which it is covered, and which contrive to find nourishment and support in the rock to which they cling. Some of these trees show their great age by their gnarled and knotted trunks and boughs. Black and impassive they stand, alike in the brightest summer or the grayest winter, sighing restlessly in the breeze, but wailing piteously when the sea-winds sweep over the hill. Partway up the little rocky eminence stands an old house, now fast falling to pieces. It is a low building, with a gambrel roof and a huge chimney. It has stood there many years, for it was built not long after the Revolution, and it might have stood many years more had it not been suffered to go to decay with a carelessness which seemed to belie the general thrift of the town.

Wandering over the hill one bright winter day, with no companion but a large dog, I stopped to look in at the window of the old house. The glass was gone from the sash, and the sash itself was broken in many places; but the obscurity was so deep within that I obtained only a partial glimpse of an interior which to my fancy had a peculiarly deserted and eerie look. I felt a desire to explore the place, attracted rather than repelled by its forlorn look of falling age; for I came from a part of the country where the most ancient relic dates back only forty years, and the aspect of everything old and quaint in the place had a charm for me which I suspect it offers to few of the natives. The front door was locked, but I obtained an entrance without difficulty at the back, and made my way through a little shed, which was evidently of more modern construction than the main part of the building. I came first into the kitchen, where was a large fireplace blackened with the smoke of long-dead fires, and a narrow, high mantelpiece. A little cupboard was let into the side of the great chimney, which projected far across the floor. The room was long and narrow, running the whole length of the house, with a window at each end. The blackened plaster was dropping from the walls and ceiling, exposing in some places the heavy beams, and the floor was dark and discolored with age and dust, although quite firm to the tread. By a low door I passed into a small room lighted by two windows--one in front, the other at the end of the house, and presenting the same appearance of desolate decay. There were four doors in this room--the one through which I had just entered, another leading to the rooms above, a third, secured by a bolt, which I did not then open, and a fourth leading into a narrow passage, in which was the locked front door. I crossed this passage, and found myself in a room of the same size as the one I had just left. It was that into which I had attempted to look from the outside. Here I missed the dog, who had hitherto followed me, though with seeming reluctance, and no persuasion could induce him to cross the threshold. This room was in rather better repair than were the other two. There was the same high mantelpiece, rather less narrow, and the same little cupboard let into the massive chimney. The floor was less discolored, but there was a deep burnt spot on it near the fireplace, as if some one had dropped a shovelful of hot coals, or rather as if some corrosive fluid had been spilled. I remained here a few moments, idly wondering what might have been the history of the former tenants, and what could have induced any one to build a house in a spot so bleak and exposed, where scarcely a pretence of soil offered itself for a garden. As I stood there, a singular impression came upon me that I was not alone. For a moment, and a moment only, I became conscious of another presence in the room. The impression passed as suddenly as it had come, but, transient as it was, it awoke me from my reverie. Smiling at myself for the fancy, I recrossed the passage and ascended the steep, narrow winding stairs to the chambers above. There were four small rooms, opening one into the other, with a closet partitioned off in each, and so low that in the highest part a tall man could but just have stood upright. Here the ruin was farther advanced. The floor creaked under my foot, the plaster had nearly all fallen from the ceiling and was peeling from the walls, while deep stains on the remaining portion showed that the rain and thawing snow had made their way through the roof. The place had a lonesome, forlorn look, even more than usually belongs to a deserted house, though such might not have been its aspect to other than my unaccustomed Western eyes.

Turning, I made my way down the short staircase, and was about to leave the house when the third door, as yet unopened, caught my eye. I drew with some difficulty the rusted bolt, and found myself at the head of a steep flight of stairs, seemingly longer than that which I had just descended. It led to the cellar, and though the afternoon was getting on, I thought I would finish my exploration, and therefore went down, though repelled by the close and peculiarly damp air. The cellar was blasted and hewn in the solid rock to a depth which, considering the extreme hardness of the stone, seemed remarkable in a house so unpretending. A dim light made its way through a narrow window at each end and fell upon the stone floor. I walked forward, looking up at the windows, but I had not taken ten steps before I recoiled with a start. At my feet lay a pit, seemingly of considerable depth, and filled with water to within four feet of the top. The cellar did not lie under the kitchen, but only under the two front rooms and the passage, and this pit occupied the whole length and fully half the breadth of the space of the rooms above, and, what was more peculiar, seemed to extend even farther forward than the house itself. Another step, and I should have fallen into it. Curious to try its depth, I picked up a little fragment of stone and dropped it in. As the stone touched the water, and the circles on the sullen surface began to widen, a current of air rushed down the stairs, and the door above shut violently. At that moment the impression which I had experienced in the room above came back upon me with tenfold distinctness, and was accompanied with a feeling of exceeding horror. It seemed as if there was closing around me some evil influence, from which I could only escape by instant flight. For one moment I resisted the unreasonable terror, and made an attempt to explain, or at least analyze, a sensation so unwonted: the next, the loathing dread grew too strong. I turned and hurried across the damp floor, up the narrow stairs, and, opening the door, made my way as quickly as possible into the outside air. The dog was waiting for me in the little shed, and seemed delighted at seeing me again. I closed the door, ashamed of my senseless fright, but nevertheless I was thankful that I had found no trouble in getting out. I am not quite prepared to say, however, that these sudden and apparently unreasonable starts are independent of external causes. The Vermont-bred horse will be thrown into an agony of fright when the closed cage of a lion passes by, though he has never learned by experience that lions will kill horses, and though the lion himself is unseen.

I walked briskly home. I had some distance to go, and had quite lost the impression of my ghostly terror when I reached the house where I was staying, a modern shingle Gothic erection, which in vain endeavored to disguise its barny appearance with sundry wooden adornments modeled after crochet-work.

"Freda," said I to my friend after tea, when she and I were sitting comfortably by the fire in the library, "do you know anything about the old yellow-gray house up on the hill?"

"Why, what of it?"

"Nothing, only I went into it to-day. What is its history?"

"Nothing particular. It was built for a Doctor Haywood. Have you read Alp's last essay on the Semi-occasional?"

"Yes, and great stuff it is."

Freda looked inexpressibly shocked. I had better have condemned law and gospel together than made light of Alp; but she put up with it, probably considering it excusable as the utterance of a savage from the wilds of New York.

"Never mind him now. He shall proclaim his figs in the name of the Prophet for all time if you will tell me about the old house. I know it has a story."

She rose and took from the drawer an old manuscript volume, which she placed in my hands. It was a little note-book, in which the entries were made not from day to day, but at irregular intervals, in a singularly clear, precise hand:

"Nov. 3, 1784. This day my neighbor Ball's cow, getting out of the pasture and running on the highway, was put in the pound. Took her out, and cautioned my neighbor to have more care of the creature. *Mem.:* To bespeak a pair of shoes for her eldest girl.

"Jan. 1, 1785. This day the wind very high.

"Jan. 10. Neighbor Ball's cow, getting among my wife's rosebushes, did do some damage, whereat she was much vexed. Caught the said cow, and begged my neighbor to keep her at home, which she promised to do, but in an hour back again. However, she is a widow.

"Jan. 13. Doctor Haywood, newly come to this place from the old country, has taken lodging with Neighbor Ball. Said to be a learned man--has much baggage, and they say some curious machines. Is curious about plants and the like. Neighbor Ball did hint to my wife that he knew about matters better let alone, whereat my wife did tell her that she wished he would give her a charm to keep her cow out of our yard.

"Jan. 15. Dr. Haywood has bought a lot on the hill, and is to build upon it. Has spoken to me about it. Have drawn the plan, and shall make the estimate.

"Feb. 1. Doctor Haywood hurries on the work--says he is in haste to get into his own house. Saw Indian Will to-day, quite drunk. With much trouble got him to our house, where my wife did let him lie in the kitchen all night. Had she not done so, the poor man might have frozen to death before morning, for it was a very cold night. Argued with him in the morning, whereat he promised amendment.

"Feb. 10. My daughter Faithful this day, with my consent, promised herself to John Clark, skipper of the Federalist schooner.

"Feb. 18. Blasting out the cellar for Haywood's house. He wants it more than common deep--says it makes the house warm.

"Feb. 21. Came this day upon a great hollow in the rock filled with water, which ran in as soon as pumped but. The doctor much displeased at first--talked of beginning over again, but finally contented himself.

"June 3. Doctor Haywood moved into his house this day. Has much curious stuff. The minister says he is a chemist.

"June 8. Went up to the doctor's house to settle with him. He came to the door and said he was too busy then, but would drop round soon. They say he lets no one inside the place since he moved. Has taken a pew in the meeting-house, and comes once of a Sabbath.

"July 22. Doctor Haywood and me did settle accounts. He beat everything down to the last penny--offered to pay part in attendance on my family if sick. Did not care to settle that way, knowing his charges. Charged James Sumner five dollars for one visit to his child, which child, nevertheless, he did greatly help.

"August 18. News came this day that the Federalist went down in the gale of the tenth, off Marblehead, with all on board. A sore affliction to my daughter Faithful. The Lord's will be done!

"August 26. Neighbor Ball's eldest girl gets lower. Doctor Cray does no good. She would call in Doctor Haywood if she dared, but his charges are so high. James

Sumner and me did consult together and agree to take the charges between us. I have heard say that he has helped several poor people free: did especially help Indian Will when he lay like to die of pleurisy at Neponset Village.

"Sept. 1. Neighbor Ball, going up the hill last night to call Doctor Haywood to her daughter Hepsey, did tell my wife that she had a look into the south room as he opened the door, and that there were queer things there, such as a brick furnace, all red with fire; and she did say, too, that she saw things like snakes, only thin like mist, twisting about in the air by the firelight, which I do hold to be her own invention or mere foolish notions.

"Sept. 2. Doctor Haywood has helped Hepsey Ball some considerable, though he says he cannot cure her, for she has consumption.

"Sept. 16. Doctor Haywood told James Sumner and me that he would ask nothing for attending Hepsey Ball, but would keep on to ease her what he could as long as she lived. He told my wife she might last a year.

"Nov. 3. Jonathan Phelps told me that Doctor Haywood had borrowed one hundred dollars of him, giving security on the house and lot.

"Nov. 8. James Sumner this day, his wife being dead a year, did ask my daughter Sophonisba to marry him, the which she did refuse, and snapped him off too short. Then he spoke to Faithful, and she burst out crying and ran up stairs, and could by no means be got to listen. Recommended James to Hannah Gardner.

"Nov. 16. Doctor Hay wood this day borrowed fifty dollars of me. If he had not been so considerate to Widow Ball should not have felt like letting it go.

"Dec. 16. Coming home from Boston last night, overtook Indian Will. He showed me a big iron tobacco-box nearly full of money--silver, with two gold-pieces, one a Spanish piece, the other an English half guinea. He got it for a lot of deer-skins in Boston. Begged him not to drink it all up, which he said he would not do, but would give it to his squaw. Did ask him to come home with me, which he refused, as he meant to go on to Neponset Village.

"Dec. 17. The wind blowing these two days to the land made it very high water, coming nearly up to Governor Stoughton's elm, and covering the road.

"Dec. 18. A great gale last night--much damage at sea, doubtless. The water very high.

"Dec. 19. Two men out in a boat found an old hat and blanket floating by the Point, said to belong to Indian Will: no one has seen him since the 16th. Likely he went to the tavern and got drunk, so missed his way and was drowned by the tide.

"Dec. 20, Last night Indian Will's body came ashore, much beaten by the rocks, but known to be his by those who knew him. The verdict was, 'Drowned by the tide.'

"Feb. 11, 1786. Doctor Haywood spent the evening at our house. He has been more social of late, going a good deal among people, especially poor people, to help them. Has never paid me the fifty dollars, but makes promises. I was led on to speak of Indian Will. The doctor said the night of the 16th he thought he heard some one cry out, but thought it some drunken person, and besides was busy with his studies, and so did not mind. My wife asked him what he studied. He said a good many different matters, but that he had given it all up now, and meant to practice. Shortly after jumped up and went away very sudden."

Here the journal came to an abrupt end. The rest of the book was filled with accounts relating to the business of a milliner and dressmaker. Slipped in between its leaves were two letters, written in a cramped, scratchy hand and rather irregular in spelling. They were directed to Sophonisba T----, Salem, Massachusetts, and seemed to be from a mother to her daughter:

"DORCHESTER, May 1, 1786.

"My Dear Child: I take my pen in hand to let you knew that we are all in good health, and hope you are enjoying the same blessing. James Sumner is married to Hannah Gardner. Most people think she will have her hands full with his children. Parson H---- married them. She wore a blue silk at two dollars the yard. Hepsey Ball is dead. She departed this life on the 29th of April, at half-past eight in the evening, being quite resigned and in good hope of her election to grace. She had not much pain at the last. Doctor Haywood called to see her in the morning, and she being then, as we thought, asleep, did start up and cry out that there was a black shadow, not his own, always following after him, which made me think her light-headed; but her mother says the doctor turned as

pale as a sheet, and made as if to go off again. Your sister Faithful is
at Mr. Trueman's, helping to make up Lorenda's wedding-clothes. I would
not have had her go, but she seemed willing to undertake it. Your loving
mother, ANNA T----."

The second was also addressed to Sophonisba, who on the 3d of June was yet
visiting friends in Salem. After a few details of domestic news, it went on:

"Doctor Haywood is missing: no one knows where he is gone. He has been
looked for in Boston, but they have found no news of him; only that a
little black boy says he saw a man like him go on board a ship bound for
the East Indies. Now he is gone, they find he owes money to a great many
besides your father. He owes to people in Boston for drugs and
medicines--some, it is said, very costly, and sent for express to the
old country. Mr. Sewell, the bookseller there, says he tried to dispose
of his books to him; and when he did not buy them, thinks he sent them
to the old country. He owes every one he could get to trust him. It is
odd what he did with all the money. It is thought Jonathan Phelps will
get the house. They went up to it and found the door unlocked. They
found nothing in the house but the furniture, and that very common and
cheap. There were none of all those things they said he had; only in the
south room a lot of bottles and jars, and a brick place built up with a
vent outside, which Parson H---- says is a furnace such as folks use
that study chemistry. There was a great heap of ashes in the fireplace,
as if he had burned papers or books there, and a great burned spot on
the floor right before it."

"Who was the writer of these?" I asked as I refolded the little old letter, "and
what became of Doctor Haywood? Was nothing more heard?"
In answer to these questions my friend gave the following narration.
The writer of the journal was my great uncle, Silas T----. Sophonisba and Faith-
ful were my mother's cousins. Both were much older than she, but I have often seen
Faithful when I was a girl, and I had all the story there is from herself. The little

house on the hill fell into the hands of the chief creditor, who took down the furnace in the south room and offered the place to rent, but no tenant ever remained there long, either because of the bleak situation or the want of a garden. There were rumors that the place was not quite canny. One woman, indeed, went so far as to declare that she had seen the doctor's figure, dim and unsubstantial, standing before the fireplace in the twilight, and that once, as she came up the cellar stairs, something followed her and laid a cold hand on her shoulder; but as she was a nervous, hysterical person, and moreover was known to be somewhat given to exaggeration, no one paid much attention to her tale.

It was certain, however, that there was a great deal of sickness in the house. One family who rented the place lost three children by fever in one summer, and it was remarkable that all three seemed to fall under the same delusion, and insisted that something or some one, coming behind them, laid upon their shoulders a cold hand. One of them, toward the last, said that a shadow kept moving to and fro in the room, and kept the sunshine all away. The woman who had seen the vision of the old doctor became a widow the next month, and so much sickness and death took place in the house that at last no one would live there, and it was shut up by its owner.

In due course of time the father and mother of Sophonisba and Faithful were laid in Dorchester burial-ground. Mr. T---- had never been a rich man by any means, and when he died there was little left for the two girls, even after the sale of the homestead. They did not, however, consider themselves poor, but with their fifteen hundred dollars in the bank and their trade of milliner and dressmaker thought themselves very well to do in the world. Sophonisba, the elder, was at that time a little under fifty--an energetic, hard-working woman, with a constitution of wrought iron and bend leather, and no more under the influence of what are called "nerves" than if they had been left out of her system entirely. If ever a woman was born into this world an old maid, it was Sophonisba T----. Her fine name was the only romantic thing about her. She had had more than one offer of marriage in her day, but she had no talent for matrimony, and had turned such a very cold shoulder on her admirers that the swains became dispirited, and betook themselves to the courtship of more impressible damsels. There was no hidden romance or tale of unreturned affection in Miss Sophonisba's experience. The simple fact was, she had never wished to be married. Miss Faithful was five years her sister's junior. She had never found room in her heart for a second love since John Clark went down in the Federalist. She had been a young and pretty girl then, and now she was a thin, silent, rather nervous little body, depending entirely upon her sister with a helpless kind of affection that was returned on Miss Sophonisba's part by a devotion which might almost be called passionate.

"I tell you what it is, Faithful," said Miss Sophonisba one evening, as they sat over their tea, "if they raise the rent on us here, I won't stay."

The sisters had lived in the house ever since the death of their mother, five years before. Their business had prospered, and they were conveniently situated, but, for all that, Miss Sophonisba had no mind to pay additional rent.

"No?" said Faithful, inquiringly.

"That I won't! We pay all it's worth now, and more too. It ain't the extra four shillings," said Miss Sophonisba, rubbing her spectacles in irritation, "but I do hate to be imposed upon."

"It will be some trouble to find a new place," suggested Miss Faithful meekly, "and we can afford it, I suppose."

"I don't care if we can afford it a dozen times over," said her sister, with increased decision. "I won't be imposed upon. If I've got either to drive or be driven, I'd rather drive."

"Of course," said Miss Faithful, who had never driven any living creature in the whole course of her life.

"I saw Peter Phelps to-day," said Miss Sophonisba, "and he says he'll let us have the old house up on the hill for anything we like to give."

Miss Faithful gave a little start: "Would you like to live there, Sophonisba?"

"Why, it's a good convenient situation, and plenty big enough for you and me and the cat."

"But you know," said Miss Faithful, timidly, "they have told such queer stories about it." "Stuff and nonsense!" said Miss Sophonisba. "You don't believe them, I hope?"

"No," hesitated her sister, "but then one remembers them, you know. Widow Eldridge always said she saw old Doctor Haywood there."

"Stuff and nonsense!" said Miss Sophonisba again. "You know perfectly well you couldn't trust a word she said about anything."

"Oh, Sophonisba, she's dead!" said Miss Faithful, shocked.

"I can't help that, child. It don't hinder her having told fibs all her lifetime."

"Her husband died the next month."

"Well, so he might anywhere. My wonder is he lived as long as he did, considering."

"And Mrs. Jones's three children died there."

"Well, and didn't Mrs. Gardner lose her two and that brother of hers? and I never heard their place was haunted; and didn't two die out of the Trueman house? and ever so many more all over town? It was a dreadful sickly summer."

"And Sarah Jane McClean was taken sick there with fever."

"Well, they had dirt enough to account for anything. Doctor Brown told me himself that they had a great heap of potatoes sprouted in the cellar, and there ain't anything so bad as that."

The last vestige of a ghost was demolished: Miss Faithful had nothing more to say.

"It's nigh twenty-five years since the old doctor went off," said Miss Sophonisba. "It ain't very probable he's alive now; and if he is, he won't be very apt to come back: and if he is dead, he certainly won't. If he did, I'd like to ask him why he never paid father that fifty dollars. I saw Peter Phelps to-day, and he says he'll fix the place all up for us if we'll have it, but of course I wouldn't say anything about it till I'd spoken to you."

"Just as you please, Sophonisba," said Miss Faithful.

"He says he'll give us a bit of ground down on the flat for a garden, and let his man dig it up for us. I went up and looked at the house. It ain't so much out of repair as you'd think."

"Did you see the burnt spot on the floor?" asked Miss Faithful with some interest.

"Yes, I saw it--a great blackened place. Most likely he spilled some of his chemical stuff on it."

Miss Sophonisba was not, as she expressed herself, one to let the grass grow under her feet. She concluded the bargain for the house next day, and informed their landlord--who, by the by, was a son of their old neighbor, Widow Ball--of their intention to move. That gentleman was not at all pleased at the idea of losing his tenants. In vain he offered to recede from the obnoxious demand of four shillings more. Miss Sophonisba told him that she had made up her mind, and that *she* wasn't in the habit of going back from her bargains when she had given her word, whatever other people might be.

"Well, Miss T----," said Mr. Ball, "I hope you won't repent. They've said queer things about that house ever since the old doctor went off so mysterious. Some folks said he drowned himself in that place in the cellar."

"Stuff and nonsense!" said Miss Sophonisba. "The old doctor never hurt any one when he was alive, except by borrowing money of them, and it ain't likely he'll want to do that now that he's dead; and if he did, I shouldn't let him have it."

"Well, my mother was in the house when Miss Eldridge came running up the stairs as pale as a sheet, and said he came behind her and caught hold of her shoulder."

"Joanna Eldridge was always a poor, miserable, shiftless, narvy thing," said Miss Sophonisba, "and half the time you couldn't believe a word she said."

"Well she was a connexion of our'n, Miss T----, and I always thought there was something in it. Narves won't account for everything."

"Well, I never trusted her a bit more for that," said Miss Sophonisba. "I know one time she told mother a long story about how you sent in a bill for shoes to Widow Sumner that James had paid you before he died, and she said you'd have made her a deal of trouble if she hadn't ha' found the receipt. A good many folks talked about it, but I always said it was just one of Joanna's stories."

Mr. Ball was put down, and took his leave.

As soon as the necessary repairs were finished the sisters moved into the house, and during that summer found reason to congratulate themselves on their change of abode. The high, airy situation was very pleasant in warm weather, and the view over the waters of the bay across to Boston and far out to sea, with the coming and departing ships, afforded much pleasure and a subject of conversation to the sisters. Their little garden on the flat throve well, and was a source of never-ending interest. They had been troubled by no ghostly visitations. Miss Sophonisba had indeed once heard a mysterious noise in the cellar, but on going down stairs she found that the cat had jumped on the hanging shelf and was helping herself out of the milk-pan.

The sisters were sitting one day toward the end of November--I think it was the twenty-fifth--in the north room, which they had made their work-room. The south room, according to the custom of our ancestors, still religiously preserved among us, was shut up "for company." The kitchen served them also for dining-room, and the largest room up stairs was their bed-chamber. Miss Sophonisba was trimming a bonnet, a task for which she had an especial gift. Ladies came to her even from Boston, saying that her work had an air and style quite its own, while her charges were not nearly so high as those of the more fashionable milliners in the city. Faithful was altering a dress of her own. Both were much engaged with their work, and neither had spoken for some time. Suddenly, Faithful started slightly, and the needle dropped from her hand.

"What's the matter?" asked her sister.

"Nothing," said Faithful, rather confused.

"Yes, there is," said Miss Sophonisba. "People don't jump that way for nothing. What is it?"

"Oh, I don't know," hesitated Miss Faithful. "I guess I pricked my finger."

"Umph!" said Miss Sophonisba in a very incredulous way, but she pushed her inquiries no farther.

As soon as her sister was silent, Miss Faithful's conscience began to chide her for her little evasion. Twice she opened her mouth to speak, and as often checked herself, but the third time the words were uttered: "If I tell you, Sophonisba, you will laugh at me."

"Well, that wouldn't kill you, child."

"No; but--well--it was only that I thought all of a sudden some one was standing behind my chair."

"How could you think so when there was no one there?"

"I don't know, but it felt as if there was."

"Nonsense, Faithful! If you didn't see any one, how did you know there was any one? Have you got eyes in the back of your head?"

"I didn't see it--I sort of felt so."

"'Sort of felt so!'" said Miss Sophonisba, with good-natured contempt. "If I was you, I'd take some catnip tea when I went to bed: you're kind of narvy."

Miss Faithful assented, and went on quietly with her sewing, but she changed the seat which she had occupied, with her back to the cellar door, for one close to her sister.

No further disturbance occurred till the middle of December. It had been a very windy day. The bay was tossing in long gray-green lines of waves crested with flying foam. The black savins sighed and wailed as they bent to the cutting blast. The wind was east, and it took a good deal of fire to keep the old house warm, but wood was cheap in those days, and Miss Sophonisba, though prudent and economical, was not given to what New England expressively calls "skrimping."

Miss Faithful, not feeling very well, had gone up stairs to bed soon after tea. A windy day always made her uncomfortable, recalling, too vividly perhaps, the gale in which the Federalist had gone down. Miss Sophonisba, having some work on hand which she was anxious to finish, was sitting up rather beyond her usual hour. Pausing for a moment in her sewing, she heard some one walking about in the room above her to and fro, with a regular though light step, as of bare or thinly-shod feet, on the boards.

"Why, what can ail the child," she said to herself, "to be walking about barefoot this time of night? She'll get her death of cold;" and she put down her work and went up stairs, intending to administer a sisterly lecture. To her surprise, Faithful was fast asleep in bed, and no other living creature was in the room. It could not have been the cat this time, for Puss was comfortably purring before the fire down stairs. Miss Sophonisba stood by the bed for a moment, candle in hand, listening for a repetition of the sound.

Suddenly a wilder gust shook the house perceptibly. Miss Faithful started from her sleep with a cry of terror. "Oh, I have had such a dream!" said she, clinging to her sister.

"What was it?" said Miss Sophonisba, soothing and quieting her like a child.

"I thought I was lying in bed just as I was, when all of a sudden I knew that Something had come in, and was going up and down, up and down the room."

"What was it like?" asked her sister, rather impressed in spite of herself.

"I couldn't see: it was all shifty and mist-like--like the shadow of smoke on the ground--and I couldn't tell if it was like a human being or not; but it seemed to me as if I ought to know it and what it was, and as if it was trying to make me understand something, and couldn't, just as it is when the cat sits and looks at you. You know the creature wants something, if she could tell what it was."

"She wants something out of the cupboard most generally," said Miss Sophonisba; "but go on."

"And finally," said Miss Faithful with a nervous shudder, "after it had gone back and forth two or three times--and I could hear it on the floor too, just like some one walking in their stocking-feet--it came close up to me and seemed to bend over me, or to be all around me in the air some way--I can't tell you how--and I was dreadfully scared, and woke up."

"It made a noise, did it?" said Miss Sophonisba.

"Yes; and somehow the noise made me feel as if I ought to know what it wanted and what it was."

"It was the wind," said Miss Sophonisba. "It got mixed up in your dreams, I expect. How it does blow!--fit to take the roof off. There! the cellar door has started open. That latch doesn't catch: I must go down and bolt it."

At that moment the cat rushed up the short staircase from the lower room, and springing on the bed, stood with bristling tail and glaring eyes, intently watching the door.

"Has she got a fit?" exclaimed Miss Sophonisba; and she put out her hand to push the cat off, but it turned to Miss Faithful, who was sitting up in bed, and crawling under the bed-clothes, lay there trembling and mewing in a very curious fashion.

"Some one has got in down stairs," said Miss Faithful, turning white. "Oh, Sophonisba, we shall all be murdered!"

"Nonsense!" said Miss Sophonisba, quite restored to herself at the thought of actual danger. She caught up a great pair of tongs and started down stairs, the candlestick in one hand, the tongs in the other, Miss Faithful, who dared not stay behind, threw a shawl over her night-dress and followed close at her sister's heels, while the cat crawled still farther under the clothes, and refused to answer to Miss Sophonisba's call. There was nothing unusual down stairs. The two outside doors were locked, the fire was burning brightly, and Miss Sophonisba's work lay on the table just as she had left it. The cellar door indeed, which latched imperfectly, stood open.

"Some one has come in and locked the door after them, and gone down cellar," was Miss Faithful's whispered suggestion.

"How could they?" said Miss Sophonisba. "We didn't hear any one; and besides, they would have left their tracks on the floor this wet night; but I'll go down and look. You stay here by the fire."

But Miss Faithful preferred to follow her sister. They found nothing out of place in the cellar, into which, if you remember, there is no outside door. Every tub and barrel and milk-pan was in its place, and the surface of the pit of water, which served the family as a cistern, was undisturbed.

"It must have been the door flying open that scared the cat," said Miss Sophonisba, "Faithful, you're as white as a sheet. I shall just heat up some elderberry wine and make you drink it;" which she did then and there, and, no further disturbance taking place, the sisters went to bed. The cat, however, whose usual place was by the kitchen fire, would not go down stairs, and when at last turned out, she mewed so piteously and scratched so persistently at the bed-room door that Miss Sophonisba gave way to her and let her in to sleep all night at the foot of the bed.

No further annoyance took place, nor was Miss Faithful troubled with a repetition of her curious dream. The next week, however, as Miss Sophonisba was in the kitchen making preparations for tea, she was startled by a scream from her sister in the next room, succeeded by the sound of a heavy fall. She hurried into the workroom. Miss Faithful lay on the floor quite insensible. It was some time before her sister's anxious exertions were rewarded by signs of returning animation. When at last she opened her eyes, she burst into a fit of hysterical sobbing and crying.

"For gracious sake, sister!" said Miss Sophonisba, really alarmed, "what is the matter?"

"Oh dear! oh dear!" sobbed Miss Faithful. "It was John! I know it was John, and I could not speak to him!"

"What?" said Miss Sophonisba, alarmed for her sister's wits. "What was John?"

"It--that--the thing that came behind me: I know it was!"

"When?" asked her sister.

"As I was sitting there in my chair something came behind me and put a hand on my shoulder. It was John--I know it was. His hand was all cold and wet: he came out of the sea to call me."

"Now just look here, Faithful!" said Miss Sophonisba. "John was one of the most careful, considerate fellows I ever knew, and he was always particular careful of you. Do you think it's likely he wouldn't have no more sense, now that he's a saint in heaven, than to come scaring you out of your wits in that way? Is it like him, now?"

"But oh, sister, if you had felt it as I did, clear into the bone!"

"Then it's over twenty-five years since the Federalist was lost. Do you suppose he's been going round the other world all this while without getting a chance to be dry? Did you see him?"

"No, but I felt it."

"Well, now if there'd been anything real there, anything material, you'd have seen it; and if it wasn't material, how could it be wet?"

Faithful was not prepared to answer, but it was evident that she had received a great shock. In vain did her sister argue, reason and coax. She could not explain, but that something had come behind her, and that this Something had touched her, she was convinced; and she added: "I do believe it was John I saw the other night. I thought then I was awake all the time, and now I know I was."

This last assertion quite overset Miss Sophonisba's patience, "If ever any one was asleep," she said, "you were when I came up stairs. I thought I heard you walking about with your bare feet, and I came up to see."

"Then you: heard it too?" said Miss Faithful, eagerly.

It was an unlucky admission, but Miss Sophonisba would not allow that she had made it.

"I heard the wind make the boards creak, I suppose; and do you think John wouldn't have more sense than to be walking about our room at half-past ten at night? What nonsense!"

"You may call it nonsense as much as you like, Sophonisba," said Miss Faithful, beginning to cry afresh, "but I know what I know, and I can't help it."

"Well, well, dear, we won't think of it any more. You're nervous and worried, and you'd just best put on your wrapper and lie down and try to go to sleep."

"I don't like to stay alone just now," said Miss Faithful, timidly.

"I don't want you to: I'll bring my work up stairs and stay with you."

Miss Sophonisba helped her sister up stairs, and began to assist her to undress.

As she took into her hand the cape of Miss Faithful's woolen dress she nearly uttered an exclamation of surprise, but checked herself in time. On the left shoulder was a wet spot, and the dress directly beneath was quite damp. Miss Sophonisba said nothing, of this matter to her sister, but she made an excuse to leave the room for a moment, and going down stairs looked to see if any water had been spilled on the floor. There was none, and Miss Sophonisba was puzzled. She remembered that when her sister was startled before she had occupied the same seat, with her back to the cellar door. She noticed that the door was slightly ajar, and it occurred to her that the cold air blowing through the crack might account for her sister's feeling of sudden chill, if not for the dampness. She went down the cellar stairs, carrying with her a lighted candle. Bold as she was, a singular sensation came over her when she saw upon each stair a print, as if some one with wet feet had ascended or descended, and that very recently. The track was not such as would be left by a person heavily shod: it was rather like that of one wearing a stocking or thin slipper.

"What under the sun--" was her perplexed exclamation as she went down, following the marks of the unknown feet until they were lost on the stone floor. It was certain that there was no one in the cellar, but as she went up again, and paused for a moment at the top of the staircase, she heard, or thought she heard, close to her ear, a long, weary sigh, as of one in pain, and a sudden breath of cold air swept past her down the stairs. She turned, and crossing the little passage went into the south room. The burned spot on the floor was covered by the neat rag carpet, but there were still some slight marks on the wall of the old doctor's brick furnace. Miss Sophonisba glanced round the room, but her eyes fell upon nothing but the familiar and well-preserved furniture; yet there came over her a strange sense that she was not alone. She saw nothing, but in spite of herself a feeling of a Presence not her own gathered about her. It was but for a moment, and then her habitual firmness and common sense reasserted themselves.

"Stuff and nonsense!" she said. "I am getting as bad as Faithful;" and leaving the room, she went back to her sister. Miss Faithful had sought comfort in her devotions, and was more composed than could have been expected. Neither felt inclined to comment on the recent disturbance. Miss Faithful's health seemed to have received no permanent harm from the sudden shock she had undergone, but she had a nervous dread of being alone, which was a source of some inconvenience to her sister.

The month of December passed, and the uncomfortable impression left by Faithful's attack was beginning to fade away from the minds of both, when it happened that the disturbance was renewed in a singular manner.

Miss Sophonisba was alone, her sister having gone to a household in the village to take the measure for some mourning garments to be made up immediately. Miss Sophonisba was busy with a black bonnet intended for a member of the same family, and was thinking of nothing but the folds of the material directly under her fingers. Gradually there came over her a feeling that she was not alone. She struggled against it, and resolutely bent her mind on her work; but the impression grew upon her, and with it a sensation of horror such as she had never before experienced. The idea that something stood behind her became so strong that she raised her eyes from her work and looked around. Was there anything actually there, or was the shapeless darkness anything more than an accidental shadow? Another instant, and something touched her cheek--something like soft, cold, moist fingers. The touch, if such it was, was very gentle, such as a child might give to attract attention. Miss Sophonisba would not give way. She took up her work and went quietly on with it, though her fingers trembled. The same long sigh fell upon her ear, the same chill breath of air swept past her, and the Presence, if such it was, was gone, and with it the shadow.

"Well," said Miss Sophonisba to herself, "some things *are* kind of curious, after all!"

There had certainly been no living creature in the house but herself, for their cat had disappeared some days before, and the loss of their favorite had been a great vexation to both sisters. The shadow behind her chair, if indeed it had been anything but fancy, had been too indistinct to allow her to say that she had really seen it before it had vanished, but what had given her the touch, the recollection of which yet caused a shiver? She put up her hand to her cheek. The place was wet--an actual drop of water adhered to her finger.

"Dear me!" said she, "I wish I did know what to think."

To one of her temperament the uncertainty was very annoying. She could not bear to think that her experience was not directly owing to natural--by which she meant, common--causes. "I am very glad Faithful was not here," she thought as she turned to her work again. She would not indulge herself by changing her seat, but kept her place with her back to the cellar door, though she could not help now and then casting a glance over her shoulder. Neither shadow nor substance, however, made itself manifest.

That same night Miss Sophonisba woke from her sleep with the feeling that some one had called her. She found herself mistaken, however, and lay quietly awake, thinking over the events of the afternoon. The more she thought the more puzzled, and even provoked, did she become. She was one of those people who cannot bear to feel themselves incapable of accounting for anything that is brought under their notice. A mystery, as such, is an exasperation to them, and they will sometimes adopt an explanation more perplexing than the phenomenon itself, rather than say, "I don't know." As she lay there thinking over the matter, and trying to make herself believe that the afternoon's experience was the effect of the wind or her own fancy, she was startled by a step on the floor of the lower room--the same light step. It crossed the floor, and she heard it on the stairs. Miss Sophonisba raised her head from her pillow and looked around. There could be no doubt that she was awake. She could see everything in the room: her sister slept quietly at her side, and the moonlight shone in brightly at the window. The slow step came up the stairs and in at the open door. She heard it on the boards: her eyes beheld the shadow of her sister's vision, so wavering and indistinct that she could not say with certainty that it wore the semblance of a human form. The blood at her heart seemed to stand still, but yet she neither screamed nor fainted, nor tried to wake her sister. She watched the Thing as it moved to and fro in the chamber. Suddenly it came toward her, and stood at the bedside, seeming indeed, as Faithful had said, to be "all around her in the air," and weigh upon her with a sense of oppression almost unendurable as the shadowy Presence obscured the moonbeams. Miss Sophonisba bent all her will to the effort, and with an heroic exertion she put out her hand to try by the sense of touch if indeed she was in her waking senses. Her fingers were met by others, soft, cold and damp. For a second, which seemed an hour, they grasped her extended hand with a close, clinging touch that some way seemed half familiar. For one instant the shapeless gloom appeared to take definite form--a tall human figure, a man in poor and ragged clothes; for one instant a pair of wistful, eager eyes looked into her own; the next, the cock without crowed loud and shrill. Her hand was released, and with the same long, weary sigh the ghostly Presence passed away. Miss Sophonisba sank back on her pillow nearly insensible. She did not know how long she lay there, but when she at last gathered her senses she saw and felt, with an involuntary shudder, that her hand was wet and cold, and that across the floor, plain in the moonlight, leading to the half-open door, were the marks of wet feet. She did not waken her sister, who still slept quietly at her side, but it was with unspeakable relief that she saw the morning dawn at last.

In spite of herself, Miss Sophonisba was forced to the conclusion that, except on the supposition that some inhabitant of another world had been permitted to approach her, her experience was wholly inexplicable. "If it comes again," said she to herself, "I'll certainly speak to it. Goodness me!" she added, somewhat irritated in spite of her terror, "if it's got anything to say, why don't it speak and be done with it?"

She said nothing of the matter to her sister, and she so far controlled herself as to preserve her usual manner.

The sisters were busily engaged all day over the mourning dresses, when toward night Miss Faithful's thread gave out and her work came to a stand-still.

"How provoking!" said she. "Three yards more would finish, and now I shall have to go down to the village and buy a whole skein, just for that."

"No," said Miss Sophonisba, who would not have acknowledged to herself her dread of being alone in the house, "I think there's some like that in the chimney cupboard in the south room: I'll get it."

She put down her work, and taking a candle went into the south room. Placing the light on a chair, she opened the cupboard door and began searching for the thread among a variety of miscellaneous matters. Some slight noise startled her. She turned, and saw standing before the fireplace an elderly gentleman, whose face was, as she thought, familiar, though she could not recall at the moment where she had seen it. It did not occur to her that her companion was not a living man, and she stood for a moment with a look of surprised inquiry, expecting him to speak. The eyes met hers in a fixed stare, like that of a corpse. She had not seen the figure move, yet the same instant it was at her side. It, was too much, even for her. She turned and sprang through the open door into the passage, but not before it had flashed across her mind that the dead face bore a horrible resemblance to the old doctor. The Thing did not follow her, and she stood still in the passage, not daring to alarm her more timid sister, and yet dreading inexpressibly to re-enter the haunted room. Her terror was not merely the oppression, the natural fear of the unknown, the sense of a nature differing from her own, which she had experienced the past night: it was all this, together with a sense of an evil influence, a feeling of loathing and horror, that made her sick in soul and in body. However strong her resolution, Miss Sophonisba felt that she could never endure, much less question, this frightful Presence. The candle was yet burning on the chair where she had left it, and, summoning all her strength, with an inward prayer she recrossed the threshold. The light still burned brightly, the thread she had come to seek lay on the floor where she had dropped it, but the figure was gone. She looked about the room: there was no trace of living presence save her own. She had even the courage to stoop down and examine the place on the carpet where the Shape had stood, and which covered the burned spot on the floor; but this time the mysterious footsteps had failed to leave their mark.

"Whatever shall I do?" said Miss Sophonisba to herself. "If Faithful was to see what I have, she'd nigh go crazy; and what excuse can we make for leaving the house?"

If no one but herself had been concerned, I think she would have stood a siege from the hosts of the unknown world rather than confess that she left the house because it was haunted. She caught herself up as the word was formed in her thoughts. "Haunted, indeed!" she said. "I'll think I'm losing my wits first. Stuff and nonsense!" But she paused, for through the middle of the room, close by her side, making an angry gesture as it passed, swept the same Shape, visible for one moment, vanishing the next. She went back into the other room, and giving her sister the thread, sat down so as to hide her face, busying herself with her work until she could in some measure regain her wonted steady composure.

Miss Faithful was much engaged with her sewing just at that moment, and her sister's unusual agitation escaped her notice. Presently she said, "Sophonisba, isn't there a bit of old black ribbon in that cupboard? I want something of the kind, just to put round inside the neck of the dress, and then it will be done."

"Yes--I don't know--I think not," said her sister, with a hesitation so unlike her usual promptness that Miss Faithful looked up surprised. "I mean, I think there is," said Miss Sophonisba. "If you'd like to look, I'll hold the candle for you."

"Oh, you needn't put down your work for that," said Miss Faithful, but Miss Sophonisba dropped the ribbon she was plaiting and followed her sister with the candle. She threw a half-frightened glance around the room as she entered, but the Vision did not reappear. It was some time before the ribbon was found. It had been pushed into the farther corner of the lower shelf, which was a wide and very thick pine board, slipping easily on the cleats by which it was upheld. One end of the roll had caught behind this shelf, and Miss Faithful pulled the board a little forward. As she did so a little roll of paper fell into the bottom of the cupboard. Miss Sophonisba picked it up. It consisted of several stained and discolored sheets of paper, seemingly torn from an account-book or journal, and covered all over with very fine and closely-written though perfectly legible characters, in a very precise hand.

"What is that?" said Miss Faithful.

"It's nothing of ours, I'm pretty sure," said her sister, looking at it. "But come, if you've got what you want: let's go into the other room--it's cold here."

As they crossed the threshold, Miss Faithful started.

"What's the matter?" said her sister, though she well knew the reason. She too had heard the same long sigh felt the same breath of chill air.

"Why, it seemed as if something breathed close to my ear," said Miss Faithful, turning white; "and what's more," she continued, as they crossed the passage and entered the work-room, "I believe you heard it too, and that you've seen things in this house you haven't told me of."

"Well, child," said Miss Sophonisba in a subdued tone, "there *are* some queer things in this world, that's a fact--queerer than ever I thought till lately."

Miss Faithful did not press for an explanation: she went quietly on with her dressmaking, and her sister, hurried though she was about her work, set herself to examine the papers.

I remember seeing the original manuscript when I was a little girl, but it was unfortunately destroyed by an accident. My father, however, had copied part of it, and this copy is yet in my possession. Miss Sophonisba could make very little of the record, which related to scientific matters of which she was quite ignorant; and as the most important words were indicated by signs and figures, she was completely puzzled. The writer seemed to have been seeking in vain some particular result.

She looked on through the dates of the year 1785, and saw here and there familiar names, and at last commenced reading at these words:

"June 3. This day took possession of my house. Busied in making arrangements. Shall build my own furnace. Am sure now that I am in the right way. Am determined no one shall come into the house."

Much followed which Miss Sophonisba could not understand, until, under the date of July 1, she found recorded:

"Being over at Neponset, looking for the plant witch-hazel, bethought myself to ask of the fellow they call Indian Will. Going to the little hovel he lives in, found him lying very ill with pleurisy. By the grace of God was able to help him. His wife told me where to find what I sought. To my surprise, discovered she knew much of its virtues. It may be these people have a knowledge of simples worth investigating.

"Sept. 3. No nearer my great end. My means fast growing less. Have borrowed from Jonathan Phelps, but the sum is but a drop for such a purpose. Most like some of these people, who complain of my price for the exercise of my skill, would give me threefold did they know what I work for, if they might share in its result. Yet I know I am in the right way. Should I die before I come to its end--Is Death the gate of knowledge?"

"Oct. 7. I advance just so far and no farther. Why is it that I see my path so plain just to the one point, and there it stops? How small our understanding of the endless mysteries around us! yet should something differing from every day's experience befall us, how quickly we speak of the *supernatural*!

"Oct. 29. No nearer, no nearer, and my money all but done. Took some of my books into Boston and offered them to sell. Refused, of course. How should they know their value? Have sent them to London. It was hard, but patience! patience!"

"Oct. 30. This day Indian Will brought the plants I wanted. Have bade him never to tell any one that he comes here. He only has ever entered. So far as I know, he has obeyed. He thinks me like one of his own powahs.

"Dec. 15. At last! I have passed the crisis, and without accident. How simple it seems, now that I know! It was my last bit of the essential metal: like from like. Each element has its seed in itself. The poor people say I have been good to them. Should success be final, I can indeed help mankind.

"Dec. 16. Last night, lifting the crucible from the furnace, spilled the liquor on the floor. Had I one particle more of the essential element! All was utterly lost: no one will lend to me.

"Dec. 18. What have I done that I should feel guilt? What was worth the life of such a useless creature to the interests of mankind? Why did he not trust my word and give me what I needed when I asked him? If he had not waked from his half-drunken sleep when I made the attempt, I would have given him threefold. I gave him his life once: why will not that atone? No one will know ever. I will devote my life to relieve distress. What is such as his, weighed in the balance with my purpose? It is strange that since then I have forgot the very essential thing in the process. I cannot read my own cipher in which I wrote it down; but it will come, it will come.

"Dec. 19. Have been all day trying to read the cipher in vain. Have lost the key, have forgotten the chief link. Until I can recall it the metal is useless. What if it should never come to me? This night went down to the Point. Threw into the sea the evidences of what I have brought to pass. The tide will soon wash them away.

"Dec. 20. Surely it is not meant this thing should be known. To-day a body came on shore, bruised and shattered, but said to be identified by those who should have known best. Now, no one will ever search this house. Twice to-day I have been to look at the place: nothing can be seen. Providence means I should live to finish my work--to complete that which I alone of mortal men have rightly understood. Why is it this link is broken off in my mind, and the cipher I myself wrote darker than before? Would the creature but have given it up quietly! It was in self-defence I struck at last. What was it to repent of? Some have held that such as he are not human--only animals a little more sagacious than the brutes about us.

"Dec. 22. Useless, useless! My memory fails me entirely. I have tried to go on in vain. What is this that is with me now these last two days?

"Dec. 25. Once I kept Christmas in another fashion than this. I had no guest but one I dare not name--

'Tumulum circumvolat umbra.'

"Dec. 27. To day it put out its hand: the soft wet fingers touched me. I will go out into the world, I will go out into the world. I will help those who are sick and in misery. Will it not be at peace then?"

Then the journal paused: there was no further entry till April 29, 1786:

"The girl, Hepsey Ball, died to-day. Her eyes were opened to see what I see all the hours in the day. I must go. I have not dared to leave, lest the awful Thing should be found in its hiding-place. They begin to press me for money. The house will go on the mortgage. Heard Phelps say if it was his he would drain the place in the cellar. To-day received fifty dollars from the sale of apparatus. Could not part with it before, thinking I should recover my lost knowledge, and should use it. Perhaps it will come back to me if I go away: it may be This will not follow me. I will drop the gold into the same place: if it is that it wants, it will rest. I cannot tell what I have done, my life is too precious. I only, of all men, have seen unveiled the mystery. I will leave This behind. When I am safe it may be found, and they will lay it to rest in the earth, if that is what it seeks. Then it will cease to persecute me with its step close at my back, its loathsome clinging touch."

Miss Sophonisba (my friend went on) looked up from her reading with such a strange expression that her sister was startled. "Put on your bonnet, Faithful," said she: "I'm going down to see the minister."

"What do you mean?" said Miss Faithful: "it's nearly nine o'clock."

"I don't care if it's midnight. I'm going to show these to him, and tell him what's happened here, and he may make what he can of it."

"Then you have seen something?" said Miss Faithful, turning pale.

Miss Sophonisba made a sign of assent; "I'll tell you all about it when we get there, but do come along now. You're work's done, and I'll take the bonnet with me and finish it there."

They lived at some distance from the parsonage, and the roads were in even worse condition than they are now. It was a tiresome walk, and Miss Faithful, clinging to her sister's side, was almost inclined to wish they had braved the terrors at home rather than ventured out into the dark. The clergyman was a middle-aged bachelor, a grandson of the Parson H---- mentioned by Mrs. T----. He heard Miss Sophonisba's story in silence, but without any sign of dissent. Faithful, in spite of her terror, could not but feel a mild degree of triumph in her sister's evident conviction that what she had seen was, to say the least, unaccountable.

Mr. H---- looked over the papers which had been found in the cupboard, and which Miss Sophonisba had brought with her. "This is undoubtedly Doctor Haywood's writing," he said at last. "I have a book purchased of him by my grandfather, and which has marginal notes in the same hand."

"What shall we do, sir?" asked Miss Sophonisba.

"If I were you I should leave the house as soon as possible. If there is anything in the air which induces such--" Mr. H---- hesitated for a word--"sensations as these, it would be better to go."

"Sensations!" said Miss Sophonisba, almost indignant. "I tell you I saw it myself; and what made the wet spot on Faithful's cape, and the rest?"

"I can't undertake to say, Miss T----; but if you like I will just come up to-morrow, and we will look into the matter a little. My cousin, Lieutenant V----, is here from his ship, and he will assist me. And meantime you had best stay here to-night: my sister will be very glad to see you."

Miss H---- was a particular friend of the sisters, but she could not but feel a little curious to know the object of their visit. Miss Sophonisba would have kept the matter to herself, but Miss Faithful, in her excitement, could not but tell the story of their experiences. Miss H----, however, was a discreet woman, and kept the tale to herself.

The next evening the clergyman, his cousin the lieutenant and Miss Sophonisba went quietly about dusk to the old house. They went down into the cellar, and the drag which the sailor had constructed brought up some bleached bones, and at the second cast a skeleton hand and a skull. As the latter was disengaged from the drag something fell glittering from it upon the cellar floor: two coins rolled to different corners. Mr. H----, picked them up. One was a Spanish piece, the other an English half guinea.

"Miss T----," said the clergyman in a low tone, "I will see that these poor relics are laid in the burial-ground; and then--really I think you had better leave the house."

Miss Sophonisba made no opposition.

The three ascended the cellar stairs, but as they entered the room they paused terror-stricken, for across the floor, making, as it passed, a wild gesture of despair, swept the Shape, living yet dead.

"What was that?" said the clergyman, who was the first to recover himself, "It," said Miss Sophonisba in a whisper.

"I have seen that face before," said the sailor. "Once on a stormy passage round the Cape we came upon a deserted wreck rolling helplessly upon the waves. I, then a young midshipman, went in the boat which was sent to board her. No living creature was there, but in the cabin we found a corpse, that of an old, old man. The look of the Thing was so awful that I could not bear it and hid my face. One of the sailors, however, took from the dead hand a paper covered with characters in cipher, which no one could read. This paper afterward fell into my possession, and I submitted it in vain to several experts, all of whom failed to read it. By an accident it was destroyed, and the secret, whatever it was, is hidden for ever; but the face of that corpse was the face I have just seen in this room."

CLARA F. GUERNSEY.

The Blood Seedling.

In a bit of green pasture that rose, gradually narrowing, to the tableland that ended in prairie, and widened out descending to the wet and willowy sands that border the Great River, a broad-shouldered young man was planting an apple tree one sunny spring morning when Tyler was President. The little valley was shut in on the south and east by rocky hills, patched with the immortal green of cedars and gay with clambering columbines. In front was the Mississippi, reposing from its plunge over the rapids, and idling down among the golden sand-bars and the low, moist islands, which were looking their loveliest in their new spring dresses of delicate green.

The young man was digging with a certain vicious energy, forcing the spade into the black crumbling loam with a movement full of vigor and malice. His straight black brows were knitted till they formed one dark line over his deep-set eyes. His beard was not yet old enough to hide the massive outline of his firm, square jaw. In the set teeth, in the clouded face, in the half-articulate exclamations that shot from time to time from the compressed lips, it was easy to see that the thoughts of the young horticulturist were far from his work.

A bright young girl came down the path through the hazel thicket that skirted the hillside, and putting a plump brown hand on the topmost rail of the fence vaulted lightly over, and lit on the soft springy turf with a thud that announced a whole-some and liberal architecture. It is usually expected of poets and lovers that they shall describe the ladies of their love as so airy and delicate in structure that the flowers they tread on are greatly improved in health and spirits by the visitation. But not being a poet or in love, we must admit that there was no resurrection for the larkspurs and pansies upon which the little boots of Miss Susie Barringer landed. Yet she was not of the coarse peasant type, though her cheeks were so rosy as to cause her great heaviness of heart on Sunday mornings, and her blue lawn dress was as full as it could afford from shoulders to waist. She was a neat, hearty and very pretty country girl, with a slightly freckled face, and rippled brown hair, and astonished blue eyes, but perfectly self-possessed, and graceful as a young quail.

A young man's ears are quick to catch the rustling of a woman's dress. The flight of this plump bird in its fluttering blue plumage over the rail-fence caused our young man to look up from his spading: the scowl was routed from his brow by a sudden incursion of blushes, and his mouth was attacked by an awkward smile.

The young lady nodded, and was hurrying past. The scowl came back in force, and the smile was repulsed from the bearded mouth with great loss: "Miss Tudie, are you in a hurry?"

The lady thus addressed turned and said, in a voice that was half pert and half coaxing, "No particular hurry. Al, I've told you a dozen times not to call me that redicklis name."

"Why, Tudie, I hain't never called you nothing else sence you was a little one so high. You ort to know yer own name, and you give yerself that name when you was a yearling. Howsom-ever, ef you don't like it now, sence you've been to Jacksonville, I reckon I can call you Miss Susie--when I don't disremember."

The frank amende seemed to satisfy Miss Susie, for she at once interrupted in the kindest manner: "Never mind, Al Golyer: you can call me what you are a-mind to." Then, as if conscious of the feminine inconsistency, she changed the subject by asking, "What are you going to do with that great hole?--big enough to bury a fellow."

"I'm going to plant this here seedlin', that growed up in Colonel Blood's pastur', nobody knows how: belike somebody was eatin' an apple and throwed the core down-like. I'm going to plant a little orchard here next spring, but the colonel and me, we reckoned this one 'ud be too old by that time for moving, so I thought I'd stick it in now, and see what come out'n it. It's a powerful thrifty chunk of a saplin'."

"Yes. I speak for the first peck of apples off'n it. Don't forget. Good-morning."

"Hold on a minute, Miss Susan, twell I git my coat. I'll walk down a piece with you. I have got something to say to you."

Miss Susie turned a little red and a little pale. These occasions were not entirely unknown in her short experience of life. When young men in the country in that primitive period had something to say, it was something very serious and earnest. Allen Golyer was a good-looking, stalwart young farmer, well-to-do, honest, able to provide for a family. There was nothing presumptuous in his aspiring to the hand of the prettiest girl on Chaney Creek. In childhood he had trotted her to Banbury Cross and back a hundred times, beguiling the tedium of the journey with kisses and the music of bells. When the little girl was old enough to go to school, the big boy carried her books and gave her the rosiest apple out of his dinner-basket. He fought all her battles and wrote all her compositions; which latter, by the way, never gained her any great credit. When she was fifteen and he twenty he had his great reward in taking her twice a week during one happy winter to singing-school. This was the bloom of life--nothing before or after could compare with it. The blacking of shoes and brushing of stiff, electric, bristling hair, all on end with frost and hope, the struggling into the plate-armor of his starched shirt, the tying of the portentous and uncontrollable cravat before the glass, which was hopelessly dimmed every moment by his eager breath,--these trivial and vulgar details were made beautiful and unreal by the magic of youth and love. Then came the walk through the crisp, dry snow to the Widow Barringer's, the sheepish talk with the old lady while Susie "got on her things," and the long, enchanting tramp to the "deestrick school-house."

There is not a country-bred man or woman now living but will tell you that life can offer nothing comparable with the innocent zest of that old style of courting that was done at singing-school in the starlight and candlelight of the first half of our century. There are few hearts so withered and old but they beat quicker sometimes when they hear, in old-fashioned churches, the wailing, sobbing or exulting strains of "Bradstreet" or "China" or "Coronation;" and the mind floats down on the current of these old melodies to that fresh young day of hopes and illusions--of voices that were sweet, no matter how false they sang--of nights that were rosy with dreams, no matter what Fahrenheit said--of girls that blushed without cause, and of lovers who talked for hours about everything but love.

I know I shall excite the scorn of all the ingenuous youth of my time when I say that there was nothing that our superior civilization would call love making in those long walks through the winter nights. The heart of Allen Golyer swelled under his satin waistcoat with love and joy and devotion as he walked over the crunching roads with his pretty enslaver. But he talked of apples and pigs and the heathen and the teacher's wig, and sometimes ventured an illusion to other people's flirtations in a jocose and distant way; but as to the state of his own heart, his lips were sealed. It would move a blase smile on the downy lips of juvenile Lovelaces, who count their conquests by their cotillons, and think nothing of making a declaration in an avant-deux, to be told of young people spending several evenings of each week in the year together, and speaking no word of love until they were ready to name their wedding-day. Yet such was the sober habit of the place and time.

So there was no troth plighted between Allen and Susie, though the youth loved the maiden with all the energy of his fresh, unused nature, and she knew it very well. He never dreamed of marrying any other woman than Susie Barringer, and she sometimes tried a new pen by writing and carefully erasing the initials S.M.G., which, as she was christened Susan Minerva, may be taken as showing the direction of her thoughts.

If Allen Golyer had been less bashful or more enterprising, this history would never have been written; for Susie would probably have said Yes for want of anything better to say, and when she went to visit her aunt Abigail in Jacksonville she would have gone *engaged*, her finger bound with gold and her maiden meditations fettered by promises. But she went, as it was, fancy free, and there is no tinder so inflammable as the imagination of a pretty country girl of sixteen.

One day she went out with her easy-going aunt Abigail to buy ribbons, the Chancy Creek invoices not supplying the requirements of Jacksonville society. As they traversed the court-house square on their way to Deacon Pettybones' place, Miss Susie's vagrant glances rested on an iris of ribbons displayed in an opposition window. "Let's go in here," she said with the impetuous decision of her age and sex.

"We will go where you like, dear," said easy-going Aunt Abigail. "It makes no difference."

Aunt Abigail was wrong. It made the greatest difference to several persons whether Susie Barringer bought her ribbons at Simmons' or Pettybones' that day. If she had but known!

But, all unconscious of the Fate that beckoned invisibly on the threshold, Miss

Susie tripped into "Simmons' Emporium" and asked for ribbons. Two young men stood at the long counter. One was Mr. Simmons, proprietor of the emporium, who advanced with his most conscientious smile: "Ribbons, ma'am? Yes, ma'am--all sorts, ma'am. Cherry, ma'am? Certingly, ma'am. Jest got a splendid lot from St. Louis this morning, ma'am. This way, ma'am."

The ladies were soon lost in the delight of the eyes. The voice of Mr. Simmons accompanied the feast of color, insinuating but unheeded.

The other young man approached: "Here is what you want, miss--rich and elegant. Just suits your style. Sets off your hair and eyes beautiful."

The ladies looked up. A more decided voice than Mr. Simmons'; whiter hands than Mr. Simmons' handled the silken bands; bolder eyes than the weak, pink-bordered orbs of Mr. Simmons looked unabashed admiration into the pretty face of Susie Barringer.

"Look here, Simmons, old boy, introduce a fellow."

Mr. Simmons meekly obeyed: "Mrs. Barringer, let me interduce you to Mr. Leon of St. Louis, of the house of Draper & Mercer."

"Bertie Leon, at your service," said the brisk young fellow, seizing Miss Susie's hand with energy. His hand was so much softer and whiter than hers that she felt quite hot and angry about it.

When they had made their purchases, Mr. Leon insisted on walking home with them, and was very witty and agreeable all the way. He had all the wit of the newspapers, of the concert-rooms, of the steamboat bars at his fingers' ends. In his wandering life he had met all kinds of people: he had sold ribbons through a dozen States. He never had a moment's doubt of himself. He never hesitated to allow himself any indulgence which would not interfere with business. He had one ambition in life--to marry Miss Mercer and get a share in the house. Miss Mercer was as ugly as a millionaire's tombstone. Mr. Bertie Leon--who, when his moustache was not dyed nor his hair greased, was really quite a handsome fellow--considered that the sacrifice he proposed to make in the interests of trade must be made good to him in some way. So, "by way of getting even," he made violent love to all the pretty eyes he met in his commercial travels--"to have something to think about after he should have found favor in the strabismic optics of Miss Mercer," he observed, disrespectfully.

Simple Susie, who had seen nothing of young men besides the awkward and blushing clodhoppers of Chaney Creek, was somewhat dazzled by the free-and-easy speech and manner of the hard-cheeked bagman. Yet there was something in his airy talk and point-blank compliments that aroused a faint feeling of resentment which she could scarcely account for. Aunt Abigail was delighted with him, and when he bowed his adieux at the gate in the most recent Planters'-House style, she cordially invited him to call--"to drop in any time: he must be lonesome so far from home."

He said he wouldn't neglect such a chance, with another Planters'-House bow.

"What a nice young man!" said Aunt Abigail.

"Awful conceited and not overly polite," said Susie as she took off her bonnet and went into a revel of bows and trimmings.

The oftener Albert Leon came to Mrs. Barringer's bowery cottage, the more the old lady was pleased with him and the more the young one criticised him, until it was plain to be seen that Aunt Abigail was growing tired of him and pretty Susan dangerously interested. But just at this point his inexorable carpet-bag dragged him off to a neighboring town, and Susie soon afterward went back to Chaney Creek.

Her Jacksonville hat and ribbons made her what her pretty eyes never could have done--the belle of the neighborhood. Non cuivis contingit adire Lutetiam, but to a village where no one has been at Paris the county-town is a shrine of fashion. Allen Golyer felt a vague sense of distrust chilling his heart as he saw Mr. Simmons' ribbons decking the pretty head in the village choir the Sunday after her return, and, spurred on by a nascent jealousy of the unknown, resolved to learn his fate without loss of time. But the little lady received him with such cool and unconcerned friendliness, talked so much and so fast about her visit, that the honest fellow was quite bewildered, and had to go home to think the matter over, and cudgel his dull wits to divine whether she was pleasanter than ever, or had drifted altogether out of his reach.

Allen Golyer was, after all, a man of nerve and decision. He wasted only a day or two in doubts and fears, and one Sunday afternoon, with a beating but resolute heart, he left his Sunday-school class to walk down to Crystal Glen and solve his questions and learn his doom. When he came in sight of the widow's modest house, he saw a buggy hitched by the gate.

"Dow Padgett's chestnut sorrel, by jing! What is Dow after out here?"

It is natural, if not logical, that young men should regard the visits of all other persons of their age and sex in certain quarters as a serious impropriety.

But it was not his friend and crony Dow Padgett, the liveryman, who came out of the widow's door, leading by the hand the blushing and bridling Susie. It was a startling apparition of the Southwestern dandy of the period--light hair drenched with bear's oil, blue eyes and jet-black moustache, an enormous paste brooch in his bosom, a waistcoat and trowsers that shrieked in discordant tones, and very small and elegant varnished boots. The gamblers and bagmen of the Mississippi River are the best-shod men in the world.

Golyer's heart sank within him as this splendid being shone upon him. But with his rustic directness he walked to meet the laughing couple at the gate, and said, "Tudie, I come to see you. Shall I go in and talk to your mother twell you come back?"

"No, that won't pay," promptly replied the brisk stranger. "We will be gone the heft of the afternoon, I reckon. This hoss is awful slow," he added with a wink of preternatural mystery to Miss Susie.

"Mr. Golyer," said the young lady, "let me interduce you to my friend, Mr. Leon."

Golyer put out his hand mechanically, after the cordial fashion of the West. But Leon nodded and said, "I hope to see you again." He lifted Miss Susie into the buggy, sprang lightly in, and went off with laughter and the cracking of his whip after Dow Padgett's chestnut sorrel.

The young farmer walked home desolate, comparing in his simple mind his own plain exterior with his rival's gorgeous toilet, his awkward address with the other's easy audacity, till his heart was full to the brim with that infernal compound of love and hate which is called jealousy, from which pray Heaven to guard you.

It was the next morning that Miss Susie vaulted over the fence where Allen Golyer was digging the hole for Colonel Blood's apple tree.

"Something middlin' particular," continued Golyer, resolutely.

"There is no use leaving your work," said Miss Barringer pluckily. "I will stay and listen."

Poor Allen began as badly as possible: "Who was that feller with you yesterday?"

"Thank you, Mr. Golyer--my friends ain't fellers! What's that to you, who he was?"

"Susie Barringer, we have been keeping company now a matter of a year. I have loved you well and true: I would have give my life to save you any little care or trouble. I never dreamed of nobody but you--not that I was half good enough for you, but because I did not know any better man around here. Ef it ain't too late, Susie, I ask you to be my wife. I will love you and care for you, good and true."

Before this solemn little speech was finished, Susie was crying and biting her bonnet-strings in a most undignified manner. "Hush, Al Golyer!" she burst out. "You mustn't talk so. You are too good for me. I am kind of promised to that fellow. I 'most wish I had never seen him."

Allen sprang to her and took her in his strong arms: she struggled free from him. In a moment the vibration which his passionate speech had produced in her passed away. She dried her eyes and said firmly enough, "It's no use, Al: we wouldn't be happy together. Good-bye! I shouldn't wonder if I went away from Chaney Creek before long."

She walked rapidly down to the river-road. Allen stood fixed and motionless, gazing at the light, graceful form until the blue dress vanished behind the hill, and leaned long on his spade, unconscious of the lapse of time.

When Susan reached her home she found Leon at the gate.

"Ah, my little rosebud! I came near missing you. I am going to Keokuk this morning, to be gone a few days. I stopped here a minute to give you something to keep for me till I come back."

"What is it?"

He took her chubby cheeks between his hands and laid on her cherry-ripe lips a keepsake which he never reclaimed.

She stood watching him from the gate until, as a clump of willows snatched him from her, she thought, "He will go right by where Al is at work. It would be jest like him to jump over the fence and have a talk with him. I'd like to hear it."

An hour or so later, as she sat and sewed in the airy little entry, a shadow fell upon her work, and as she looked up her startled eyes met the piercing glance of her discarded lover. A momentary ripple of remorse passed over her cheerful heart as she saw Allen's pale and agitated face. He was paler than she had ever seen him, with that ghastly pallor of weather-beaten faces. His black hair, wet with perspiration, clung clammily to his temples. He looked beaten, discouraged, utterly fatigued with the conflict of emotion. But one who looked closely in his eyes would have seen a curious stealthy, half-shaded light in them, as of one who, though working against hope, was still not without resolute will.

Dame Barringer, who had seen him coming up the walk, bustled in: "Good-morning, Allen. How beat out you do look! Now, I like a stiddy young man, but don't you think you run this thing of workin' into the ground?"

"Wail, maybe so," said Golyer with a weary smile--"leastways I've been a-running this spade into the ground all the morning, and--"

"You want buttermilk--that's your idee: ain't it, now?"

"Well, Mizzes Barringer, I reckon you know my failin's."

The good woman trotted off to the dairy, and Susie sewed demurely, waiting with some trepidation for what was to come next.

"Susie Barringer," said a low, husky voice which she could scarcely recognize as Golyer's, "I've come to ask pardon--not for nothing I've done, for I never did and never could do you wrong--but for what I thought for a while arter you left me this morning. It's all over now, but I tell *you* the Bad Man had his claws into my heart for a spell. Now it's all over, and I wish you well. I wish your husband well. If ever you git into any trouble where I can help, send for me: it's my right. It's the last favor I ask of you."

Susceptible Susie cried a little again. Allen, watching her with his ambushed eyes, said, "Don't take it to heart, Tudie. Perhaps there is better days in store for me yet."

This did not appear to comfort Miss Barringer in the least. She was greatly grieved when she thought she had broken a young man's heart: she was still more dismal at the slightest intimation that she had not. If any explanation of this paradox is required, I would observe, quoting a phrase much in vogue among the witty writers of the present age, that Miss Susie Barringer was "a very female woman."

So pretty Susan's rising sob subsided into a coquettish pout by the time her mother came in with the foaming pitcher of subacidulous nectar, and plied young

Golyer with brimming beakers of it with all the beneficent delight of a Lady Bountiful.

"There, Mizzes Barringer! there's about as much as I can tote. Temperance in all things."

"Very well, then, you work less and play more. We never get a sight of you lately. Come in neighborly and play checkers with Tudie."

It was the darling wish of Mother Barringer's heart to see her daughter married and settled with "a stiddy young man that you knowed all about, and his folks before him." She had observed with great disquietude the brilliant avatar of Mr. Bertie Leon and the evident pride of her daughter in the bright-plumaged captive she had brought to Chaney Creek, the spoil of her maiden snare. "I don't more'n half like that little feller." (It is a Western habit to call a well-dressed man a "little feller." The epithet would light on Hercules Farnese if he should go to Illinois dressed as a Cocodes.) "No honest folks wears beard onto their upper lips. I wouldn't be surprised if he wasn't a gamboller."

Allen Golyer, apparently unconscious in his fatigue of the cap which Dame Barringer was vicariously setting for him, walked away with his spade on his shoulder, and the good woman went systematically to work in making Susie miserable by sharp little country criticisms of her heart's idol.

Day after day wore on, and, to Dame Barringer's delight and Susie's dismay, Mr. Leon did not come.

"He is such a businessman," thought trusting Susan, "he can't get away from Keokuk. But he'll be sure to write." So Susie put on her sun-bonnet and hurried up to the post-office: "Any letters for me, Mr. Whaler?" The artful and indefinite plural was not disguise enough for Miss Susie, so she added, "I was expecting a letter from my aunt."

"No letters here from your aunt, nor your uncle, nor none of the tribe," said old Whaler, who had gone over with Tyler to keep his place, and so had no further use for good manners.

"I think old Tommy Whaler is an impudent old wretch," said Susie that evening, "and I won't go near his old post-office again." But Susie forgot her threat of vengeance the next day, and she went again, lured by family affection, to inquire for that letter which Aunt Abbie *must* have written. The third time she went, rummy old Whaler roared very improperly, "Bother your aunt! You've got a beau somewheres--that's what's the matter."

Poor Susan was so dazzled by this flash of clairvoyance that she hurried from that dreadful post-office, scarcely hearing the terrible words that the old gin-pig hurled after her: "And he's forgot you!--that's what's the matter."

Susie Barringer walked home along the river-road, revolving many things in her mind. She went to her room and locked her door by sticking a pen-knife over the latch, and sat down to have a good cry. Her faculties being thus cleared for action, she thought seriously for an hour. If you can remember when you were a school-girl, you know a great deal of solid thinking can be done in an hour. But we can tell you in a moment what it footed up. You can walk through the Louvre in a minute, but you cannot see it in a week.

Susan Barringer (sola, loquitur): "Three weeks yesterday. Yes, I s'pose it's so. What a little fool I was! He goes everywheres--says the same things to everybody, like he was selling ribbons. Mean little scamp! Mother seen through him in a minute. I'm mighty glad I didn't tell her nothing about it." [Fie, Susie! your principles are worse than your grammar.] "He'll marry some rich girl--I don't envy her, but I hate her--and I am as good as she is. Maybe he will come back--no, and I hope he won't;--and I wish I was dead!" (Pocket handkerchief.)

Yet in the midst of her grief there was one comforting thought--nobody knew of it. She had no confidante--she had not even opened her heart to her mother: these Western maidens have a fine gift of reticence. A few of her countryside friends and rivals had seen with envy and admiration the pretty couple on the day of Leon's arrival. But all their poisonous little compliments and questions had never elicited from the prudent Susie more than the safe statement that the handsome stranger was a friend of Aunt Abbie's, whom she had met at Jacksonville. They could not laugh at her: they could not sneer at gay deceivers and lovelorn damsels when she went to the sewing-circle. The bitterness of her tears was greatly sweetened by the consideration that in any case no one could pity her. She took such consolation from this thought that she faced her mother unflinchingly at tea, and baffled the maternal inquest on her "redness of eyes" by the school-girl's invaluable and ever-ready headache.

It was positively not until a week later, when she met Allen Golyer at choir-meeting, that she remembered that this man knew the secret of her baffled hopes. She blushed scarlet as he approached her: "Have you got company home, Miss Susie?"

"Yes--that is, Sally Withers and me came together, and--"

"No, that's hardly fair to Tom Fleming: three ain't the pleasantest company. I will go home with you."

Susie took the strong arm that was held out to her, and leaned upon it with a mingled feeling of confidence and dread as they walked home through the balmy night under the clear, starry heaven of the early spring. The air was full of the quickening breath of May.

Susie Barringer waited in vain for some signal of battle from Allen Golyer. He talked more than usual, but in a grave, quiet, protecting style, very different from his former manner of worshiping bashfulness. His tone had in it an air of fatherly caressing which was inexpressibly soothing to his pretty companion, tired and lonely with her silent struggle of the past month. When they came to her gate and he said good-night, she held his hand a moment with a tremulous grasp, and spoke impulsively: "Al, I once told you something I never told anybody else. I'll tell you something else now, because I believe I can trust you."

"Be sure of that, Susie Barringer."

"Well, Al, my engagement is broken off."

"I am sorry for you, Susie, if you set much store by him."

Miss Susie answered with great and unnecessary impetuosity, "I don't, and I am glad of it!" and then ran into the house and to bed, her cheeks all aflame at the thought of her indiscretion, and yet with a certain comfort in having a friend from whom she had no secrets.

I protest there was no thought of coquetry in the declaration which Susan Barringer blurted out to her old lover under the sympathetic starlight of the May heaven. But Allen Golyer would have been a dull boy not to have taken heart and hope from it. He became, as of old, a frequent and welcome visitor at Crystal Glen. Before long the game of chequers with Susie became so enthralling a passion that it was only adjourned from one evening to another. Allen's white shirts grew fringy at the edges with fatigue-duty, and his large hands were furry at the fingers with much soap. Susie's affectionate heart, which had been swayed a moment from its orbit by the irresistible attraction of Bertie Leon's diamond breastpin and city swagger, swung back to its ancient course under the mild influence of time and the weather and opportunity. So that Dame Barringer was not in the least surprised, on entering her little parlor one soft afternoon in that very May, to see the two young people economically occupying one chair, and Susie shouting the useless appeal, "Mother, make him behave!"

"I never interfere in young folks' matters, especially when they're going all right," said the motherly old soul, kissing "her son Allen" and trotting away to dry her happy tears.

I am almost ashamed to say how soon they were married--so soon that when Miss Susan went with her mother to Keokuk to buy a wedding-garment, she half expected to find, in every shop she entered, the elegant figure of Mr. Leon leaning over the counter. But the dress was bought and made, and worn at wedding and *infair* and in a round of family visits among the Barringer and Golyer kin, and carefully laid away in lavender when the pair came back from their modest holiday and settled down to real life on Allen's prosperous farm; and no word of Bertie Leon ever came to Mrs. Golyer to trouble her joy. In her calm and busy life the very name faded from her tranquil mind. These wholesome country hearts do not bleed long. In that wide-awake country eyes are too useful to be wasted in weeping. My dear Lothario Urban us, those peaches are very sound and delicious, but they will not keep for ever. If you do not secure them to-day, they will go to some one else, and in no case, as the Autocrat hath said with authority, can you stand there "mellering 'em with your thumb."

There was no happier home in the county, and few finer farms. The good sense and industry of Golyer and the practical helpfulness of his wife found their full exercise in the care of his spreading fields and growing orchards. The Warsaw merchants fought for his wheat, and his apples were known in St. Louis. Mrs. Golyer, with that spice of romance which is hidden away in every woman's heart, had taken a special fancy to the seedling apple tree at whose planting she had so intimately assisted. Allen shared in this, as in all her whims, and tended and nursed it like a child. In time he gave up the care of his orchard to other hands, but he reserved this seedling for his own especial coddling. He spaded and mulched and pruned it, and guarded it in the winter from rodent rabbits and in summer from terebrant grubs.

It was not ungrateful. It grew a noble tree, producing a rich and luscious fruit, with a deep scarlet satin coat, and a flesh tinged as delicately as a pink seashell. The first peck of apples was given to Susie with great ceremony, and the next year the first bushel was carried to Colonel Blood, the Congressman. He was loud in his admiration, as the autumn elections were coming on: "Great Scott, Golyer! I'd rather give my name to a horticultooral triumph like that there than be Senator."

"You've got your wish, then, colonel," said Golyer. "Me and my wife have called that tree The Blood Seedling sence the day it was transplanted from your pastur'."

It was the pride and envy of the neighborhood. Several neighbors asked for scions and grafts, but could do nothing with them.

"Fact is," said old Silas Withers, "those folks that expects to raise good fruit by begging graffs, and then layin' abed and readin' newspapers, will have a good time waitin'. Elbow-grease is the secret of the Blood Seedlin', ain't it, Al?"

"Well, I reckon, Squire Withers, a man never gits anything wuth havin' without a tussle for it; and as to secrets, I don't believe in them, nohow."

A square-browed, resolute, silent, middle-aged man, who loved his home better than any amusement, regular at church, at the polls, something richer every Christmas than he had been on the New Year's preceding--a man whom everybody liked and few loved much--such had Allen Golyer grown to be.

*　　*　　*　　*　　*

If I have lingered too long over this colorless and commonplace picture of rural Western life, it is because I have felt an instinctive reluctance to recount the startling and most improbable incident which fell one night upon this quiet neighborhood, like a thunderbolt out of blue sky. The story I must tell will be flatly denied and easily refuted. It is absurd and fantastic, but, unless human evidence is to go for nothing when it testifies of things unusual, the story is true.

At the head of the rocky hollow through which Chaney Creek ran to the river, lived the family who gave the brook its name. They were among the early pioneers of the county. In the squatty yellow stone house the present Chaney occupied his grandfather had stood a siege from Black Hawk all one summer day and night, until relieved by the garrison of Fort Edward. The family had not grown with the growth of the land. Like many others of the pioneers, they had shown no talent for keeping abreast of the civilization whose guides and skirmishers they had been. In the progress of a half century they had sold, bit by bit, their section of land, which kept intact would have proved a fortune. They lived very quietly, working enough to secure their own pork and hominy, and regarding with a sort of impatient scorn every scheme of public or private enterprise that passed under their eyes.

The elder Chaney had married, some years before, at the Mormon town of Nauvoo, the fair-haired daughter of a Swedish mystic, who had come across the sea beguiled by dreams of a perfect theocracy, and who on arriving at the city of the Latter-Day Saints had died, broken-hearted from his lost illusions.

The only dowry that Seraphita Neilsen brought her husband, besides her delicate beauty and her wide blue eyes, was a full set of Swedenborg's later writings in English. These became the daily food of the solitary household. Saul Chaney would read the exalted rhapsodies of the Northern seer for hours together, without the first glimmer of their meaning crossing his brain. But there was something in the majesty of their language and the solemn roll of their poetical development that irresistibly impressed and attracted him. Little Gershom, his only child, sitting at his feet, would listen in childish wonder to the strange things his silent, morose and gloomy father found in the well-worn volumes, until his tired eyelids would fall at last over his pale, bulging eyes.

As he grew up his eyes bulged more and more: his head seemed too large for his rickety body. He pored over the marvelous volumes until he knew long passages by heart, and understood less of them than his father--which was unnecessary. He looked a little like his mother, but while she in her youth had something of the faint and flickering beauty of the Boreal Lights, poor Gershom never could have suggested anything more heavenly than a foggy moonlight. When he was fifteen he went to the neighboring town of Warsaw to school. He had rather heavy weather among the well-knit, grubby-knuckled urchins of the town, and would have been thoroughly disheartened but for one happy chance. At the house where he boarded an amusement called the "Sperrit Rappin's" was much in vogue. A group of young folks, surcharged with all sorts of animal magnetism, with some capacity for belief and much more for fun, used to gather about a light pine table every evening, and put it through a complicated course of mystical gymnastics. It was a very good-tempered table: it would dance, hop or slam at the word of command, or, if the exercises took a more intellectual turn, it would answer any questions addressed to it in a manner not much below the average capacity of its tormentors.

Gershom Chaney took all this in solemn earnest. He was from the first moment deeply impressed. He lay awake whole nights, with his eyes fast closed, in the wildest dreams. His school-hours were passed in trancelike contemplation. He cared no more for punishment than the fakeer for his self-inflicted tortures. He longed for the coming of the day when he could commune in solitude with the unfleshed and immortal. This was the full flowering of those seeds of fantasy that had fallen into his infant mind as he lay baking his brains by the wide fire in the old stone house at the head of the hollow, while his father read, haltingly, of the wonders of the invisible world.

But, to his great mortification, he saw nothing, heard nothing, experienced nothing but in the company of others. He must brave the ridicule of the profane to taste the raptures which his soul loved. His simple, trusting faith made him inevitably the butt of the mischievous circle. They were not slow in discovering his extreme sensibility to external influences. One muscular, black-haired, heavy-browed youth took especial delight in practicing upon him. The table, under Gershom's tremulous hands, would skip like a lamb at the command of this Thomas Fay.

One evening, Tom Fay had a great triumph. They had been trying to get the "medium"--for Gershom had reached that dignity--to answer sealed questions, and had met with indifferent success. Fay suddenly approached the table, scribbled a phrase, folded it and tossed it, doubled up, before Gershom; then leaned over the table, staring at his pale, unwholesome face with all the might of his black eyes.

Chaney seized the pencil convulsively and wrote, "Balaam!"

Fay burst into a loud laugh and said, "Read the question?"

It was, "Who rode on your grandfather's back?"

This is a specimen of the cheap wit and harmless malice by which poor Gershom suffered as long as he stayed at school. He was never offended, but was often sorely perplexed, at the apparent treachery of his unseen counselors. He was dismissed at last from the academy for utter and incorrigible indolence. He accepted his disgrace as a crown of martyrdom, and went proudly home to his sympathizing parents.

Here, with less criticism and more perfect faith, he renewed the exercise of what he considered his mysterious powers. His fastings and vigils, and want of bodily movement and fresh air, had so injured his health as to make him tenfold more nervous and sensitive than ever. But his faintings and hysterics and epileptic paroxysms were taken more and more as evidences of his lofty mission. His father and mother regarded him as an oracle, for the simple reason that he always answered just as they expected. A curious or superstitious neighbor was added from time to time to the circle, and their reports heightened the half-uncanny interest with which the Chaney house was regarded.

It was on a moist and steamy evening of spring that Allen Golyer, standing by his gate, saw Saul Chaney slouching along in the twilight, and hailed him: "What news from the sperrits, Saul?"

"Nothing for you, Al Golyer," said Saul, gloomily. "The god of this world takes care of the like o' you."

Golyer smiled, as a prosperous man always does when his poorer neighbors abuse him for his luck, and rejoined: "I ain't so fortunate as you think for, Saul Chaney. I lost a Barksher pig yesterday: I reckon I must come up and ask Gershom what's come of it."

"Come along, if you like. It's been a long while since you've crossed my sill. But I'm gitting to be quite the style. Young Lawyer Marshall is a-coming up this evening to see my Gershom."

Before Mr. Golyer started he filled a basket, "to make himself welcome and pay for the show," with the reddest and finest fruit of his favorite apple tree. His wife followed him to the gate and kissed him--a rather unusual attention among Western farmer-people. Her face, still rosy and comely, was flushed and smiling: "Al, do you know what day o' the year it is?"

"Nineteenth of Aprile?"

"Yes; and twenty years ago to-day you planted the Blood Seedlin' and I give you the mitten!" She turned and went into the house, laughing comfortably.

Allen walked slowly up the hollow to the Chaney house, and gave the apples to Seraphita and told her their story. A little company was assembled--two or three Chaney Creek people, small market-gardeners, with eyes the color of their gooseberries and hands the color of their currants; Mr. Marshall, a briefless young barrister from Warsaw, with a tawny friend, who spoke like a Spaniard.

"Take seats, friends, and form a circle o' harmony," said Saul Chaney. "The me'jum is in fine condition: he had two fits this arternoon."

Gershom looked shockingly ill and weak. He reclined in a great hickory armchair, with his eyes half open, his lips moving noiselessly. All the persons present formed a circle and joined hands.

The moment the circle was completed by Saul and Seraphita, who were on either side of their son, touching his hands, an expression of pain and perplexity passed over his pale face, and he began to writhe and mutter.

"He's seein' visions," said Saul.

"Yes, too many of 'em," said Gershom, querulously. "A boy in a boat, a man on a shelf, and a man with a spade--all at once: too many. Get me a pencil. One at a time, I tell you--one at a time!"

The circle broke up, and a table was brought, with writing materials. Gershom grasped a pencil, and said, with imperious and feverish impatience, "Come on, now, and don't waste the time of the shining ones."

An old woman took his right hand. He wrote with his left very rapidly an instant, and threw her the paper, always with his eyes shut close.

Old Mrs. Scritcher read with difficulty, "A boy in a boat--over he goes;" and burst out in a piteous wail, "Oh, my poor little Ephraim! I always knowed it."

"Silence, woman!" said the relentless medium.

"Mr. Marshall," said Saul, "would you like a test?"

"No, thank you," said the young gentleman. "I brought my friend, Mr. Baldassano, who, as a traveler, is interested in these things."

"Will you take the medium's hand, Mr. What's-your-name?"

The young foreigner took the lean and feverish hand of Gershom, and again the pencil flew rapidly over the paper. He pushed the manuscript from him and snatched his hand away from Baldassano. As the latter looked at what was written, his tawny cheek grew deadly pale. "Dios mio!" he exclaimed to Marshall. "This is written in Castilian!"

The two young men retired to the other end of the room and read by the tallow candle the notes scrawled on the paper. Baldassano translated: "A man on a shelf-

-table covered with bottles beside him: man's face yellow as gold: bottles tumble over without being touched."

"What nonsense is that?" said Marshall.

"My brother died of yellow fever at sea last year."

Both the young men became suddenly very thoughtful, and observed with great interest the result of Golyer's "test." He sat by Gershom, holding his hand tightly, but gazing absently into the dying blaze of the wide chimney. He seemed to have forgotten where he was: a train of serious thought appeared to hold him completely under its control. His brows were knit with an expression of severe almost fierce determination. At one moment his breathing was hard and thick--a moment after hurried and broken.

All this while the fingers of Gershom were flying rapidly over the paper, independently of his eyes, which were sometimes closed, and sometimes rolling as if in trouble.

A wind which had been gathering all the evening now came moaning up the hollow, rattling the window-blinds, and twisting into dull complaint the boughs of the leafless trees. Its voice came chill and cheerless into the dusky room, where the fire was now glimmering near its death, and the only sounds were those of Gershom's rushing pencil, the whispering of Marshall and his friend, and old Mother Scritcher feebly whimpering in her corner. The scene was sinister. Suddenly, a rushing gust blew the door wide open.

Golyer started to his feet, trembling in every limb, and looking furtively over his shoulder out into the night. Quickly recovering himself, he turned to resume his place. But the moment he dropped Gershom's hand, the medium had dropped his pencil, and had sunk back in his chair in a deep and deathlike slumber. Golyer seized the sheet of paper, and with the first line that he read a strange and horrible transformation was wrought in the man. His eyes protruded, his teeth chattered, he passed his hand over his head mechanically, and his hair stood up like the bristles on the back of a swine in rage. His face was blotched white and purple. He looked piteously about him for a moment, then crumpling the paper in his hand, cried out in a hoarse, choking voice, "Yes, it's a fact: I done it. It's no use denying on't.. Here it is, in black and white. Everybody knows it: ghosts come spooking around to tattle about it. What's the use of lying? I done it."

He paused, as if struck by a sudden recollection, then burst into tears and shook like a tree in a high wind. In a moment he dropped on his knees, and in that posture crawled over to Marshall: "Here, Mr. Marshall--here's the whole story. For God's sake, spare my wife and children all you can. Fix my little property all right for 'em, and God bless you for it!" Even while he was speaking, with a quick revulsion of feeling he rose to his feet, with a certain return of his natural dignity, and said, "But they sha'n't take me! None of my kin ever died that way: I've got too much sand in my gizzard to be took that way. Good-bye, friends all!"

He walked deliberately out into the wild, windy night.

Marshall glanced hurriedly at the fatal paper in his hand. It was full of that capricious detail with which in reverie we review scenes that are past. But a line here and there clearly enough told the story--how he went out to plant the apple tree; how Susie came by and rejected him; how he passed into the power of the devil for the time; how Bertie Leon came by and spoke to him, and patted him on the shoulder, and talked about city life; how he hated him and his pretty face and his good clothes; how they came to words and blows, and he struck him with his spade, and he fell into the trench, and he buried him there at the roots of the tree.

Marshall, following his first impulse, thrust the paper into the dull red coals. It flamed for an instant, and flew with a sound like a sob up the chimney.

They hunted for Golyer all night, but in the morning found him lying as if asleep, with the peace of expiation on his pale face, his pruning-knife in his, heart, and the red current of his life tinging the turf with crimson around the roots of the Blood Seedling.

JOHN HAY.

The Marquis.

Mrs. Ruggles lived near Crawfish Creek. Crawfish Creek ran near Thompson City. Thompson City was in a Western State, but now is in a Middle one. It was always in the midst of a great country--accepting local testimony and a rank growth of corn and politicians as the tests of greatness. The earth there was monotonously parched in summer, and monotonously muddy at all other times. The forests were gigantic, the air carbonic, and when the citizens wished to give Thompson City the highest commendation, they did so by saying that "fevernagur" was worse in some other places.

In the parlor of Mrs. Ruggles, which was also her kitchen and dining-hall, hung a frame containing a seven-by-nine mirror, which was the frame's excuse for being, although a compartment above and one below held squares of glass covered with paint instead of mercury. The lower one was colored like the contents of a wash-tub after a liberal use of indigo; and in the centre was a horizontal stroke of red, surmounted by a perpendicular dash of white, intersected by an oblique line of black--all of which represented a red boat, with a white sail and black spar, making an endless voyage across the lake of indigo. The black crosses in the sky were birds. The black lines on the left were bulrushes. And among these bulrushes a certain gloomy little object was either a Hebrew prophet or a muskrat.

Above the mirror was painted a long-tailed coat, from behind which extended a hand holding a bell-crowned hat, to whose scarlet lining the holder seemed inviting the spectator's particular attention. There were also a pair of legs and boots, a heavy shock of hair, a labyrinth of neckcloth and a florid human face. Under the boots were the words,

MARQUIS DE LA FAYETTE.

And the beholder was ever in doubt whether the marquis was trying to stand exclusively upon this title or was unconsciously trampling it into the ground.

Mrs. Ruggles admired this picture. Her knowledge of French was not great, but her ear was delicate; and thinking the words "sounded handsome," she had deliberately conferred them in full on her first-born. When in good-humor she was content with calling him "Marquis-dee." In fact, it was only when chasing him into the street with a lilac bush in her hand that she insisted on addressing him by his full name. At such times, between each flourish of the lilac bush and each yell of the young nobleman, she pronounced with significant fullness, with fearful exactness, the handsome-sounding name of Marquis de la Fayette Ruggles. His playmates, however, had not the delicate ear of the mother, and as the son had brown specks on his face, he was popularly known as "Frecky Rug."

Mrs. Ruggles and her late husband were pioneers in the Crawfish Valley. Subsequent settlers knew little, and apparently cared less, about her. They knew, however, that she had been a Peables, and that Peables blood was still doing its duty in her veins. And from her independence and reserve they argued that the Peableses must have been "high up"--at least in the estimation of Mrs. Ruggles. After Mr. Ruggles had been overcome by malaria in clearing the creek bottoms the pride of the Peables blood had sustained her in a long, brave fight with circumstances.

It was while he lay one night upon his deathbed, mistaking a watching neighbor for his wife, that he started up, saying, "Becky, if I could prove it to you afore I died!"

"Out of his head," was the quiet remark of Mrs. Ruggles to the watching neighbor by the bedside. There was no further sign of delirium. That exclamation of the dying Mr. Ruggles was a mystery to the women of Crawfish Creek, and remains so to this day.

It may be that the pride of Mrs. Ruggles was in excess of her wisdom. It may be if that pride had been a little more respected by the irreverent Crawfish settlers, they would not have had occasion to wonder, as they did wonder, how a heart so true, an honesty so stoical, a discrimination so acute could exist with an independence so absurd, a mind so uncultured, a sense of dignity so ridiculous as were found united in her character. It may be that the Peables blood was worthy of receiving honor as great as the ridicule it did receive. It may be if the world had known the

Peableses it would have been as proud of them as she was.

She was a person of scrupulous neatness, careful never to be seen by strangers except in a tidy dress, and with her hair in a Grecian knot, gracefully secured by a leather string and a wooden peg. "Weak creepings" were her main reliance in the way of disease. She was also troubled, at times, with a "fullness of the head." In addition, there were other times when her right side "felt separate." But she seldom complained of anything belonging to herself. Even her maladies, she took pleasure in knowing, were very different from those enjoyed by certain other women. Unwilling to be too familiar with any one baser than a Ruggles, she usually dined, as she lived, alone with her noble son.

On a certain summer evening she stirred her tea a long time in silence. She stirred it vigorously, creating a maelstrom inside her cup, where, very like a whale in the story-books, a little crust of bread disappeared and reappeared, and sailed round and round as if very much perplexed. Then she unconsciously reversed the current of the maelstrom, sending the baked and buttered whale to the bottom.

"I never see that air Miller, no odds how well I be," she remarked mechanically to the tea-pot, "but what I feel weak creepin's come over me. He puts dye-stuff on his baird. An' when a man's whiskers is gray an' his head keeps black, it's a sign he uses his jaw more'n he does his brains. An' that yaller-headed doll-baby o' his'n--the peert thing:--I'll lay fifty cents she never washed a dish. To think o' her sayin' a thing like that about Markis-dee!--an' there's more o' the Peables in him to-day--But I s'pose she don't know no better." And Mrs. Ruggles rose from the table, while the corner of her apron made a sudden journey to the corner of her eye. It was evident her moral nature had received a wound that rankled.

A year before this time the marquis and his playmates had watched several vigorous fellows plant a theodolite on the bank of Crawfish Creek, very much as the natives must have watched the Spaniards plant their first cross on San Salvador. The contract for grading the new railway bed was in the hands of a stranger named Miller, who was said to have known better days, and in the time of his prosperity had been thought a proper person to be called Colonel. He was a bluff man of forty years, who appeared to have known both the ups and downs of life, and whose determination to wear a black beard was equaled only by its determination to be gray. Rumor said that he had been a railroad president, that he made and spent vast sums of money, and that his home was somewhere in the East.

His only child, Alice, ten or twelve years old, bright, fair, full of animal spirits, who was indulged to the last degree by the roughly generous colonel, sometimes accompanied him about the half-developed country, searching for strange birds and blossoms in the woods or watching demurely the laborers ply their picks and shovels while he inspected their work.

The two rode almost daily between Thompson City and the line of excavation, passing the house of Mrs. Ruggles and a cool spring by the roadside near it, whence that lady had obtained the water which made the tea which was stirred into the maelstrom which has been described. While obtaining it, clad in her working garb, the patter of hoofs and a clear girlish laugh--sweet as the carol of a meadow lark-- came ringing along the road. As the colonel and Alice halted to let her high-mettled pony and his heavier Morgan drink, Mrs. Ruggles, who could not otherwise escape observation, with becoming pride and modesty stepped behind the thick willows, leaving the marquis with a pail of water between his legs and a bunch of mottled feathers in his hand.

He stood dumb before the lovely girl, with her face sparkling from exercise and enjoyment, and her golden hair escaping from its prison of blue ribbons. While the horses drank she espied a cluster of cool violets brightening the damp grass near the spring. The marquis had presence of mind enough left to step forward and pluck them. Her "Thank you!" added greatly to his embarrassment, which he expressed by vigorously twisting the mottled feathers.

"What bird are those from?" asked Alice.

The question so increased his embarrassment that now the marquis could express it only by chewing his cap, and she smilingly waited a moment for the composure of the young naturalist's feelings.

"She was a low, chunky hen," said he, at length--"she was a low, chunky hen, an' she laid a hundred an' seven eggs, an' then she had spazzums an' whirled roun' till she died."

A burst of irrepressible laughter escaped Alice, with the exclamation, "Did anybody ever see such a boy?" as she and her father rode away. And those were the exceptionable words concerning her son which so rankled that evening in the heart of Mrs. Ruggles.

The marquis gazed with hungry eyes after the airy little figure as it dashed down the unlovely, worm-fenced road. The golden hair, overflowing its boundaries of blue ribbon, was more glorious to him than the golden sunshine overflowing the blue sky. They met no more at the spring, but several times a week, from a respect-ful distance, he watched her riding by. From Thompson City to the little log bridge over Crawfish Creek the road lay for four miles through heavy woods. Then came cleared fields, and soon the house of Mrs. Ruggles.

So the summer days went by. The season was waning, the grading was almost done, and soon the contractor would be elsewhere. Then came one particularly warm and sultry day. The screams of locusts everywhere suggested that they were frying. The colonel, riding once more slowly out toward the workmen with his daughter, was near the middle of the forest. The trees on either hand were tall, and the road was so straight and narrow that the sunlight scarcely touched it. The mar-quis, in the top of a tall chestnut that overhung the road near the edge of the wood, was overhauling a nest of flying squirrels--perhaps in the hope of finding mottled feathers on their wings. From his elevation he could see for a great distance down the level, dusty road between the trees, and far across the surrounding country.

The sun did not shine bright, yet no cloud was in the sky. The atmosphere, thick, oppressive, opaque, veiled the horizon with strange gloom. Not a leaf could stir in the vast forest. Not a dimple nor the semblance of a current broke the surface of the sluggish creek. Not a sound, save the interminable frying of the locusts.

The colonel slackened his pace, surprised that his horse should so soon begin to drip and pant--Alice, familiar with the road, in the mean time riding a mile ahead. The marquis clung to the topmost branches, looking at the still sky far above him, the still stream far below him, the still tree-tops far around him, till he caught a glimpse of the only interesting object to be seen--a black pony bearing its usual burden, if Alice Miller could be called a burden, and pacing leisurely up the road beneath him. He gazed as far as the palisade of trees permitted, but her father was not yet in sight.

Suddenly, in the west, a single vein of lightning darted down the sky. A few trees shuddered as if to shake the gathering shadows from their bosoms. Then ten-fold stillness. A bird flew past with a scream of terror, the marquis looking in vain to see a hawk pursuing it. The distant moan of a cow came from the fields. Not another sound, it seemed, was in the world.

In an instant the south-west was black. A strange, remote murmur smote the colonel's ear. Overhead he could see but a strip of hot, hazy sky. Had he seen the whole heavens, he could have done nothing but go on. Quickly the murmur became an awful muttering, then a deafening roar. The clatter, the rush, the crash of a tornado were behind him. The groans of the very earth were about him. The darkness of twilight was upon him. Alice and Death were before him. A cloudy demon, towering high as the heavens, in whose path nothing could live, was striding near and nearer.

Farm-houses were overthrown. Trees were twisted off from their roots and torn to pieces. Wild animals and birds were dashed to death. Streams were emptied of their waters. Human beings and horses and cattle were lifted into the air, hurled hither and thither and thrown dead upon the earth.

The whirlwind was following the line of the road! Colonel Miller had no opportunity to see this, nor could he ride aside from that line if he chose. He could but cry aloud, "My darling! O God! Alice!" and lash his horse forward. The high, close forest would keep the wind from lifting his horse from the ground or himself from the saddle. But the great trees crashed like thunder behind him. Their fragments whirled above him. Their branches fell before him. The limb of a huge oak grazed his face, crushed his horse, and both rolled to the ground, blinded with dust, imprisoned within a barricade of splintered trunks and shattered tree-tops.

The marquis, from his high lookout, saw, before any one else, the approaching tornado, and, descending like a flash, he yet noted its direction. As Alice reached the foot of his tree he was on the ground, had seized the pony's mane, was half seated and half clinging in front of her, had snatched the reins from her hand, and was urging the frightened animal to its utmost speed. Overcome with terror and confusion, Alice clung instinctively to the saddle and to him, without hearing his hurried advice to "stick like a old burdock."

They shot like an arrow up the road. The noise of the tempest was audible. Closer it was coming, crushing, rending, annihilating all before it. The way grew darker. The terrified pony scarce touched the ground. His only will was to go forward, and he still obeyed a firm use of the bit. But who could hope to outrun a hurricane? Twelve miles an hour against eighty! The marquis heeded nothing. Not far behind, the road was but a slash of fallen, writhing tree-tops. The sweat dropped from his face. He dared not look behind.

They reached it--the lane, by the log bridge, running at right angles to the road--and in a moment, behind them, that lane was choked with whirling debris.

But in that moment they had cleared the track of the whirlwind. For the first time Alice comprehended the conduct of the marquis. For the first time he turned to see. A quarter of a mile each side the road the hurricane had carried complete desolation. But after passing the heavy timber it had veered several degrees, and was sparing the house of Mrs. Ruggles.

With a white face she met them at the gate. A word of explanation from the marquis--an ejaculation of mental anguish from the girl. Two fugitive tie-choppers from the woods turned back to find the colonel's body. Mrs. Ruggles, carrying Alice in her arms to the door--the yaller-headed doll-baby that never washed a dish--did what she could to soothe her, but did it as silently as possible.

Mrs. Ruggles intercepted the returning tie-choppers in the lane. A look of eager joy was in their faces. The bruised colonel, assisted to the threshold, sank into the big arm-chair, and Alice was in his arms. Mrs. Ruggles did not see their meeting, not at all. No, her back was toward them, but the corner of her apron made another journey to the corner of her eye as the father folded his lost child once more to his heart.

His desire to express his gratitude to Mrs. Ruggles and her boy was equaled only by her fears that he would do so. As a last resort he called the marquis to him, and, while a tear stood on his rough cheek, drew a handful of money from his pocket. But a bony hand appeared majestically between them, and a voice said, "Not by no means. We're not them kind o' persons. Markis-dee, put away the camfire."

Then a rickety gig rattled up to the gate: "Contusion--severe--no danger--there!--be lame a while--so!--the other bandage--bridge gone--creek half dry--bend your leg--so!--current turned up-stream--now the shoulder--not strange Crawfish Creek should run backward--he! he!" And the rickety gig rattled merrily off in search of broken bones.

Alice, meeting the marquis outside the door, approached him in a way that made him tremble. What was said will never be known, but she placed her white little hand upon his shoulder, the golden head bowed for a moment and her sweet lips touched his sunburnt face.

By remaining quiet that night the colonel would be able to get back to Thompson City in the morning. Before nine o'clock he was at rest in the bed-room. A couch for Alice had been prepared in the same room. In the other--kitchen, parlor and dining-hall--a blanket was thrown down for the marquis, and two chairs fixed for the bed of Mrs. Ruggles. Before retiring, however, she sat down at her lonely table, where, notwithstanding the tea she drank to keep them off, an unusual number of weak creepings came over her.

"I couldn't help it," was all she said to the tea-pot. Whether she referred to the tornado, or her kindness to the sufferers, or to the manner of rendering the kindness, no one knows. That was all she said to the tea-pot, but to her son, who sat for a while beside her, she spoke in a low tone: "Markis-dee, you could never c'verse with her. You're better'n she is. Put her out o' yer head. She laughed at ye."

"But she kissed me wi' tears in 'er eyes afterward," was his answer as he turned toward his bed on the floor.

An hour later the tea was exhausted, but Mrs. Ruggles yet sat at her lonely table, as still as the sleepers around her. The clock struck ten: she nervously drew a soiled paper from her bosom. Eleven: she rose with hesitation and set the tallow candle behind the door. Then she softly entered the bed-room and stood before the window where Alice lay. The sky was clear again. The moon shone on the face and form of the sleeping girl, making softer their graceful lines, richer the shadows in the golden hair, tenderer the tint of cheek and lip.

She stepped again into the shade and stole to the colonel's bedside. His disturbed mind had turned backward over the path of life from the sudden death escaped, and, sleeping or waking, his memory had been busy with the people and events of other days.

"John Miller!" she said, in a suppressed tone. He started. "John Miller, I know ye. Common name--I wa'n't sure afore to-day. When you pulled that money out o' yer pocket I see that in yer face that satisfied me. It's fer the good name o' the dead I've come. Elseways I never'd ha' troubled ye." The astonished colonel shifted his position painfully, prepared to speak or to listen. "There yer girl lies in the light o' heaven. Nex' room my boy lies in the shadder an' dark. He don't know, an' he never will. John Miller, I married as honest an' as good a man as ever you see. Folks has come to me in sickness an' trouble, an' gone behin' my back to talk. Some said I done right to take him--'twas Christian in me. Some said I must ha' been a fool. Some said we wa'n't married a-tall. Wasn't I a Peables? Didn't I know 'twould be flung up to my face? Wasn't I prouder'n any on 'em?"

A moment's confusion and doubting of senses: then, as the suppressed voice went on, the colonel remembered. A dozen years ago; before he had meddled with railroads; back in the old town; soon after taking his father's shop; he was plaintiff; Ruggles worked in the first room; Porter's testimony; Becky Peables the sweetheart of both; burglary; loss trifling; George Ruggles, for one year; came back and married when released; went West. The old case had scarce crossed his mind for years.

"Yes, you sent him, an' I waited fer him. The day he come out I married him. We had to dig hard. I'd do it ag'in. Now his boy's saved yer girl's life to pay ye fer puttin' his father'n State's pris'n. Two year ago didn't Bill Porter--sick an' a-dyin'--hunt till he foun' me here? Didn't he go an' swear? Done fer spite. Didn't he sen' me the affydavy?--an' I've got it safe. Got it swore to by him, with the justice o' the peace's name signed, an' two witnissis, an' the judge's red seal on top o' that. Could I go back an' show that paper'n tell how 'twas? Too late! George was dead. I couldn't go. My folks a'most disowned me when I took him. I said then I never'd step my foot into their doors. Them that gives me the col' shoulder once don't do it no more. Come to me?--well an' good. Go to them?--never."

The bewildered colonel, promising every possible reparation, would have thrown himself at her feet, could he have done so, for the part he had taken in the prosecution. But she permitted no interruption, and continued: "He lay by the winder where yer girl lies. The moon come in on his bed as it does on her'n. In the night, when I see the light o' the sky shine there where he died, I feel his sperit in the room. I moved the bed to this corner, where it's darker. I wa'n't good enough to lie there. But 'twas on his mind. He said, 'Becky, if I could prove it to you afore I died!' An' I say, George's sperit sent Bill Porter here, an' sent you here, an' sent me into this room to-night. Now, fer the sake o'him an' Markis-dee, go back an' tell the truth!"

Speaking the word "truth," she vanished across the light to her dark place of rest.

Next morning the colonel examined and copied the confession while a buggy waited for him at the door. Respecting the evident wishes of Mrs. Ruggles, he went away with no attempt to express the feelings that were uppermost in his heart.

She sleeps beside her husband in the orchard. Her old log-house has been replaced by a large white box, of which her son the marquis is proprietor. Each year adds to his acres or his stock. An able-bodied wife, whose industry and English are equal to his own, sits near him at the door on a summer evening, while he smokes his pipe, takes an oakum-headed child upon his knee, and gazes quietly in the direction of the spring and across the grain-fields where once he saw--or rather heard, without waiting to see--a forest swept down in a moment. He smokes and gazes as he sees again a dazzling creature ride down the dreary road, and wonders where on earth that face can be, and how much it has changed, and whether, through so many years, any memory of him can linger in her heart. He says nothing. But he hugs closer the oakum-headed child as he remembers the one romance in his hard, humdrum life.

CHAUNCEY HICKOX.

Under False Colors.

Chapter I.
Hoisting The Flag.

A dreary, murky November day brooded over Southampton, and an impenetrable fog hung over sea and shore alike, penetrating the clothing, chilling the blood and depressing the spirits of every unlucky person who was so unfortunate as to come within the range of its influence. The passengers on the steamship America, from Bremen for New York via Southampton, found the brief period of their stay at the latter port almost unendurable; and while some paced the wet decks impatiently, others grumbled both loudly and deeply in the cabins, or shut themselves up in their state-rooms in sulky discomfort. Those who remained on deck had at least the amusement of watching for the steamboat which was to bring the Southampton passengers--a pastime which, however, being indefinitely prolonged, began to grow wearisome. It came at last--a wretched little vessel, rather smaller than the smallest of the noisy tugs that puff and paddle on our American rivers--and the wet, sick, unsheltered passengers were gradually transferred to the deck of the ship.

Among those who appeared to have suffered most severely from the rocking of the miserable little steamboat was a young, fair-haired girl, apparently about seventeen years of age, who seemed almost insensible. She would have fallen had not one of her fellow-travelers, a lady evidently not much her senior, thrown her arm around her; thus aided, she managed to reach the steamer's deck and to totter down the staircase leading to the ladies' cabin. The active, busy steward at once bustled up to the two young girls:

"Your names, ladies, if you please. I will point out your state-rooms in a moment. Miss Marion Nugent--Miss Rhoda Steele? Miss Nugent, berth No. 20, stateroom G--"

"Cannot I occupy the same state-room with this young lady?" interrupted the taller girl, who was still lending the support of her arm to sustain her half-fainting companion.

"Do not leave me, please," murmured the sufferer.

The steward threw a compassionate glance upon the pair, went away, and after a short consultation with the unseen powers, returned and said that the arrangement had been effected, and that they could take possession at once of their stateroom, into which he proceeded to usher them. It was more spacious than such apartments usually are, and abounded with all those little contrivances for comfort and convenience for which the steamers of the North German Lloyds are justly famed. The invalid sank down on the soft-cushioned little sofa and gasped painfully for breath.

"For Heaven's sake, get me some wine or some brandy!" exclaimed her companion. "This poor thing seems very ill; and do tell the doctor to come here at once."

With a quick, energetic movement, as she spoke she unclasped the heavy waterproof cloak of the sufferer and threw it back, thus revealing a fair, pallid face, framed in loosened curls of silky golden hair. It was a face that must have looked singularly lovely when tinted with the rosy hues of health, so delicate were the features and so large and blue the half-closed eyes, but it was ghastly pale, and a livid, bluish tinge had settled around the small mouth, whose ruby hues had fled to give place to a sickly purple. The steward speedily returned with some brandy, the bull's-eye was thrown open, and the cold sea air and potent spirit soon asserted their restorative powers. She sat up, a more natural color over-spreading her countenance, and she murmured inarticulately a few words of thanks, while the kindhearted steward hastened away again in search of the doctor.

"I am subject to these attacks," she said, faintly; to her companion when they were again left alone. "Only feel how my heart is beating."

The ship's surgeon soon made his appearance. He was a young, light-haired, solemn-looking German, who shook his head and looked very grave as he listened to the labored breathing and felt the bounding, irregular pulse of the sufferer.

"It is a pity that the ship has started," he said in very good English, "for I hardly think you are fitted to bear the fatigues of a sea-voyage at this season of the year; and had we been still at anchor, I should have counseled you to return to shore. But it is too late now, and you must try to keep as quiet as possible. I would advise you to retire to your berth at once: it will probably be a stormy night, and you had better settle yourself comfortably before the motion begins to be unpleasant. I will see you again in the morning, and if you feel worse meanwhile, let me know at once."

The doctor and the steward then quitted the state-room, and its two occupants, being left alone, surveyed each other curiously.

The active and energetic girl who had acted as spokeswoman and directress throughout the brief scene we have just described had let fall her waterproof cloak and stood arrayed in a black velvet jacket and dark silk skirt, both much the worse for wear, and contrasting sadly with the neat but simple traveling costume of her companion. But about her slender, finely-proportioned figure there was an air of style and grace which lent an elegance even to her shabby and faded finery, and which was wanting in the owner of the fresher and more appropriate attire. Her face was beautiful, with a singular and weird beauty which owed nothing of its fascinations to the ordinary charms of delicate outlines and dainty coloring. Her features were small and attenuated, and her complexion was of a sallow paleness, whose lack of freshness seemed caused by dissipation and late hours or by the ravages of illness. Heavy masses of soft silken hair, black as midnight, with bluish reflections on its lustrous waves (bleu a force d'etre noir, as Alexandre Dumas describes such tresses), untortured by crimping-pins or curling-tongs, were rolled back in plain folds above her low, broad brow. Her eyes would have lent beauty to a plainer face. Large almost to a fault, of that dark, clear blue which is too perfect and too transparent ever to look black even under the shadow of such long, thick eyelashes as shaded them in the present instance, they were perfectly magnificent; and their lustrous azure and ever-varying expression lent to the mobile countenance of their possessor its most potent and peculiar charm.

She was the first to speak. "Do you not think you had better retire to your berth?" she asked. "The rocking of the ship is increasing, and we had better, early as it is, settle ourselves for the night, before it becomes so violent as to prevent us from moving."

At this moment two porters made their appearance laden with packages. Two small new trunks--one marked R.S., the other M.N.--were deposited on the floor and identified by their possessors. The sick girl then attempted, with trembling hands, to disembarrass herself of her apparel, but it was not without much assistance from her companion that she was enabled to remove her traveling costume and make her preparations for retiring. At last, however, she was ready, and was about to make an attempt to reach the upper berth, which was the one allotted to her by number, when a quick, imperative gesture from her companion stopped her.

"No, no," she said: "you must take the lower berth. I can reach the upper one without any trouble, and you are not strong enough for so much exertion."

"You are very, very kind," said the invalid, gratefully. She sank back on the pillow and watched the other for some minutes in silence, as she quietly and quickly gathered up and put in order the scattered articles with which the state-room was strewn.

"Will you not give me that little black bag?" she said at last. "Thanks! that is it. I wished to be certain that I had put my letter of introduction in it. Ah! here it is, quite safe. It would never do for me to lose that letter, for the lady with whom I am going to live as governess has never seen me, and she might take me for an impostor were I to come without it. An English lady who was her most intimate friend engaged me for her. I wonder what New York is like?--very rough, and wild, no doubt, and I am afraid I shall be much annoyed by the rattlesnakes. You are going to New York too, are you not?"

"I am."

"Have you friends there?"

"None."

"I wish I had some acquaintances among our fellow-passengers, but I do not know a single one. Do you?"

"No."

"You have not told me your name yet. Mine is Marion Nugent; and yours--"

"Is not so pretty a one--Rhoda Steele."

There was something in the tone of these replies that quelled the invalid's disposition to talk, and she remained silent while her companion finished her arrangements and prepared to take possession of her berth. It was time that she did

so. The threatened gale was by this time blowing in earnest, and the ship was com-
mencing to roll fearfully; so, after securing all the boxes and bags as well as possible,
and hanging up all the scattered garments, she made a hasty retreat to her couch,
and lay there only half undressed, but utterly prostrate, and as unable to touch the
tea and biscuits brought by the attentive stewardess as was her more delicate and
suffering room-mate.

Time passed on: the daylight faded from the sky, a feeble glimmering lamp
shed its faint rays into the state-room, and the great steamship went steadily on,
though rocked and tossed like a plaything by the whistling winds and angry sea.
Then midnight came: the lights in the state-rooms were extinguished and a profound silence reigned throughout the cabins, broken only by the ceaseless throb of
the mighty engines and the noisy clanking of the screw.

The state-room was wrapped in profound darkness when Rhoda Steele awoke
with a start as from some troubled dream. Was she still dreaming, or did she indeed
hear a strange choking sound proceeding from the lower berth? She sprang to the
floor at once, heeding neither the darkness nor the violent motion, and clinging
to the side of the berth she called aloud. There was no answer: even the gurgling,
choking sound she had at first heard had ceased. She put out her hand, and it en-
countered her companion's face. It was deathly cold, and the features quivered as
if convulsed under her touch. Again she called aloud--still no answer; and then,
thoroughly frightened, she caught up a cloak from the sofa, threw it around her,
and opening the state-room door, she rushed into the cabin. It was almost deserted.
The lamps swung heavily overhead, swayed by the unceasing rolling of the ship; a
drowsy waiter slumbered at one of the tables, his head resting on his folded arms;
and one or two sleepy passengers tried to maintain a recumbent posture on the
broad sofas that lined the sides. The cries of the terrified girl soon brought several
of the waiters to her assistance, and Captain Wessels himself, who had not retired
to rest, owing to the stormy weather, came to ascertain the cause of the unusual
disturbance. Her story was quickly told: lights were brought, and the captain accompanied her back to the state-room.

It was a pitiful sight that met their eyes. The young girl lay motionless in her
berth, her face tinged with a livid bluish hue, her eyes closed, and her small hands
clenched as if in agony.

"The doctor!--run for the doctor!" was the instant and universal exclamation. The doctor came. One look at the pallid face, one touch on the slender wrist, and he turned with a grave face to the bystanders.

"There is nothing to be done," he said. "She is dead. I feared some such catastrophe when I saw her last evening. She was in the last stages of heart disease."

"And who was she?--what was her name?" asked kind-hearted Captain Wessels, looking down with pitying eyes at the fair pale face.

The steward brought his lists.

"Berth No. 22," he read--"Miss Rhoda Steele."

"And this young lady?" continued the captain, turning to the other occupant of the state-room, who had sunk back as if exhausted on the sofa, still enveloped in the shrouding folds of her large waterproof cloak.

She raised her head. The answer came after a moment's hesitation--came with a strange, defiant ring in its tone:

"My name is Marion Nugent."

Chapter II.
Under Full Sail.

More than a year has passed away since the events narrated in our first chapter took place, and the curtain now rises on a far different scene--a dinner-party in one of the most splendid of the gorgeous mansions on Madison avenue, New York.

Mrs. Walton Rutherford, the giver of the entertainment in question, was a member of a class unhappily now fast dying out of New York society--one of those ladies of high social position and ancient lineage who adorn the station which they occupy as much by their virtues as by their social talents. A high-minded, pure-souled matron, a devoted wife and mother, as well as a queen of society, inheriting the noble qualities of her Revolutionary forefathers as well as their great estates--such was the lady who presided over the brilliant festivity we are about to describe. She had been left for many years a widow, and her surviving children--two sons, Clement and Horace--were both of mature age; Horace, the younger, being just thirty years old, and Clement, the elder, some seven years his senior. Mrs. Rutherford herself was a few years over sixty. A year or two before the period at which our story opens a terrible misfortune had befallen her. Amaurosis--that most insidious and unmanageable of diseases of the eye--had attacked her vision, and in a few months after it declared itself she was totally, hopelessly blind. But, although debarred by her infirmity from going into society, she still received her friends in her own home; and her evening receptions and elegant dinners were always cited as being among the most agreeable and successful entertainments of the season.

Another sorrow had recently come to trouble the calm of her honored and tranquil existence--the marriage of her eldest son. Clement Rutherford, unlike any other member of the family, was a cold, reserved man, unpleasant in temper and disagreeable in manner. When he was still quite a boy, his mother's only sister, Miss Myra Van Vleyden, had died, and had bequeathed to him the large fortune which she had inherited conjointly with Mrs. Rutherford from her father, the two sisters being the only children of Schuyler Van Vleyden. She was a soured, morose old maid, and probably saw some congeniality of disposition in her eldest nephew which caused her to single him out as her heir. After he attained to years of manhood, he always manifested a decided antipathy to ladies' society, and was generally looked upon as a confirmed old bachelor; so that when he announced to his mother the fact of his engagement to Mrs. Archer's pretty governess, Miss Nugent, her distress of mind was fully equaled by her astonishment. The match met with her strongest disapproval, as was to have been expected; for it was hardly probable that she, the oldest surviving representative of the old Knickerbocker family the Van Vleydens, an acknowledged leader of society by the triple right of wealth, birth and intellect, should be inclined to welcome very warmly as a daughter-in-law the penniless beauty who had been occupied for some months past in teaching Mrs. Archer's little daughters the rudiments of French and music. Moreover, the investigations and inquiries respecting the young lady's origin which she had at once caused to be instituted on hearing of her son's engagement, had revealed a state of affairs which had placed Miss Nugent in a very unenviable light. Her parents were well born, though poor. She was the daughter of a curate in the North of England, who had lost his young wife by heart disease when Marion was but a few months old, and two years later Mr. Nugent died of consumption, leaving his little daughter to the care of his unmarried and elderly brother, the Reverend Walter Nugent, who, though the living he held was but a small one, contrived to rear and educate his niece as his own child. He had only allowed her to leave him and become a governess on the assurance of the village physician that her health was seriously impaired, and that a sea voyage and complete change of scene would prove the best and surest of restoratives. But the pained though manly tone of the letter in which he replied to Mrs. Rutherford's inquiries had prepossessed that warm-hearted, high-minded lady most strongly against her future daughter-in-law. "I loved Marion always as though she were my own child," wrote Mr. Nugent, "and I cannot but look upon her total neglect of me since her arrival in America as being wholly inexcusable. She has never even written me one line since her departure, and I learned of her safe arrival only by the newspapers. I can but infer from her obstinate and persistent silence that she wishes to sever all ties between herself and me, and I have resigned myself to the prospect of a lonely and cheerless old age. I trust that she may be happy in the brilliant marriage which, you say, she is about to make, and I can assure her that her old uncle will never disturb her in her new prosperity."

Mrs. Rutherford had one long, stormy interview with her eldest son, and learning therein that his determination to marry Miss Nugent was fixed and unalterable, she had with commendable wisdom accepted the situation, and resolved to so order the conduct of herself and her relatives as to give the scandalous world no room for that contemptuous pity and abundant gossip which an open rupture between herself and her son would doubtless have occasioned.

The manner of the wooing had been in this wise: John Archer, a sober, staid gentleman of great wealth, was Clement Rutherford's most intimate friend, and naturally, when the Archers moved into their new and splendid villa at Newport, Clement was invited to spend a few weeks with them--an invitation which he readily accepted. A few days after his arrival, Mrs. Archer, who was a pretty, lively little coquette, not in the least sobered by some thirteen years of married life, offered to drive him out in her little phaeton. "John has just given me a new pair of ponies," she said--"such perfect beauties and so gentle that I long to drive them." So the pretty, stylish equipage, with its fair driver and faultless appointments, made its first appearance on the avenue that afternoon, and also, I am sorry to say, its last; for the "gentle beauties" afore-said, excited to emulation by the number of spirited steeds around them, became ambitious of distinction, and sought for and decidedly obtained it by running away, thereby overturning the phaeton, breaking the harness, bruising Mrs. Archer severely and dislocating Mr. Rutherford's ankle.

Mrs. Archer was as well as ever in a few days, but the injuries received by her guest proved sufficiently serious to compel him to maintain a recumbent position for a long time, and prevented him from walking for several weeks. She made every arrangement possible for his comfort, and she had a charming little reception-room on the ground floor, adjoining the library, fitted up as a bed-chamber, and installed him there; so that as soon as he was able to quit his bed for a sofa, he could be wheeled into the latter apartment, and there enjoy the distractions of literature and society. For a few days after he made his first appearance there his lovely hostess was all attention and devotion; but, finding that he was anything but an agreeable or impressionable companion, she soon wearied of his society. Mr. Archer, shortly after the accident had taken place, had been summoned from home by important business connected with some mining property which he possessed, and which necessitated his presence in the interior of Pennsylvania; so Mrs. Archer, thus left with the entertainment of her most uncongenial guest exclusively confided to her care, came speedily to the conclusion that he was a nuisance, and began to look about for a substitute to relieve her from her unwelcome duties. She decided that her pretty governess, who spoke French so well, and sang little French *chansonettes* so sweetly, and got herself up in such a charming manner, giving so much "chic" and style even to the simplest of toilettes, was just the person to take upon herself the task of amusing the uninteresting invalid.

"Do look after Mr. Rutherford a little, there's a dear, good creature," whispered Mrs. Archer confidentially to Miss Nugent. "He is dreadfully tiresome, to be sure, but John thinks the world of him, you know, and it would not exactly do to leave him alone all the time. I wish him to receive every attention while he is in the house, of course; but as for sitting for hours at a time with him in that stuffy little library--just in the height of the season, too--why, I cannot think of doing it. If you will just go and sit with him sometimes, and read to him a little, it will be an absolute charity to me. I'll see that Alice and Emily do not get into any mischief."

Which, considering that the young ladies in question were, one twelve, the other ten years of age, and both much addicted to flirtation and dancing the "German," was rather a rash promise and inconsiderately made.

So Miss Nugent was definitely installed as reader and *garde malade* in general, and Clement Rutherford soon learned to await her coming with impatience and to welcome her with delight. All his life long will he remember those summer days, when her voice and the low plash of the far-off ocean waves wove themselves together into music as she read, and when the blue splendors of her lustrous eyes lent a new meaning to the poet's story as it flowed in melodious verses from her lips. Then came a day when the book was laid aside, and the impassioned utterances of poetry gave place to the more prosaic but not less fervent accents of a newly-awakened passion. Cold, silent and morose as Clement Rutherford had always been, it had so happened that but few women had ever attempted to attract him, notwithstanding his wealth and social position; and the interested motives of those few had been so apparent that he had been repelled and disgusted, instead of being fascinated, by their wiles; so that Miss Nugent's grace and beauty and syren charms proved all too potent for his unoccupied though icy heart to resist; and thus it chanced that the day before Mr. Rutherford left Newport he astonished his hostess by requesting a private interview with her, and therein announcing his engagement to her governess.

"You could have knocked me down with a feather," Mrs. Archer said afterward to an intimate friend. "I never should have suspected that such a quiet, stupid man as he was would fall in love in that ridiculous kind of a way. Good gracious! how indignant old Mrs. Rutherford will be! and I shall be blamed for the whole affair, no doubt. I wish John had never brought the man here--I never *did* like him; and then, too, it is so provoking to lose Miss Nugent just now, while we are at Newport. Of course I can find no one to replace her till we return to New York. Well, I always *was* an unlucky little woman."

The marriage took place in the latter part of September, only a few weeks after the engagement had been first announced. Mrs. Rutherford, true to her resolution of making the best of the affair, was careful that none of the usual courtesies and observances should be neglected. The bridal gifts from the Rutherford family, if less splendid, were as numerous as they would have been had Mr. Rutherford married a member of his mother's decorous, high-bred "set," and all his immediate relatives called most punctiliously on the bride when the newly-wedded pair arrived in New York after their six weeks' trip to Philadelphia and Washington.

Mr. Rutherford decided to take rooms at the Brevoort House till he could purchase a suitable residence. His mother's splendid home was not thrown open to receive him and his unwelcome bride, as it would have been had he made a choice more consonant with her wishes.

But we have wandered far from the dinner given by Mrs. Rutherford in honor of her new daughter-in-law, and with which our chapter commences.

It was a superb entertainment, as the Rutherford dinners usually were. The service of gold plate purchased by Schuyler Van Vleyden when he was minister to Austria adorned the table, which was also decorated with three splendid pyramids of choicest flowers. An exquisite bouquet bloomed in front of each lady's plate, and the painted blossoms on the peerless dinner-service of rare old Sevres vied in every respect save fragrance with their living counterparts. An unseen orchestra, stationed in the conservatory, sent forth strains of music, now grave, now gay, as Gounod or Offenbach ruled the tuneful spirit of the hour. Twelve guests only were present, including Mrs. John Archer, to whom Mrs. Rutherford had in this fashion testified her forgiveness, and who had accepted the proffered olive-branch with delight, wearing, in order to do honor to the occasion, an exquisite dress, fresh from one of the most renowned *ateliers* of Parisian fashion. Mrs. Rutherford, as usual, notwithstanding her infirmity, presided with unfailing grace and dignity; and in her splendid dress of black satin, brocaded with bouquets of flowers in their natural hues, her cap and collar of priceless old point lace, and her antiquely set but magnificent ornaments of sapphires and diamonds, she still looked a queen of society. A well-trained servant was stationed behind her chair, who from time to time placed before her suitably-prepared portions of the various delicacies of the entertainment, of which she slightly partook, in order to obviate the restraint which her presence at the festivity without participating in it would have occasioned. On her left hand sat her younger son, Horace, whose watchful eyes followed her every movement, and whose loving care anticipated her every wish. He was a tall, stalwart-looking young man, fair-haired and blue-eyed, like his elder brother, but his frank, joyous expression and winning manners bore no resemblance to the sullen countenance and surly demeanor of Clement.

The bride was, of course, the, cynosure of all eyes. Attired in rich, creamy-white satin, the corsage shaded with folds of delicate lace, with coral ornaments on her neck and arms, and with the heavy masses of her dark hair interwoven with coral beads, she looked extremely beautiful, and was pronounced by the ladies present to be "handsome and stylish-looking, but decidedly dull." This latter accusation was more truthful than such charges usually are. Mrs. Clement Rutherford did feel unusually stupid. She was *ennuye* by the long, formal, stately dinner; she knew but few of the persons present; and her point-lace fan was frequently called into requisition to conceal her yawns. The game had been served before her next neighbor, a sprightly young New Yorker, who had been rather fascinated by her beauty, contrived to arouse her into something like animation. He succeeded at last, however, and it was not long before an unusually brilliant sally drew a merry laugh from her lips. Her laugh was peculiar--a low, musical, trilling sound, mirthful and melodious as the chime of a silver bell.

As its joyous music rang on the air, Mrs. Rutherford turned ghastly pale. She gasped convulsively, half rose from her seat and fell back in a deathlike swoon.

Of course all was instantly confusion and dismay. The guests sprang up, the waiters hurried forward--Horace was instantly at his mother's side.

"She has only fainted," he said in his clear, decided tones. "She will be better in a few moments. Let me beg of you, my friends, to resume your seats. Clement, will you oblige me by taking our mother's post?"

With the help of Mrs. Rutherford's special attendant, Horace supported the already reviving sufferer from the room. They conveyed her to her sleeping apartment, where restoratives and cold water were freely used, and she soon regained perfect consciousness. But returning animation seemed to bring with it a strange and overwhelming sorrow. When the servant had retired, leaving her alone with her son, she refused to answer any of his queries, and burying her face in her pillow, she wept with convulsive and irrepressible violence. At length the very vehemence of her grief seemed, by exhausting itself, to restore her to comparative calm: her tears ceased to flow, her heavy sobs no longer shook her frame, and she remained for some time perfectly quiet and silent. At length she spoke:

"Horace!"

"What is it, mother?"

"Describe to me the personal appearance of your brother's wife--minutely, as though a picture were to be painted from your words."

It was no unusual request. Horace was in the habit of thus minutely describing persons and places for his mother's benefit.

"She is rather below the middle height, and her form, though slender, is finely moulded and of perfect proportions. Her hands and feet are faultless, and her walk is extremely graceful, resembling more the gait of a French-woman than that of an English girl. Her complexion is pale and rather sallow, and her countenance is full of expression, which varies constantly when she talks. The lower part of her face is somewhat too thin for perfect beauty, and the chin is inclined to be pointed, and the cheeks are rather hollow, but the upper part is superb. Her brow is low and broad, and she folds back from it the heavy waves of her black hair in the plainest possible style. Her eyes are her chief beauty, and would transfigure any face into loveliness. They are very large, and of a dark, transparent blue, of so lustrous and so perfect an azure that not even in shadow do they look black. Stay--I can give you a better idea of her appearance than by multiplying words. Did you, when you were in Munich, visit the Gallery of Beauties in the Royal Palace?"

"I did."

"Do you remember the portrait of Lola Montez?"

"Certainly--as though I had seen it yesterday."

"Marion resembles that portrait very strikingly, particularly in the shape and carriage of her head."

"I am not mistaken--it is she. Would that I had never lived to see this day!" And Mrs. Rutherford wrung her hands in an agony of helpless, hopeless distress.

"It is she?" repeated Horace, in perplexity. "Whom do you mean, mother? Who was Marion Nugent?"

"She is not Marion Nugent--this impostor who has thrust herself into our midst, bringing scandal and dishonor as her dower."

"And who, then, is she?"

Mrs. Rutherford turned toward him and fixed on his face her tear-bathed eyes, as though sight were restored to her, and she were trying to read his thoughts in his countenance.

"Why should I tell you?" she said, after a pause: "why reveal to you the shameful secret, and tell of a misfortune which is without a remedy? Clement is married: what words of mine can divorce him? And who will believe the evidence of a blind woman? If I were not blind, I might openly denounce her, but now--" And again she wrung her hands in unspeakable anguish.

Horace knelt beside his mother's couch and folded her hands in his own.

"I will believe you, mother," he said, earnestly. "Trust me--tell me all. If this woman whom my brother has married be an impostor, he may yet be freed from the matrimonial chain."

"Could that be possible?"

"It may be. Let me try, at least. I will devote myself to your service if you will but confide in me."

"Close the door, and then come near me, Horace--nearer still. I *will* tell you all."

Two days later the steamship Pereire sailed from New York for Brest, numbering among her passengers Horace Rutherford.

Chapter III.
Striking the Flag.

The events narrated in our last chapter took place early in November, and it was not till the following March that the astonished friends of Horace Rutherford saw him reappear amongst them as suddenly and as unexpectedly as he had departed. "Business of importance" was the sole explanation he vouchsafed to those who questioned him respecting the motive of his brief European tour; and with that answer public curiosity was perforce obliged to content itself. Society had, in fact, grown weary of discussing the affairs of the Rutherford family. Clement Rutherford's *mesalliance*, his mother's sudden illness at that memorable dinner-party, her subsequent seclusion from the world, and Horace's inexplicable absence, had all afforded food for the insatiable appetite of the scandal-mongers. Then Gossip grew eloquent respecting the flirtations and "fast" manners of Clement Rutherford's wife, and whispered that the old lady's seizure had been either apoplexy or paralysis, brought on by her distress of mind at her son's marriage, and that she had never been herself since. Next, the elegant establishment of the newly-wedded pair on Twenty-sixth street, with its gorgeous furniture and costly appointments, furnished a theme for much conversation, and doubts were expressed as to whether the "Upper Ten" would honor with its august presence the ball which Mrs. Clement Rutherford proposed giving on Shrove Tuesday, which in that year came about the middle of March. But as to that, it was generally conceded that they would. Youth, beauty, wealth and the shadow of an old family name could cover a multitude of such sins as rapid manners, desperate flirtations and a questionable origin; and notwithstanding her fastness, and, worse still, her ***ci-devant*** governess-ship, Mrs. Clement Rutherford was a decided social success.

On the day succeeding that oh which he had arrived, Horace made his appearance at his brother's house. Clement had not heard of his return, and received him with a cordiality strikingly at variance with his usual manner.

"Come into the library," he said, after the first greetings had been exchanged. "I have some fine cigars for you to try, and you can tell me something about your travels."

"Thank you, Clement: I believe I must decline your offer. I have a message for your wife: can I see her?"

A cloud swept over the brow of the elder brother.

"I suppose you can," he said, coldly, looking at his watch as he spoke. "Two o'clock. She took breakfast about half an hour ago, so she is probably at home. You had better go up stairs to her ***boudoir***, as she calls it, and Christine, her maid, will tell her that you wish to see her."

He turned away, and was about to leave the room when Horace caught his hand.

"Clement! brother! Answer me one question: Are you happy in your married life?"

"Go ask the scandal-mongers of New York," was the bitter reply: "they are eloquent respecting the perfection of my connubial bliss."

"If she had been a kind and affectionate wife, if she had made him happy," muttered Horace as he ascended the stairs, "my task would have been a harder one. Now my duty is clear, and my course lies smooth and straight before, me."

The room into which he was ushered by Christine, the pretty French maid, was a perfect marvel of elegance and extravagance. It was very small, and on every part of it had been lavished all that the combined efforts of taste and expenditure could achieve. The walls had been painted in fresco by an eminent Italian artist, and bevies of rosy Cupids, trailing after them garlands of many-hued flowers, disported on a background of a delicate green tint. The same tints and design were repeated in the Aubusson carpet, and on the fine Gobelin tapestry which covered the few chairs and the one luxurious couch that formed the useful furniture of the tiny apartment. Etageres of carved and gilded wood occupied each corner, and, together with the low mantelshelf (which was upheld by two dancing nymphs in Carrara marble), were crowded with costly trifles in Bohemian glass, Dresden and Sevres porcelain, gilded bronze, carved ivory and Parian ware. An easel, drawn toward the centre of the room, supported the one painting that it contained, the designs on the walls being unsuited for the proper display of pictures. This one picture had evidently been selected on account of the contrast which it afforded to the gay coloring and *riante* style of the decorations. It was a superb marine view by Hamilton--a cloudy sunset above a stormy sea, the lurid sinking sun flinging streaks of blood-red light upon the leaden waters that, in the foreground, foamed and dashed themselves wildly against the rocks of a barren and precipitous shore.

Horace stood lost in contemplation before the easel, when the door opened and his sister-in-law entered. He turned to greet her, and her beauty, enhanced as it was by the elegance of her attire, drew from him an involuntary glance of admiration. Her dress was an exemplification of how much splendor may be lavished on a morning-costume without rendering it absolutely and ridiculously inappropriate. She wore a robe of turquoise-blue Indian cashmere, edged around the long train and flowing sleeves with a broad border of that marvelous gold embroidery which only Eastern fingers can execute or Eastern imaginations devise. A band of the same embroidery confined the robe around her slender, supple waist, and showed to advantage the perfection of her figure. A brooch and long ear-pendants of lustreless yellow gold, and a fan of azure silk with gilded sticks, were the adjuncts to this costume, whose rich hues and gorgeous effects would have crushed a less brilliant and stylish-looking woman, but which were wonderfully becoming to its graceful wearer.

"Welcome home, Horace!" she said in that low sweet voice which was one of her most potent charms. "How kind it is of you to pay me a visit so soon after your return!"

She placed herself on the couch and motioned to him to take a seat near her. He drew up his chair, and a short, embarrassed pause succeeded.

Mrs. Rutherford toyed with her fan and stole glances from under her long black lashes at her visitor, who sat twisting one of his gloves and wishing most ardently that Providence had entrusted the painful task before him to some one of a more obdurate and less chivalrous nature.

Wearied of silence, the lady spoke at last.

"Have you nothing of interest respecting your travels to tell me?" she asked.

Her voice seemed to break the spell which paralyzed him. He turned toward her with the look of one who nerves himself up to take a desperate resolution:

"Yes: I have a story to relate to you, and one of more than common interest."

"Really!" She yawned behind her fan. "Excuse me, but I was at Mrs. Houdon's ball last evening, and the 'German' was kept up till five o'clock this morning. I am wretchedly tired. Now do go on with your story: I have no doubt but that I shall find it amusing, but do not be much surprised if I fall asleep."

"I think you will find it interesting, and I have no fear of its putting you to sleep. But you must make me one promise. I am but a poor narrator, and you must engage not to interrupt me."

"I have no hesitation in promising to remain perfectly quiet, no matter how startling your incidents or how vivid your descriptions may be."

She leaned back among the cushions with another stifled yawn and shaded her eyes with her fan. Without heeding the veiled impertinence of her manner, Horace commenced his narrative:

"Some twenty-five years ago a friendless, penniless Englishwoman died at one of the cheap boarding-schools in Dieppe, where she had officiated for some time as English teacher and general drudge. She left behind her a little girl about five years of age--a pretty, engaging child, whose beauty and infantile fascinations so won the heart of Madame Tellier, the proprietress of the establishment, that she decided to take charge of the little creature and educate her, her project being to fit her for the post of English teacher in her school. But the pretty child grew up to be a beautiful but unprincipled girl, with an inborn passion for indolence and luxury. At the age of seventeen she eloped from the school with a young Parisian gentleman, who had been spending the summer months at one of the seaside hotels in Dieppe, and her benefactress saw her and heard of her no more.

"We will pass over the events of the next few years. It would hardly interest you to follow, as I did, each step by which the heroine of my history progressed ever downward on the path of vice. We find her at last traveling in Italy under the protection of the Count von Erlenstein, an Austrian noble of great wealth and dissolute character. She has cast aside the name she once bore, and, anticipating the jewel-borrowed cognomens of Cora Pearl and La Reine Topaze, she adopts a title from the profusion of pink coral jewelry which she habitually wears, and Rose Sherbrooke is known as Rose Coral."

Horace paused. A short, sharp sound broke the momentary silence: it was caused by the snapping of one of the gilded fan-sticks under the pressure of the white, rigid fingers that clasped it. But the listener kept her face hidden, and but for that convulsive motion the speaker might have fancied that she slept, so silent and motionless did she remain. After a short pause Horace continued:

"The attachment of Count von Erlenstein proved to be a lasting one, and we find Rose Coral at a later period installed in a luxurious establishment in Vienna, and one of the reigning queens of that realm of many sovereigns, the ***demi-monde*** of the gay capital of Austria. But the count falls ill; his sickness speedily assumes a dangerous form; his death deprives Rose Coral of her splendor; and the sunny streets of Vienna know her fair face no more. I will not retrace for you, as I could do, each step in her rapid descent from luxury to poverty, from splendor to vice, from celebrity to ruin. But one day she makes her appearance, under the name of Rhoda Steele, on board the steamship America, bound for New York. The state-room which she occupies is shared by a young girl named Marion Nugent, whose future career is to be that of a governess in the United States. On the first night out one of the occupants of the state-room is taken suddenly ill and dies, the corpse is committed to the deep, and it is reported throughout the ship that the name of the deceased is Rhoda Steele. The tale was false: it was Marion Nugent who died--it was Rose Sherbrooke, ***alias*** Rose Coral, ***alias*** Rhoda Steele, who lived to rob the dead girl of her effects and to assume her name!"

The broken fan was flung violently to the floor, and Mrs. Rutherford sprang to her feet, her face livid with passion and her blue eyes blazing with a steel-like light.

"How dare you come here to assert such falsehoods?" she cried. "You have always hated me--you and all the rest of your haughty family--because it pleased Clement Rutherford to marry me--me, a penniless governess. But I am your sister-in-law, and I *demand* that you treat me with proper respect. You came here to-day simply to insult me. Well, sir, I will summon my husband, and he shall protect me from your insolence."

She turned toward the door as she spoke, but he motioned her back with an imperative and scornful gesture.

"Softly, Rose Coral," he said, with a sneer: "the manners of the Quartier Breda are not much to my taste, nor do they suit the character you have been pleased to assume. Do you think me so void of common sense as to return home without full proof of your identity? I have in my possession a large colored photograph of you, taken some years ago by Hildebrandt of Vienna, and endorsed by him on the back with a certificate stating that it is an accurate likeness of the celebrated Rose Coral. Secondly, I have brought home with me two witnesses--one is Jane Sheldon, late housekeeper for the Rev. Walter Nugent, and formerly nurse to the deceased Marion Nugent; and the other is a French hairdresser who lived many years in Vienna, and who, for several months, daily arranged the profuse tresses of Rose Coral. One will prove who you are *not*, and the other will as certainly prove who you *are*."

"Who I *was*" she said, defiantly. "I will deny it no longer: I am Rose Sherbrooke, once known as Rose Coral, and, what is more to the purpose, I am the wife of Clement Rutherford. Have a care, my brother Horace, lest you reveal to the world that your immaculate relatives have been touching pitch of the blackest hue and greatest tenacity. Prove me to be the vilest of my sex, I remain none the less a wedded wife--your brother's wife--and I defy you. The game is played out, and I have won it."

She threw herself back in her chair and cast on him a glance of insolent disdain. Horace Rutherford looked at her with a scornful smile.

"The game is *not* played out," he said, calmly. "One card remains in my hand, and I produce it. It is the Ace of Diamonds, and its title is The Rose of the Morning."

A livid paleness overspread Mrs. Rutherford's features, and a stifled cry escaped from her lips. She half rose from her seat, but, seeming to recollect herself, she sank back and covered her face with her hands. Horace continued, after a momentary pause:

"My investigations into the history of the Count Wilhelm von Erlenstein during the last years of his life revealed the fact that he had lost the most valuable of the jewels of his family. It had been stolen. It was a pink diamond of great size and beauty, known to gem-connoisseurs by the name of The Rose of the Morning--one of those remarkable stones which have a history and a pedigree, and which are as well known by reputation to diamond-fanciers as are Raphael's Transfiguration and the Apollo Belvidere to the lovers of art. This gem was worn by Count Wilhelm as a clasp to the plume in his toque at a fancy ball given by one of the Metternich family, at which he appeared in the costume of Henri III. of France. He afterward, with culpable carelessness, placed it, amongst his studs, pins, watch-chains and other similar bijouterie, in a small steel cabinet which stood in his bed-chamber. His illness and the dismissal of Rose Coral occurred soon after the fancy ball in question, and it was not till his heir, the present count, had been for some time in possession of the estates that it was discovered that the great diamond was missing. It was not to be found, and suspicion immediately fell upon the late count's valet, a Frenchman named Antoine Lasalle; who was found to have been mysteriously possessed of a large sum of money after the count's death. He was arrested, and it was conclusively proved that he had stolen a number of valuable trinkets from his dying master, but still no trace of The Rose of the Morning could be discovered, and Lasalle strenuously denied all knowledge respecting it. The family offered large rewards for its recovery, and the detectives of all the large cities of Europe have been for some time on the alert to discover it, but in vain. As soon as I heard this story, I thought that I could make a tolerably shrewd guess as to the whereabouts of the missing jewel; and I caused investigations to be set on foot in New York by a trusty agent, which resulted in the discovery that The Rose of the Morning had been sold some six months before to a jeweler in Maiden lane for about one-twenty-fifth of its value, the peculiar tint of the stone, and the purchaser's ignorance of the estimation in which it is held by the gem-fanciers of Europe, having militated against the magnitude of the valuation set upon it. It was secured for me at a comparatively trifling price. The person who sold it to the jeweler some six months ago, in spite of a partial disguise and an assumed name, was easy to recognize, from the description given, as that lady of many names, Mrs. John Archer's governess. Now, Rose Coral, what say you? You may be Mrs. Clement Rutherford, my brother's lawful wife, but you are not the less a thief and a criminal, for whom the laws have terrible punishment and bitter degradation."

"This is but a poor invention: where are your proofs?" she cried, looking up as she spoke, but her faltering voice and quivering lips contradicted her words.

"Here is my chief witness." He drew off his left-hand glove as he spoke, and extended his hand toward her. On the third finger blazed the beautiful gem of which he had spoken, its great size and purity fully displayed in the pale afternoon sunlight that flashed back in rosy radiance from its bright-tinted depths.

"It is almost too large to wear as a ring," he said with great coolness, looking at the jewel, "but I wish it to run no further risks till I can transfer it to its lawful owner, which will be as soon as it has played its talismanic part by freeing my brother from his impostor-wife."

The lady rose from her seat, pale, calm and resolved.

"Further insults are useless, sir," she said. "The game is ended now, and you have won it. What is it that you wish me to do?"

"You must sail for Europe in one of next week's steamers, leaving behind you such a confession of guilt as will enable my brother to procure a divorce without revealing the shameful fact that he was the innocent means of introducing an impostor--a *ci-devant* lorette--to his family and friends as his wife. Better this scandal of an elopement than the horror of having such a story made public. An income amply sufficient for your wants will be settled upon you, on condition that you never return to the United States, and never, in any way, proclaim the fact that Mrs. Clement Rutherford and Rose Coral were one and the same person."

"I accept your conditions," she said, wearily. "I will go, never to return. Now leave me. But stay: will you not answer me one question?"

"I will, certainly."

"Who was it that discovered my secret?"

"My mother--my blind mother. Some years ago, before she lost her sight, I accompanied her on a short European tour, in which we visited England, France, Switzerland, and finally Italy. While we were at Rome I fell ill with the fever of the country, and my physicians gave orders that as soon as I was well enough to travel

I should leave Italy for a more bracing climate. We had not visited Naples, and I was anxious that my mother should not return home without seeing the wonders of that city; so as soon as I became convalescent I prevailed upon her to leave me in the care of some friends and to join a party who were going thither. During her stay she went frequently to the opera. One evening she was greatly disturbed by the loud talking and laughing of some persons in the box next to the one she occupied, and she was much struck with the beauty, the brilliant toilette and the boisterous conduct of one of the female members of the party. She inquired the name of the person she had thus remarked. It was yourself, and she learned not only your name, but your whole history. When at her own dinner-table she heard the sweet and singular laugh that had so struck her on that occasion, the sensitiveness of hearing peculiar to the blind caused her to recognize the sound at once; and the description which I afterward gave her of your personal appearance only changed torturing doubt into agonizing certainty."

"Thanks for your courtesy: I will detain you no longer."

Horace bowed and approached the door. Suddenly, as if moved by a sudden impulse, he turned back.

"Believe me, this task has been a hard one," he said, earnestly. "And remember, if hereafter you may need pecuniary aid, do not hesitate to apply to me. For Heaven's sake, do not return to the life you once led. There was one redeeming feature in the imposture which you practiced: it showed that some yearning for a pure name and an innocent life was yet possible to you."

"I want no sermons," she answered, abruptly. "Only leave me at peace. Go: I am sick of the sight of you."

As he closed the door he cast one parting glance on the room and its occupant. She stood leaning against the back of a large arm-chair, her clasped hands resting on the top, and her white, rigid face set in the fixed calmness of total despair.

Thus left alone, she remained standing for some time as motionless as though she were a marble statue and not a living woman. Suddenly she seemed to take some desperate resolve: she threw back her head with a bitter, mirthless laugh, and going to the bell she rang it. Her maid quickly appeared.

"I have a wretched headache, Christine," she said. "I shall not come down to dinner, and do not disturb me till nine o'clock: that will give me time enough to dress for Mrs. Winchester's ball. I will wear the pale-blue satin and my point-lace tunic. Be sure you change the white roses that loop it for pink ones, and lay out my parure of pearls and diamonds, and my point-lace fan and handkerchief. Now bring me the two phials that stand on the third shelf of the closet in my bed-chamber."

Christine departed on her errand and soon returned, bringing with her two bottles, the smallest of which was labeled "Solution of Morphia--POISON. Dose for an adult, ten drops;" while the largest Was simply inscribed "Sulphuric Ether." These she placed on the chimney-piece, and then proceeded to arrange the cushions of the lounge and to draw the curtains. "I will now leave madame to her repose," she said. "Does madame need anything more?"

"No, I shall want nothing more," was the reply. The door closed upon the maid's retreating form, and Mrs. Rutherford instantly shot the bolt.

She cast a sad and wistful glance around the dainty room and on its glittering contents. "J'etais si bien ici," she said regretfully. "I had found here the existence which suited me, and now the end has come. It is not in my nature to remain satisfied with a life of poverty and respectability, and I will not return to one of degradation and vice. But, after all, what does it matter? My fate would have found me sooner or later, and this soft couch is better than a hospital bed or the slabs of La Morgue: this draught is more soothing than the cold waters of the Thames or the Seine. Life is no longer a game that is worth the candle: let us extinguish the lights and put the cards away."

She took up the phial of morphia, drew the little sofa nearer to the fireplace and extended herself upon it. The daylight faded from the sky and night came, and with the night came sleep--a sleep whose dream was of Eternity, and whose wakening light would be the dawn of the resurrection morning.

"Accidental death" was the verdict of the coroner and the newspapers, and, in fact, of the world in general--a conclusion much assisted by the evidence of Christine, who testified that her mistress was in the habit of using narcotics and anaesthetics in large quantities to relieve the pain of the neuralgic headaches from which she was a constant sufferer. Society said, "How sad! Dreadful, is it not?" and went on its way--not exactly rejoicing, for the death of Mrs. Rutherford deprived its members of her long-promised, long-talked-of Shrove-Tuesday ball, and consequently the gay world mourned her loss very sincerely for a short time; in fact, till a well-known leader of fashion announced her intention of giving a fancy-dress party on the night thus left vacant, whereupon Society was consoled, and Mrs. Rutherford's sad fate was forgotten.

Only two persons--Horace Rutherford and his mother--suspected that her death was not an accidental one; but they guarded their secret carefully, and Clement Rutherford will never learn that his dead wife was other than the innocent English girl she represented herself to be. Walter Nugent wrote a pathetic letter to Mrs. Rutherford, begging that a lock of his lost and now forgiven darling's hair might be sent to him; and it cost Horace a sharp pang of regret when he substituted for the black, wavy tress furnished by Clement a golden ringlet purchased from one of the leading hairdressers of New York.

"Heaven forgive me!" he said to himself, remorsefully, as he sealed the little packet; "but I really think that this is one of the cases wherein one cannot be blamed for not revealing the truth."

A few months later, Horace Rutherford stood in Greenwood Cemetery contemplating with curiosity and interest the inscription on a recently-erected monument of pure white marble.

"Sacred to the memory of Marion Nugent, beloved wife of Clement Rutherford," he read. "Well, this is consistent at least. She wears the disguise of a virtuous woman in her very tomb. Marion Nugent rests beneath the waves of the Atlantic ocean, and here Rose Sherbrooke sleeps in an honored grave beneath the shelter of the dead girl's stainless name. But the deception has power to harm no longer, so let us leave her in peace. It is well for our family that, even as a sunken wreck, we still find this pirate bark Under False Colors,"

LUCY HAMILTON HOOPER.

The Hungry Heart.

A village on the coast of Maine; in this village a boarding-house; in this boarding-house a parlor.

This parlor is, strictly speaking, a chamber: it is in the second story, and until lately it contained a bed, washstand, etc.; but a visitor from New York has taken a fancy to change it to a reception-room. In the rear, communicating with it, is a sleeping-closet.

The room is what you might expect to find in a village boarding-house: the floor of liliuptian extent; the ceiling low, uneven, cracked and yellow; the originally coarse and ugly wall-paper now blotched with age; the carpet thin, threadbare, patched and stained; the furniture of various woods and colors, and in various stages of decrepitude.

But a tiny bracket or two, three or four handsome engravings, two fresh wreaths of evergreens, two vases of garden flowers, a number of Swiss and French knick-knacks, and a few prettily-bound books, give the little nest an air of refinement which is almost elegance.

You judge at once that the occupant must be a woman--a woman moreover of sensibility and taste; a woman of good society. Of all this you become positive when you look at her, take note of her gracious manner and listen to her cultured voice.

Her expression is singularly frank and almost childlike: it exhibits a rapid play of thoughts, and even of emotions: it is both vivacious and refined, both eager and sweet. It would seem as if here were the impossible combination, the ideal union, so often dreamed of by poets and artists, of girlish simplicity and innocence with womanly cleverness and feeling.

In a large easy-chair reclines her rather small, slender and willowy form, starting slightly forward when she speaks, and sinking back when she listens. Her sparkling eyes are fixed on the eyes of her one visitor with an intentness and animation of interest which should be very fascinating.

He, a young man, not five years older than herself, very gentle in manner and with a remarkably sweet expression of face, evidently is fascinated, and even strongly moved, if one may judge by the feverish color in his cheeks, the eager inquiry of his gaze and the tremor of his lips.

The first words of hers which we shall record are a strange utterance to come from a woman:

"Let me tell you something which I have read lately. It sounds like a satire, and yet there is too much truth in it: 'Every woman in these days needs two husbands-- one to fill her purse, and one to fill her heart; one to dress her, and one to love her. It is not easy to be the two in one.' That is what I have read, and it is only too true. Remember it, and don't marry."

A spasm of intense spiritual pain crossed the young man's fine and kindly face.

"Don't say such things, I beg of you!" he implored. "I am sure that in what you have quoted there is a slander upon most women. I know that it slanders you."

Her lips parted as if for a contradiction, but it was evidently very pleasant to her to hear such words from him, and with a little childlike smile of gratification she let him proceed.

"I have perfect confidence in you," he murmured. "I am willing to put all my chances of happiness in your hands. My only fear is that I am not half worthy of you--not a thousandth part worthy of you. Will you not listen to me seriously? Will you not be so kind?"

A tremor of emotion slightly lifted her hands, and it seemed for a moment as if she would extend them to him. Then there was a sudden revulsion: with a more violent shudder, evidently of a painful nature, she threw herself backward, her face turned pale, and she closed her eyes as if to shut him from her sight.

"I ought to ask your pardon," she whispered. "I never thought that it would come to this. I never meant that it should. Oh, I ask your pardon." Recovering herself with singular quickness, a bright smile dancing along the constantly changing curves of her lips, like sunbeams leaping from wavelet to wavelet, she once more leaned cordially toward him, and said in a gay yet pleading tone, "Let us talk of something else. Come, tell me about yourself--all about yourself, nothing about me."

"I cannot speak of anything else," he replied, after looking at her long in silence. "My whole being is full of you: I cannot think of anything else."

A smile of gratitude sweetly mastered her mouth: then it suddenly turned to a smile of pity; then it died in a quiver of remorse.

"Oh, we cannot marry," she sighed. "We must not marry, if we could. Let me tell you something dreadful. People hate each other after they are married. I know: I have seen it. I knew a girl of seventeen who married a man ten years older--a man who was Reason itself. Her friends told her, and she herself believed it, that she was sure of happiness. But after three years she found that she did not love, that she was not loved, and that she was miserable. He was too rational: he used to judge her as he would a column of figures--he had no comprehension for her feelings."

There was a momentary pause, during which she folded her hands and looked at him, but with an air of not seeing him. In the recollection of this heart-tragedy of the past and of another she had apparently forgotten the one which was now pressing upon herself.

"It was incredible how cold and unsympathizing and dull he could be," she went on. "Once, after she had worked a week in secret to surprise him with a dressing-gown made by her own hands--labored a week, waited and hoped a week for one word of praise--he only said, 'It is too short.' Don't you think it was cruel? It was. I suppose he soon forgot it, but she never could. A woman cannot forget such slights: they do not seem little blows to her; they make her very soul bleed."

"Don't reproach **me** for it," whispered the young man with a pleading smile. "You seem to be reproving me, and I can't bear it. I am not guilty."

"Oh, not you," she answered quickly. "I am not scolding you. I could not."

She did not mean it, but she gave him a smile of indescribable sweetness: she had had no intention of putting out her hands toward him, but she did it. He seized the delicate fingers and slowly drew her against his heart. Her face crimson with feeling, her whole form trembling to the tiniest vein, she rose to her feet, turning away her head as if to fly, and yet did not escape, and could not wish to escape. Holding her in his arm, he poured into her ear a murmur which was not words, it was so much more than words.

"Oh, *could* you truly love me?" she at last sobbed. "Could you *keep* loving me?"

After a while some painful recollection seemed to awaken her from this dream of happiness, and, drawing herself out of his embrace, she looked him sadly in the eyes, saying, "I must not be so weak. I must save myself and you from misery. Oh, I must. Go now--leave me for a while: do go. I must have time to think before I say another word to you."

"Good-bye, my love--soon to be my wife," he answered, stifling with a kiss the "No, no," which she tried to utter.

Although he meant to go, and although she was wretchedly anxious that he should go, he was far from gone. All across the room, at every square of the thread-bare carpet, they halted to renew their talk. Minutes passed, an hour had flown, and still he was there. And when he at last softly opened the door, she herself closed it, saying, "Oh no! not yet."

So greedy is a loving woman for love, so much does she hate to lose the breath of it from her soul: to let it be withdrawn is like consenting to die when life is sweetest.

Thus it was through her, who had bidden him to go, and who had meant that he should go, that he remained for minutes longer, dropping into her ear whispers of love which at last drew out her confession of love. And when the parting moment came--that moment of woman's life in which she least belongs to herself--there was not in this woman a single reservation of feeling or purpose.

These people, who were so madly in love with each other, were almost strangers. The man was Charles Leighton, a native of Northport, who had never gone farther from his home than to Boston, and there only to graduate in the Harvard College and Medical School.

The lady was Alice Duvernois: her name was all that was known of her in the village--it was all that she had told of herself. Only a month previous to the scene above described she had arrived in Northport to obtain, as she said, a summer of quiet and sea-bathing. She had come alone, engaged her own rooms, and for a time seemed to want nothing but solitude.

Even after she had made herself somewhat familiar with the other inmates of the boarding-house, nothing positive was learned of her history. That she had been married was probable: an indefinable something in her face and carriage seemed to reveal thus much: moreover, her trunks were marked "James Duvernois."

And yet, so young did she sometimes look, so childlike was her smile and so simple her manner, that there were curious ones who scouted the supposition of wifehood. People addressed her both as "Miss" and "Mrs."; at last it was discovered that her letters bore the latter title: then she became popularly known as "the beautiful widow."

It would be a waste of time to sketch the opening and ripening of the intimacy between Doctor Leighton and this fascinating stranger. On his part it was as nearly a case of love at first sight as perhaps can occur among people of the Anglo-Saxon race. From the beginning he had no doubts about giving her his whole heart: he was mastered at once by an emotion which would not let him hesitate: he longed with all his soul for her soul, and he strove to win it.

Well, we will not go over the story: we know that he had triumphed. Yes, in spite of her terror of the future, in spite of some withholding mystery in the past, she had granted him--or rather she had not been able to prevent him from seizing--her passionate affection. She had uttered a promise which, a month before, she would not have dreamed herself capable of making.

In so doing she had acquired an almost unendurable happiness. It was one of those mighty and terrible joys which are like the effect of opium--one of those joys which condense life and abbreviate it, which excite and yet stupefy, which intoxicate and kill. With this in her heart she lived ten of her old days in one, but also she drew for those ten days upon her future.

After one of her interviews with Leighton, after an hour of throbbing, of trembling, of vivid but confused emotions, her face would be as pale as death, and her weakness such that she could hardly speak. The hands which, while they clung to his, had been soft and moist, became dry and hot as with fever, and then cold as ice. At night she could scarcely sleep: for hours her brain throbbed with the thought of him, and of what stood between him and her. In the morning she was heavy with headache, dizzy, faint, hysterical; yet the moment she saw him again she was all life, all freshness.

From the point of confession there was no more resistance. She would be his wife; she would be married whenever he wished; she seemed mad to reward him for his love; she wanted somehow to sacrifice herself for his sake. Yet, although she hesitated no longer, she sometimes gazed at him with eyes full of anxiety, and uttered words which presaged evil.

"If any trouble springs from this, you must pardon me," she more than once whispered. "I cannot help it. I have never, never, never been loved before; and oh, I have been so hungry, so famished for it, I had begun to despair of it. Yes, when I first met you, I had quite despaired of there being any love in the world for me. I could not help listening to you: I could not help taking all your words and looks into my craving heart; and now I am yours--forgive me!"

Stranger as she was in Northport, everybody trusted the frank sweetness in her face, and sought no other cause for admiring her and wishing her happiness. The whole village came to the church to witness her marriage and to doat upon a bridal beauty which lay far more in expression than in form or feature. A few words of description--inadequate notes to represent the precious gold of reality--must be given to one who could change the stare of curiosity to a beaming glance of sympathy.

Small, slender, fragile; neither blonde nor brunette; a clear skin, with a hectic flush; light chestnut hair, glossy and curling; eyes of violet blue, large, humid and lustrous, which at the first glance seemed black because of the darkness, length and closeness of the lashes, and capable of expressing an earnestness and sweetness which no writer or artist might hope to depict; a manner which in solitude might be languid, but which the slightest touch of interest kindled into animation; in fine, white teeth that sparkled with gayety, and glances that flashed happiness.

She was married without bridal costume, and there was no wedding journey. Leighton was poor, and must attend to his business; and his wife wanted nothing from him which he could not spare--nothing but his love. Impossible to paint her pathetic gratitude for this affection; the spiritual--it was not passionate--fondness which she bore him; the softness of her eyes as she gazed for minutes together into his; the sudden, tremulous outreachings of her hands toward him, as she just touches him with her finger and draws back, then leans forward and lies in his arms, uttering a little cry of happiness. Here was a heart that must long have hungered for affection--a heart unspeakably thankful and joyous at obtaining it.

"I have been smiling all day," she sometimes said to him. "People have asked me why I looked so gay, and what I had heard that was funny. It is just because I am entirely happy, and because the feeling is still a surprise. Shall I ever get over it? Am I silly? No!"

Her gladness of heart seemed to make her angelic. She rejoiced in every joy around her, and grieved for every sorrow. She visited the poor of her husband's patients, watched with them when there was need, made little collections for their relief, chatted away their forebodings, half cured them with her smile. There was something catching, comforting, uplifting in the spectacle of that overbrimming content.

The well were as susceptible to its influence as the sick. Once, half a dozen men and twice as many boys were seen engaged in recovering her veil out of a pond into which the wind had blown it; and when it was handed to her by a shy youth on the end of a twenty-foot pole, all felt repaid for their labors by the childlike burst of laughter with which she received it. Now and then, however, shadows fell across this sunshine. In those dark moments she frequently reverted to the unhappy couple of whom she had told Leighton when he first spoke to her of marriage. She was possessed to describe the man--his dull, filmy, unsympathetic black eyes, his methodical life and hard rationality, his want of sentiment and tenderness.

"Why do you talk of that person so much?" Leighton implored. "You seem to be charging me with his cruelty. I am not like him."

The tears filled her eyes as she started toward him, saying, "No, you are ***not*** like him. Even if you should become like him, I couldn't reproach you. I should merely die."

"But you know him so well?" he added, inquiringly. "You seem to fear him. Has he any power over you?"

For a moment she was so sombre that he half feared lest her mind was unstrung on this one subject.

"No," she at last said. "His power is gone--nearly gone. Oh, if I could only forget!"

After another pause, during which she seemed to be nerving herself to a confession, she threw herself into her husband's arms and whispered, "He is my--uncle."

He was puzzled by the contrast between the violence of her emotion and the unimportance of this avowal; but as he at least saw that the subject was painful to her, and as he was all confidence and gentleness, he put no more inquiries.

"Forget it all," he murmured, caressing her; and with a deep sigh, the sigh of tired childhood, she answered, "Yes."

The long summer days, laden with happiness for these two, sailed onward to their sunset havens. After a time, as August drew near its perfumed death, Alice began to speak of a journey which she should soon be obliged to make to New York. She *must* go, she said to Leighton--it was a matter of property, of business: she would tell him all about it some day. But she would return soon; that is, she would return as soon as possible: she would let him know how soon by letter.

When he proposed to accompany her she would not hear of it. To merely go on with her, she represented, would be a useless expense, and to stay as long as she might need to stay would injure his practice. In these days her gayety seemed forced, and more than once he found her weeping; yet so innocent was he, so simple in his views of life, so candid in soul, that he suspected no hidden evil: he attributed her agitation entirely to grief at the prospect of separation.

His own annoyance in view of the journey centred in the fact that his wife would be absent from him, and that he could not incessantly surround her with his care. Whether she would be happy, whether she would be treated with consideration, whether she would be safe from accidents and alarms, whether her delicate health would not suffer, were the questions which troubled him. He had the masculine instinct of protection: he was as virile as he was gentle and affectionate.

The parting was more painful to him than he had expected, because to her it was such an undisguised and terrible agony.

"You will not forget me?" she pleaded. "You will never, never hate me? You will always love me? You are the only person who has ever made the world pleasant to me; and you have made it so pleasant! so different from what it was! a new earth to me! a star! I will come back as soon as this business will let me. Some day I will come back, never to go away. Oh, will not that be delightful?"

Her extreme distress, her terror lest she might not return, her forebodings lest he should some day cease to love her, impressed him for a moment--only for a truant moment--with doubts as to a mystery. As he left the railway station, full of gratitude for the last glance of her loving eyes, he asked himself once or twice, "What is it?"

What was it?

We will follow her. She is ominously sad during the lonely journey: she is almost stern by the time she arrives in New York. In place of the summer's sweetness and gayety, there is a wintry and almost icy expression in her face, as if she were about to encounter trials to which she had been long accustomed, and which she had learned to bear with hardness if not with resentment.

No one meets her at the railway station, no one at the door of the sombre house where her carriage stops--no one until she has passed up stairs into a darkling parlor.

There she is received by the man whom she has so often described to Deighton--a man of thin, erect form, a high and narrow forehead, regular and imperturbable features, fixed and filmy black eyes, a mechanical carriage, an icy demeanor.

At sight of her he slightly bowed--then he advanced slowly to her and took her hand: he seemed to be hesitating whether he should give her any further welcome.

"You need not kiss me," she said, her eyes fixed on the floor. "You do not wish to do it."

He sighed, as if he too were unhappy, or at least weary; but he drew his hand away and resumed his walk up and down the room.

"So you chose to pass your summer in a village?" he presently said, in the tone of a man who has ceased to rule, but not ceased to criticise. "I hope you liked it."

"I told you in my letters that I liked it," she replied in an expressionless monotone.

"And I told you in my letters that I did not like it. It would have been more decent in you to stay in Portland, among the people whom I had requested to take care of you. However, you are accustomed to have your own way. I can only observe that when a woman will have her own way, she ought to pay her own way."

A flush, perhaps of shame, perhaps of irritation, crossed her hitherto pale face, but she made no response to the scoff, and continued to look at the floor.

After a few seconds, during which neither of them broke the silence, she seemed to understand that the reproof was over, and she quietly quitted the room.

The man pushed the door to violently with his foot, and said in an accent of angry scorn, "That is what is now called a wife."

Well, we have reached the mystery: we have found that it was a crime.

In the working of social laws there occur countless cases of individual hardship. The institution of marriage is as beneficent as the element of fire; yet, like that, it sometimes tortures when it should only have comforted.

The sufferer, if a woman, usually bears her smart tamely--with more or less domestic fretting and private weeping indeed, but without violent effort to escape from her bed of embers. Divorce is public, ugly and brutal: her sensibility revolts from it. Moreover, mere unhappiness, mere disappointment of the affections, does not establish a claim for legal separation. Finally, there is woman's difficulty of self-maintenance--the fact that her labor will not in general give her both comfort and position.

What then? Unloved, unable to love, yet with an intense desire for affection, and an immense capacity for granting it, her heart is tempted to wander beyond the circle of her duty. A flattering shape approaches her dungeon-walls; a voice calls to her to come forth and be glad, if only for a moment; there seems to be a chance of winning the adoration which has been her whole life's desire; there is an opportunity of using the emotions which are burning within her. Shall she burst open the gate on which is written LEGALITY?

Evidently the temptation is mighty. Laden with a forsaken, wounded and perhaps angry heart, she is so easily led into the belief that her exceptional suffering gives her a right to exceptional action! She feels herself justified in setting aside law, when law, falsifying its purpose, violating its solemn pledge, brings her misery instead of happiness. She will not, or cannot, reflect that special hardships must occur under all law; that it is the duty of the individual to bear such chance griefs without insurrection against the public conscience; that entire freedom of private judgment would dissolve society.

Too often--though far less often than man does the like--she makes of her sorrow an armor of excuse, and enters into a contest for unwarrantable chances of felicity. Only, in general, she is so far conscious of guilt, or at least so far fearful of punishment, as to carry on her struggle in the darkness. Few, however maddened by suffering, openly defy the serried phalanx of the world. Still fewer venture the additional risk of defying it under the forms of a legality which they have ventured to violate.

Why is it that so few women, even of a low and reckless class, have been bigamists? It is because the feminine soul has a profound respect, a little less than religious veneration, for the institution of marriage; because it instinctively recoils from trampling upon the form which consecrates love; because in very truth it regards the nuptial bond as a sacrament. I believe that the average woman would turn away from bigamy with a deeper shudder than from any other stain of conjugal infidelity.

But there are exceptions to all modes of feeling and of reasoning.

Here is Alice Duvernois: she is a woman of good position, of intellectual quickness, of unusual sensitiveness of spirit; yet she has thought out this woeful question differently from the great majority of her sex. To her, thirsty for sympathy and love, bound to a man who gives her neither, grown feverish and delirious with the torment of an empty heart, it has seemed that the sanctity of a second marriage will somehow cover the violation of a first.

This aberration we can only explain on the ground that she was one of those natures--mature in some respects, but strangely childlike in others--whom most of us love to stigmatize as unpractical, and who in fact never become quite accustomed to this world and its rules.

On the very evening of her arrival home she put to her husband a question of infantile and almost incredible simplicity. It was one of the many observations which made him tell her from time to time that she was a fool.

"What do they do," she asked, "to women who marry two husbands?"

"They put them in jail," was his cool reply.

"I think it is brutal," she broke out indignantly, as if the iron gates were already closing upon her, and she were contesting the justice of the punishment.

"You are a pretty simpleton, to set up your opinion against that of all civilized society!" was the response of incarnate Reason.

From that moment she trembled at her danger, and quivered under the remorse which terror brings. At times she thought of flying, of abandoning the husband who did not love her for the one who did; but she was afraid of being pursued, afraid of discovery. The knowledge that society had already passed judgment upon her made her see herself in the new light of a criminal, friendless, hunted and doomed. The penalty of her illegal grasp after happiness was already tracking her like a bloodhound.

Yet when she further learned that her second marriage was not binding because of the first, her heart rose in mutiny. Faithful to the only love that there had been for her in the world, she repeated to herself, a hundred times a day, "It *is* binding--it *is*!"

She was in dark insurrection against her kind; at times she was on the point of bursting out into open defiance. She stared at Duvernois, crazy to tell him, "I am wedded to another."

He noticed the wild expression, the longing, wide-open eyes, the parted and eager lips, the trembling chin. At last he said, with a brutality which had become customary with him, "What are you putting on those airs for? I suppose you are imagining yourself the heroine of a romance."

With a glare of pain and scorn she walked away from him in silence.

It is shocking indeed to be fastened speechless upon a rack, and to be charged by uncomprehending souls with counterfeiting emotion. She was so constituted that she could not help laying up this speech of her husband's against him as one of many stolid misdoings which justified both contempt and aversion. In fact, his inability or unwillingness to comprehend her had always been, in her searching and sensitive eyes, his chief crime. To be understood, to be accepted at her full worth, was one of the most urgent demands of her nature.

The life of this young woman, not only within but without, was strange indeed. She fulfilled that problem of Hawthorne's--an individual bearing one character, living one life in one place, and a totally different one in another place--upon one spot of earth angelic, and upon another vile.

Stranger still, her harsher qualities appeared where her manner of life was lawful, and her finer ones where it was condemnable. At Northport she had been like sunlight to her intimates and like a ministering seraph to the poor. In New York she avoided society: she had no tenderness for misery.

The explanation seems to be that love was her only motive of feeling and action. Not a creature of reason, not a creature of conscience--she was only a creature of emotion, an exaggerated woman.

Unfortunately, her husband, methodical in life, judicial in mind, contemptuous of sentiment, was an exaggerated man. Here was a beating heart united to a skeleton. The result of this unfortunate combination had been a wreck of happiness and defiance of law.

Duvernois had not a friend intelligent enough to say to him, "You **must** love your wife; if you cannot love her, you must with merciful deception make her believe that you do. You must show her when you return from business that you have thought of her; you must buy a bouquet, a toy, a trifle, to carry home to her. If you do these things, you will be rewarded; if not, you will be punished."

But had there been such a friend, Duvernois would not have comprehended him. Ho would have replied, or at least he would have thought, "My wife is a fool. She is not worth the money that I now spend upon her, much less the reflection and time that you call upon me to spend."

Two such as Alice and Duvernois could not live together in peace. Notwithstanding her old dread of him, and notwithstanding the new alarm with which she was filled by the discovery that she was a felon, she could not dissemble her feelings when she looked him in the face. Sometimes she was silently contemptuous--sometimes (when her nerves were shaken) openly hostile. Rational, impassive, vigorous as he was, she made him unhappy.

The letters of Leighton were at once a joy and a sorrow. She awaited them impatiently; she went every day to the delivery post-office whither she had directed them to be sent; she took them from the hands of the indifferent clerk with a suffocating beating of the heart. Alone, she devoured them, kissed them passionately a hundred times, sat down in loving haste to answer them. But then came the necessity of excusing her long absence, of inventing some lie for the man she worshiped, of deterring him from coming to see her.

During that woeful winter of terror, of aversion, of vain longing, her health failed rapidly. A relentless cough pursued her, the beautiful flame in her cheek burned freely, and a burst of blood from the lungs warned her that her future was not to be counted by years.

She cared little: her sole desire was to last until summer. She merely asked to end her hopeless life in loving arms--to end it before those arms should recoil from her in horror.

No discovery. Her husband was too indifferent toward her to watch her closely, or even to suspect her. As early in June as might be she obtained permission to go to the seaside, and with an eagerness which would have found the hurricane slow she flew to Northport.

Leighton received her with a joy which at first blinded him to her enfeebled health.

"Oh, how could you stay so long away from me?" were his first words. "Oh, my love, my darling wife! thank you for coming back to me."

But after a few moments, when the first flush and, sparkle of excitement had died out of her cheeks and eyes, he asked eagerly, "What is the matter with you? Have you been sick?"

"I am all well again, now that I see you," she answered, putting out her arms to him with that little start of love and joy which had so often charmed him.

It absolutely seemed that in the presence of the object of her affection this erring woman became innocent. Her smile was as simple and pure as that of childhood: her violet eyes reminded one of a heaven without a cloud. It must have been that, away from punishment and from terror, she did not feel herself to be guilty.

But the day of reckoning was approaching. She had scarcely begun to regain an appearance of health under the stimulus of country air and renewed happiness, when a disquieting letter arrived from Duvernois. In a tone which was more than usually authoritative, he directed her to meet him at Portland, to go to Nahant and Newport. Did he suspect something?

She would have given years of life to be able to show the letter to Leighton and ask his counsel. But here her punishment began to double upon her: the being whom she most loved was precisely the one to whom she must not expose this trouble--the one from whom she was most anxious to conceal it.

In secret, and with unconfided tears, she wrote a reply, alleging (what was true) that her feeble health demanded quiet, and praying that she might be spared the proposed journey. For three days she feverishly expected an answer, knowing the while that she ought to go to Portland to meet Duvernois, should he chance to come, yet unable to tear herself away from Leighton, even for twenty-four hours.

In the afternoon of the third day she made one of her frequent visits of charity. At the house of a poor and bed-ridden widow she met, as she had hoped to meet, her husband. When they left the place he took her into his gig and carried her home.

It was a delicious day of mid June: the sun was setting in clouds of crimson and gold; the earth was in its freshest summer glory. In the beauty of the scene, and in the companionship of the heart which was all hers, she forgot, or seemed to forget, her troubles. One hand rested on Leighton's arm; her face was lifted steadily to his, like a flower to the light; her violet eyes were dewy and sparkling with happiness. There were little clutches of her fingers on his wrist whenever he turned to look at her. There were spasms of joy in her slender and somewhat wasted frame as she leaned from time to time against his shoulder.

Arrived at the house, she was loth to have him leave her for even the time required to take his horse to the stable.

"Come soon," she said--"come as quick as you can. I shall be at the window. Look up when you reach the gate. Look at the window all the way from the gate to the door."

In an instant, not even taking off her bonnet, she was sitting by the window waiting for him to appear.

A man approached, walking behind the hedge of lilacs which bordered the yard, and halted at the gate with an air of hesitation. She turned ghastly white: retribution was upon her. It was Duvernois.

With that swift instinct of escape which sensitive and timorous creatures possess, she glided out of the room, through the upper hall, down a back stairway, into the garden behind the house, and so on to an orchard already obscure in the twilight. Here she paused in her breathless flight, and burst into one of her frequent coughs, which she vainly attempted to smother.

"I was already dying," she groaned. "Ah, why could he not have given me time to finish?"

From the orchard she could faintly see the road, and she now discovered Leighton returning briskly toward the house. Her first thought was, "He will look up at the window, and he will not see me!" Her next was, "They will meet, and all will be known!"

Under the sting of this last reflection she again ran onward until her breath failed. She had no idea where she should go: her only purpose was to fly from immediate exposure and scorn--to fly both from the man she detested and the man she loved. Her speed was quickened to the extent of her strength by the consideration that she was already missed, and would soon be pursued.

"Oh, don't let them come!--don't let them find me!" she prayed to some invisible power, she could not have said what.

Mainly intent as she was upon mere present escape from reproachful eyes, she at times thought of lurking in the woods or in some neighboring village until Duvernois should disappear and leave her free to return to Leighton. But always the reflection came up, "Now he knows that I have deceived him; now he will despise me and hate me, and refuse to see me; now I can never go back."

In such stresses of extreme panic and anguish an adult is simply a child, with the same overweight of emotions and the same imperfections of reason. During the moments when she was certain that Leighton would not forgive her, Alice made wild clutches at the hope that Duvernois might. There were glimpses of the earlier days of her married life; cheering phantoms of the days when she believed that she loved and that she was beloved--phantoms which swore by altars and bridal veils to secure her pardon.

She imagined Duvernois overtaking her with the words, "Alice, I forgive your madness: do you also forgive the coldness which drove you to it?"

She imagined herself springing to him, reaching out her hands for reconciliation, putting up her mouth for a kiss, and sobbing, "Ah, why were you not always so?"

Then of a sudden she scorned this fancy, trampled it under her weary, aching feet, and abhorred herself for being faithless to Leighton.

At last she reached a sandy, lonely coast-road, a mile from the village, with a leaden, pulseless, corpselike sea on the left, and on the right a long stretch of black, funereal marshes. Seating herself on a ruinous little bridge of unpainted and wormeaten timbers, she looked down into a narrow, sluggish rivulet, of the color of ink, which oozed noiselessly from the morass into the ocean. Her strength was gone: for the present farther flight was impossible, unless she fled from earth--fled into the unknown.

This thought had indeed followed her from the house: at first it had been vague, almost unnoticed, like the whisper of some one far behind; then it had become clearer, as if the persuading fiend went faster than she through the darkness, and were overtaking her. Now it was urgent, and would not be hushed, and demanded consideration.

"If you should die," it muttered, "then you will escape: moreover, those who now abhor you and scorn you, will pity you; and pity for the dead is almost respect, almost love."

"Oh, how can a ruined woman defend herself but by dying?" She wept as she gazed with a shudder into the black rivulet.

Then she thought that the water seemed foul; that her body would become tangled in slimy reeds and floating things; that when they found her she would be horrible to look upon. But even in this there was penance, a meriting of forgiveness, a claim for pity.

Slowly, inch by inch, like one who proposes a step which cannot be retraced, she crept under the railing of the bridge, seated herself on the edge of the shaky planking and continued to gaze into the inky waters.

A quarter of an hour later, when the clergyman of Northport passed by that spot, returning from a visit to a dying saint of his flock, no one was there.

We must revert to the two husbands. Duvernois had long wondered what could keep his wife in a sequestered hamlet, and immediately on her refusal to join him in a summer tour he had resolved to look into her manner of life.

At the village hotel he had learned that a lady named Duvernois had arrived in the place during the previous summer, and that she had been publicly married to a Doctor Leighton. He did not divulge his name--he did not so much as divulge his emotions: he listened to this story calmly, his eyes fixed on vacancy.

At the door of the boarding-house he asked for Mrs. Duvernois, and then corrected himself, saying, "I mean Mrs. Leighton."

He must have had singular emotions at the moment, yet the servant-girl noticed nothing singular in his demeanor.

Mrs. Leighton could not be found. None of the family had seen her enter or go out: it was not known that she had been in the house for an hour.

"But there comes Doctor Leighton," remarked the girl as the visitor turned to leave.

Even in this frightful conjuncture the characteristic coolness of Duvernois did not forsake him: after a moment's hesitation and a quick glance at his rival, he said, "I do not know him: I will call again."

On the graveled walk which led from the yard gate to the doorstep the two men met and passed without a word--the face of the one as inexpressive of the strangeness and horror of the encounter as the mind of the other was unconscious of them.

Leighton immediately missed Alice. In a quarter of an hour he became anxious: in an hour he was in furious search of her.

Somewhat later, when Duvernois came once more to the house, accompanied by a fashionably-dressed youth, who, as it subsequently appeared, was his younger brother, he found the family and the neighborhood in wild alarm over the disappearance of Mrs. Leighton. The two at once returned to the hotel, procured saddle-horses and joined in the general chase.

It was ten o'clock at night, and the moon was shining with a vaporous, spectral light, when the maddest of chances brought the two husbands together over a body which the tide, with its multitudinous cold fingers, had gently laid upon the beach.

Leighton leaped from his horse, lifted the corpse with a loud cry, and covered the white wet face with kisses.

Duvernois leaned forward in his saddle, and gazed at both without a word or a movement.

"Oh, what could have led her to this?" groaned the physician, already too sure that life had departed.

"Insanity," was the monotoned response of the statue on horseback.

The funeral took place two days later: the coffin-plate bore the inscription, "Alice Leighton, aged 23." Duvernois read it, and said not a word.

"If you don't claim her as your wife," whispered the brother, "you may find it difficult to marry again."

"Do you think I shall want to marry again?" responded the widower with an icy stare.

He was aware that he had lost a shame and a torment, and not aware that she might have been an honor and a joy, if only he had been able to love.

J. W. DE FOREST.

"How Mother Did It."

The year 1839--that is, the year in which I was born--is of no manner of importance to myself or anybody else. The year 1859--that is, the year in which I began to *live* (Charlie and I got married that year)--is of considerable importance to myself and to somebody else. The two decades forming the interim between those years constitute my Dark Age, in which I teethed and measled and whooping-coughed, and went to school, and wore my hair in two long pig-tails, and loved molasses candy, and regarded a school-room as purgatory, a ball-room as heaven--when I sang and danced and grew as the birds and grasshoppers and flowers sing and dance and grow, because they having nothing else to do.

Then came my Golden Age. That means, then came Charlie into my life, when I felt for the first time that there was music in the birds' voices and perfume in the flowers--that there was light in the heavens above and on the earth beneath, for God was in heaven and Charlie was on earth--when I, who had all along been hardly more than a human grasshopper, became the happiest of happy women--so much happier, I thought, than I deserved. For who was I, and what great thing had I ever done, that I should be crowned with such a crown of glory as--Charlie? why should I, insignificant I, be so blest among women as to be taken to wife by Charlie?

I was insanely sentimental enough to rather resent the fact that Charlie was prosaically well off: his circumstances were distressingly easy. It would have been so much nicer, so deliciously romantic, if there had been an opportunity afforded me to show how ready, nay, eager, I was to sacrifice friends, home and country for his dear sake. But Charlie didn't want me to sacrifice my friends; nor did it require any great amount of heroism to exchange my modestly comfortable home for his decidedly luxurious one; and as for country, nothing on earth could have induced Charlie to leave his own country, much less his own parish, much less his own plantation. So we were married without any talk of sacrifice on either side, and moved quietly enough from father's small plantation to Charlie's large one.

There was but one drawback to the perfectness of my happiness: there was so little hope of my ever having an opportunity to air those magnanimous traits of character upon the possession of which I so plumed myself. I felt sure that I could meet the most adverse circumstances with the most smiling patience, but circumstances obstinately refused to be adverse. I was inwardly conscious that the most trying emergency could not shake my heroic but purely feminine fortitude; but, alas! my fortitude was likely to rust while waiting for the emergency. Injury and wrong should be met with sublime dignity, but the most wildly speculative imagination could not look upon Charlie's placidly handsome face and convert him into a possible tyrant.

To tell how the longed-for opportunity to exercise my powers of endurance, and my dignity, and all the rest of it, did finally come about, and to tell how I bore the test, is the object of this paper.

For the first six months of our married life, Charlie and I were simply ridiculously happy--selfishly happy too. We resented a neighbor's visit as an act of barbarous invasion, and the necessity of returning such visits was acknowledged with a sublimity of resignation worthy of pictorial representation in that exquisite parlor manual, Fox's ***Book of Martyrs***. If Charlie left the house for an hour or two, I looked upon his enforced absence as a cruel dispensation of Providence, which I did ***not*** bear with "fortitude and sublime dignity," but pouted over like the ridiculous baby I was. Bare conjugal civility required that on leaving the house Charlie should kiss me three times, and on returning six times: anything short of that I should have considered a pre-monitory symptom of approaching separation. If Charlie had ever been so savage as to call me plain "Lulie," I should have felt certain he was sick and tired of me, and was repenting of having married me instead of that spectacled basbleu, Miss Minerva Henshaw, who read Buckle and talked dictionary. I believe I was intoxicated with my own happiness, and was a little nonsensical because I was so happy.

Fortunately for the comfort of both Charlie and myself, his domestic cabinet consisted of a marvelously well-trained set of servants, who were simply perfect--as perfect in their way as Charlie was in his. They had been trained by Charlie's mother, who had been the head of affairs in his house up to the hour of her death--an event which had occurred some dozen years before my first meeting with Charlie. Everybody said she had been a celebrated housekeeper, and Charlie's devotion to her had been the talk of the country-side. There were people malicious enough to say that if Charlie's mother had never died, he would never have married, but I take the liberty of resenting such an assertion as a personal insult; for, although I don't doubt the dear old lady was a perfect jewel in her way, yet, looking at the portrait of her which hangs over our parlor mantelpiece, I see the face of a hard, determined-looking woman with cold gray eyes and rigidly set mouth, in a funny-looking black dress, neither high-necked nor low-necked, having a starchy white ruffle round the edge, in vivid white contrast to the yellow skin; with grizzly, iron-gray curls peeping out from under a cap that is fearfully and wonderfully made, with a huge ruffled border radiating in a circumference of several feet, while its two black-and-white gauze ribbon strings lie in rigid exactness over her two rigidly exact shoulders. Looking on this portrait, I do not thank anybody for saying that it was only because death chose that shining mark that I had found favor in Charlie's eyes.

We had been married, I suppose, about six months, when, sitting one evening over a cozy wood-fire in our cozy little parlor, just under the work of art I have described at such length, Charlie committed his first matrimonial solecism. He yawned, actually gaped--an open-mouthed, audible, undeniable yawn!

Glancing up at him from my work (which consisted of the inevitable worked slippers without which no woman considers her wifehood absolutely asserted), I caught him in the act. "Are you tired, Charlie?" I asked in accents of wifely anxiety.

Tired! Poor fellow! he ought to have been, for he had ridden all over the plantation that day, had written two business letters, and smoked there's no telling how many cigars, and had only taken one little cat-nap after dinner.

He was leaning back in his arm-chair, with his eyes fixed in mournful meditation upon his mother's portrait (at least I thought so), when I asked him if he was tired, and I fancied he was thinking sad thoughts of the mother who had not been dead so very long as never to trouble the thoughts of the living; so, laying down my slippers, I crossed the rug and perched myself on Charlie's knee.

"Talk to me about her, Charlie dear."

"About whom, little one?" asked Charlie, turning his eyes toward me with a little lazy look of inquiry.

"About your mother, Charlie: weren't you thinking about her just now?"

"I don't know--maybe I was. Dear mother! you don't find many women like her now-a-days."

Reader, that was my first glimpse of Charlie's hobby. And from the luck-less moment when I so innocently invited him to mount it, up to the time when I forcibly compelled him to dismount from it, I had ample opportunity to exercise my "smiling patience, sublime dignity and heroic fortitude." Whether or not I improved my opportunities properly, I will leave you to judge for yourself. But for two whole years "how mother did it" seemed to be the watchword of Charlie's existence, and was the ***bete noir*** of mine.

So long as Charlie and I were in Paradise the house kept itself, and very nicely it did it too, but by the time we were ready to come back to earth the perfect servants, who had been taking such good care of themselves, and our two daft selves into the bargain, were found to be sadly demoralized. The discovery came upon us gradually. I think my husband noticed the decadence as soon as I did, but I wasn't going to invite his attention to the fact; and he, I suppose, thought that I thought that everything was just as it should be.

One of Charlie's inherited manias was for early rising--a habit which would have been highly commendable and undeniably invaluable in a laboring man, but which struck me, who had an equally strong mania for not rising early, as extremely inconvenient and the least little bit absurd. Charlie got up early simply because "mother did it" before him; and after he had risen at earliest dawn and dressed himself, he had nothing better to do than walk out on the front gallery, locate himself in a big wicker chair, tilt his chair back and elevate his feet to the top of the banisters, and stare out over the cottonfields. This position he would maintain, probably, about twenty minutes. Then the pangs of hunger would render him restless, and he would draw out his watch to note the time of day. The next step in the formula would bring him back to my room door while I was still sleepily trying to reconnect the broken links of a dream, from which vain effort he would startle me into wide-awake reality by a stentorian "Lulie, Lulie! Come, wife--it's breakfast-time."

Upon which, instead of "heroic fortitude," I would treat him to a little cross

"Please yell at the cook, Charlie, and not at me. I'm sure if people *will* get up at such unearthly hours, they should expect to be kept waiting for their breakfast."

Then the spirit of unrest would impel Charlie toward the back door, where I would hear him commanding, exhorting, entreating.

Mentally registering a vow to give my husband a dose of Mrs. Winslow's Soothing Syrup on the coming night, I would relinquish all hope of another nap, get up and dress myself, and join my roaring lion on the front gallery, where we would both sit meekly waiting for the allied forces of kitchen and dining-room to decide upon the question of revictualing us.

"Lulie," said Charlie to me one morning at the breakfast-table, "things are getting all out of gear about this house, somehow or other."

I put down the coffee-pot with a resigned thump and asked my lord, with an injured air, to please explain himself.

"Well, when mother was alive I never knew what it was to sit down to my breakfast later than six o'clock in summer or seven in winter."

"How did she manage it, Charlie?" I asked, very meekly.

"Why, by getting up early herself. No servant on the face of the globe is going to get up at daybreak and go to work in earnest when she knows her mistress is sound asleep in bed. I will tell you how mother did: she had a pretty good-sized bell, that she kept on a table by her bedside, and every morning, as soon as her eyes were open, she would give such a peal with that old bell that all the servants on the premises knew that 'Mistress was awake and up,' and bestirred themselves accordingly. There was no discount on mother: that was the way she made father a rich man, too."

"But, Charlie, you're already a rich man, and why on earth should we get out of bed at daybreak just because your mother and father did so before us?"

"Of course, Lulie," said Charlie, the least little bit coldly, "I have no desire in the world to force you to conform to my views: I only told you how mother did it."

Reader, you know how I loved Charlie, and after that I out-larked the lark in early rising; and although Charlie and I did little more than gape in each other's faces for an hour or two, and wish breakfast would come, and wonder what made them take so long, he was perfectly satisfied that we were both on the road that was to make us healthier, wealthier and wiser.

Among other points on which my husband and I were mutually agreed was a liking for good strong coffee, and we also held in common one decided opinion, and that was, that our coffee was gradually becoming anything but good and strong.

Charlie broached the subject first. "Lulie, our coffee is getting to be perfectly undrinkable," said he one morning, putting his cup down with a face of disgust.

"It is indeed, Charlie: it's perfectly villainous. Milly ought to be ashamed of herself: I shall speak to her again after breakfast."

"Maybe you don't give out enough coffee?" suggested Charlie.

"I don't know how much Milly takes," I replied, innocently.

"Takes! Do you mean to say that you don't know how much coffee goes out of your pantry, Lulie? I don't wonder we never have any fit to drink!"

If I had been of an argumentative turn, I would have asked Charlie to explain how giving the cook carte blanche in the matter of quantity should have had such a disastrous effect in the matter of quality. But I was not of an argumentative turn, so I took no notice of his queer logic.

"Why should I bother about every spoonful of coffee, Charlie? You assured me, when I first came here, that every servant you had was as honest as you or I, and I'm sure Milly knows better than I do how much coffee she *ought* to take."

"Well," said Charlie with a sigh of mock resignation, "that may be the way they do things now-a-days, but I remember exactly how mother managed to have good coffee." Here the hobby broke into a brisk canter: "I recollect she had a little oval wooden box, that held, I suppose, about a quart--or two, maybe--of roasted coffee, and that box stood on the mantelpiece in her room; and every morning, as soon as her bell rang, Milly would come with a cup and spoon, and mother would measure out two table-spoonfuls of coffee with her own hands and give it to the cook, and the cook knew better than not to have good coffee, I can tell you."

"Are you sure it was only two spoonfuls, Charlie?"

"I am sure," responded Charlie, solemnly.

As good-luck would have it, while rummaging in the store-room a day or two after that coffee talk, I came upon a little old oval wooden box, the lid of which I detached with some difficulty, and as the scent of the roses hung round it still, I had no difficulty in identifying my treasure-trove with the wooden box that had played such a distinguished part in the good old times when cooks "knew better than not to have good coffee, I can tell you."

Hoping that some relic of my dead predecessor might prove more awe-inspiring to contumacious Milly than my own despised monitions, I exhumed the wooden box, had it thoroughly cleansed, filled with roasted coffee and placed upon my mantelpiece, giving Milly orders to come to *me* hereafter, every morning, for the coffee.

Charlie gave me a grateful little kiss when he saw the old box in the old place, either as a reward for my amiable endeavor to do things as mother did, or because he took the old wooden box for an outward and visible sign of the inward and spiritual grace that was to move Milly to make good coffee.

But somehow or other, in spite of the unsightly old wooden box on my mantelshelf, the coffee didn't improve in the least. Maybe the charm failed to work because Charlie had forgotten which end of the mantelpiece his mother used to keep it on, or I used the wrong spoon. I'm inclined to lay it on the spoon myself, but there's no telling.

The first cotton-picking season that came round after my marriage seemed to afford Charlie no end of opportunities for riding his hobby at a fast and furious pace. It seemed as if there was no end to the things that mother used to do at that important season. I suppose she really was a wonderful woman, and I humbly hope that by the time I have lived as long as she did, and get to looking as she does in her portrait, and can wear a wonderful-looking cap with the wonderful composure she wore it with, and have little iron-gray curls hanging round my iron-gray visage, I may be only half as wonderful.

"Would I see to the making of the cotton sacks? That was one thing mother always did." Thus Charlie.

Of course I would: why should I object to doing anything that would forward my husband's interests? Besides, I was actually pining for some healthful occupation: I was tired of playing at living. I resolved on a brilliant plan. I would out-mother mother, for she only *saw* to the making of the sacks: I would make them myself, every one of them, on my sewing-machine. If I couldn't make cotton-sacks on it, what was the use of having it?

Charlie had informed me that he would send me down seven or eight women from the quarters to make the sacks. I informed him with a flourish that I should need but one: I should want her to cut the sacks out. Charlie thanked me, and Martha and I and "Wheeler & Wilson" made the sacks.

Was I to blame that the wretched things burst in twenty places at once the first time they were used? Was I to blame that two women were kept busy mending my sacks until they ceased to be sacks? Charlie might think so, but I did not.

He reported the failure of my cotton-sack experiment with very unbecoming levity, as it struck me, accompanying his report with a somewhat unjust comment upon new-fangled notions, such as sewing-machines, etc., etc., winding up with--"Now, when mother was alive" (I fairly winced), "the house was not considered too good for the darkies to sit on the back gallery with their work and make the sacks right under mother's eye--sewing them with good strong thread, too, that was spun for the purpose. I can remember the old spinning-wheel: it used to sit right at that end of the gallery."

Like Captain Cuttle, I "made a note of it" for future use.

I often had occasion to wonder, during the early years of my married life, how it happened that the son of such an exceptionally perfect woman as I was compelled to presume my respected mother-in-law to have been, should have grown up with such shockingly disorderly habits as had my Charlie. The wretched creature would stalk into my bed-room--which I was particularly dainty about--fresh from shooting or fishing, with pounds of mud clinging to his boots, bristling all over with cockleburs, his hands grimed with gunpowder; and helping himself to water from my ewer, he would begin dabbling in my china basin until he had reduced its originally pure contents into a compound of mud and ink, and would wind up by making a finish of my fresh damask towel, and throwing it on the bed or a chair instead of returning it to the rack, as he should have done.

"Charlie," said I one day, saucily inviting a dose of "what mother did," "what did mother used to do when you came into her room and turned it into a pig-stye, and then left it for her to clean up again?"

"She never let me do it," said Charlie with a laugh. "I'll tell you how she did. She had a tin basin on a shelf on the back gallery, and one of those great big rolling towels that lasted about a week; and after her washstand was fixed up in the morning, we knew better than to upset it, I can tell you."

"Very well, sir: I intend you shall know better than to upset mine, I'll show you."

In fact, things had come to that pass that I had mentally resolved to "show" Charlie a great many things. I firmly believed that the secret of the power that Charlie's mother had exercised over her household, and still exercised over him in memory, lay in the fact that she made them all afraid of her: so I firmly resolved that they should all be afraid of me, poor little me! It is true, I was but twenty, and she was fifty; I was but a pocket edition of a woman, and she was a **Webster Unabridged**; I had little meek blue eyes, that dropped to the ground in the most shamefaced manner if a body did but look at me, and she had hard, cold gray eyes, that not only looked straight at you, but right through you. Still, I hoped, notwithstanding these trifling drawbacks, to make myself very awe-inspiring by dint of a grand assumption of spirit.

To put it into very plain language, I resolved to bully Charlie off his hobby. He had thrown his mother at my head (figuratively speaking, of course) until, if she had been present in ***propria persona***, I should have been tempted to try Hiawatha's remarkable feat with his grandmother, and throw her up against the moon. But as I could not revenge myself upon her personally, I began to lay deep and subtle plans for inducing Charlie to leave her to her repose.

As the veritable bell which, in the days when "mother did it," had acted as a sort of Gabriel's trump, was still extant, minus clapper and handle, I was enabled to provide myself with its fac-simile. Armed with this instrument of retribution, I laid me down to sleep by Charlie's side, gloating in anticipation over my ripening scheme of vengeance.

It was a rare thing for me to wake up before Charlie, but I did manage to do so on the morning in question, by dint, I think, of a powerful mental resolution to that effect made the night before. I raised myself very softly, so as not to disturb my husband's gentle slumbers, and, possessing myself of my big bell, I laid on with a will, raising such a clatter in the quiet morning air that Charlie fairly bounded into the middle of the room before he in the least comprehended where it came from.

"In the name of God, Lulie, what is the meaning of that?" he exclaimed, looking at me as if he half doubted my sanity.

"That's the way mother did it, Charlie," I replied placidly enough, and, replacing my big bell on the table, I settled myself on my pillow once more, ostensibly to go to sleep again--in reality to have my laugh out in a quiet fashion, for it was enough to have made the very bed-posts laugh to see Charlie's funny look of astonishment and indignation. But of course he couldn't say a word, you know.

For two more mornings I clattered my bell about his precious old head, and then he paid me to quit, and after that began riding his hobby at a little slower gait.

The next direct intimation he gave that his faith in inherited ideas was growing shaky was a plaintive little request that I would not stick so close to the old wooden box, but give out enough coffee to ensure him something to drink for his breakfast.

Now, I had no wish that my husband should drink bad coffee just because Providence had seen fit to remove his mother from this sublunary sphere: I merely wanted to cure him of telling me how mother did it; so as soon as he thus tacitly acknowledged that his suggestion had not been a success, I took matters into my own hands, and proved to him that coffee could be made as well by young wives as by old mothers.

In the due revolution of the seasons King Cotton donned his royal robes of ermine once more, and sacks again became the one thing needful. It was the very rainiest, wettest, muddiest picking-season that had ever been seen. In pursuance of my plan, I had seven or eight women down from the quarters, and a spinning-wheel also, which was set to humming right under our bed-room window.

The rainy weather had kept Charlie in the house, and he was lounging on a couch in my room, enjoying a pleasant semi-doze, when the monotonous whirr-r-r of the spinning-wheel first attracted his attention. "Lulie," he asked, rising into a sitting posture, "what is that infernal noise on the back gallery?"

"The spinning-wheel, Charlie. They are spinning thread to make the sacks with," I answered, without looking up from my work.

"Oh!" and Charlie subsided for a while. "Ahem! Lulie, my dear, how long is that devilish spinning to be kept up?"

"Devilish! Why, Charlie, that's the way mother did it."

"Well," said Charlie, scratching his head and looking foolish, "I know she did, Lulie, but I'll be confounded if I can stand it much longer."

"Why, Charlie, you used to stand it when mother did it," I answered maliciously.

"I was hardly ever about the house in those days, Lulie: I suppose that was why I didn't mind it."

"Why weren't you about the house much in those days, Charlie?"

"Because you weren't in it, you witch, I suppose."

This was such a decided triumph over the old lady of the portrait that I could afford to be amiable; so, giving him a spasmodic little hug and an energetic little kiss, I went out and stopped the spinning nuisance immediately.

After that the hobby went slower and slower, feebler and feebler. One more energetic display of my bogus spirit and "the enemy was mine."

Winter came on in its duly-appointed time, bringing with it the usual quantity of wild ducks and more than the usual degree of severe cold. Charlie was an inveterate duck-shooter, and with the return of the season came the return of mud and dirt in my bowls.

I determined to do as mother did. A tin basin made its appearance on the back gallery, four yards of crash sewed together at the end were made to revolve over the roller, and by way of forcing the experiment to a successful issue orders were given that my own pitchers should be filled only after nightfall.

I was sitting in my bed-room sewing away, in placid unconsciousness of outside cold and discomfort, when Charlie got home from his first hunt of the season.

"No water, Lulie?" and the monster took hold of my nice pitcher with a pair of muddy, half-frozen hands.

"On the gallery, dear, just where mother used to keep it;" and I smiled up at him angelically.

With a muttered something or other, poor Charlie bounded out to the back gallery. He came back in a minute, his hands as muddy and cold as ever.

"Look here, Lulie: the water's all frozen in that confounded tin basin out there."

"I'll have it thawed out for you," I said sweetly, rising as I spoke.

"I say, wifey"--and the great, handsome fellow came close up to me with his mud and his burs--"do you think it's exactly fair, when a fellow's been out all the morning shooting ducks for your dinner, to make him stand out on the gallery such a day as this and scrub the mud off his frozen hands?"

"That's the way mother did," was all my answer.

"Look here, Lulie, I cry quits. If you'll only let a body off this once, you may keep house on your own plan, little lady, and I'll never tell you how mother did it again so long as I live."

"Well, then, don't, that's a dear," I replied, "for you'll only make me dislike her memory, without doing any good. Just be patient with me, Charlie, and maybe after a while I'll be as good a housekeeper as your mother was before me. The mistake you and all other men make is, in comparing your wives at the end of their first year of housekeeping with your mothers, whose housekeeping you knew nothing about until it was of ever so many years' duration. I'm young yet, but I'm improving in that matter every day, Charlie."

With which little moral lecture I gave Charlie a kiss, and some water to wash the mud from his poor red hands.

Moral.--My dear girls, don't you ever marry a man that cannot take his affidavit he never had a mother, unless it is expressly stipulated in the marriage contract that he is never to tell you how his mother did it.

J.R. HADERMANN.

The Red Fox: A Tale of New Year's Eve.

It was New Year's Eve, 184-. I and my two little boys, children of five and seven, were alone in the house. My husband had been unexpectedly called away on business, and the servant had gone to her friends to spend the coming holiday.

It was drawing toward night. The cold shadows of the winter twilight were already falling. A dull red glow in the west told where the sun was going down. Over the rest of the sky hung heavy gray clouds. A few drops of rain fell from time to time, and the wind was rising, coming round the corner of the house with a long, mournful howl like that of a lost hound.

I am not a very nervous person, but I did not like the idea of spending by myself the long evening that would come after the children's bed-time.

We were living then in a very new place in Michigan, which I shall call Maysville. My husband, an ex-army officer, had resigned the sword for the saw-mill. Our house was the oldest in the village, which does not speak much for its antiquity, as five years before Maysville had been unbroken forest. The house stood outside the cluster of houses that formed the little settlement: it was a quarter of a mile to our nearest neighbor.

Now, Maysville calls itself a city, has an academy and a college, and a great quantity of church in proportion to its population. Then, we "went to meeting" in a little white-painted, pine box of a thing, like a barn that had risen in life. The stumps stood about the street: the cows wandered at will and pastured in the "public square," an irregular clearing running out into indefinite space. Here also the Indians would encamp when they came to town from their reservation about five miles away, and here also, I regret to say, they would sometimes get drunk, and add what Martha Penney calls "a revolving animosity to the scenery." The squaws, however, would generally secure the knives and guns before the quarrelsome stage was reached. Not unfrequently the ladies would bring the weapons to Mrs. Moore or myself to hide away till their lords and masters should be sober. Then, feeling secure that no great harm could happen, they would look on with the utmost placidity at the antics of their better halves until they dropped down to sleep off their liquor.

There were no Indians in town that night, however, and if there had been, I was not at all afraid of them, for we were on excellent terms with the whole reservation. My feeling about staying alone was merely one of those unreasonable sensations that sometimes overtake people of ill-regulated minds.

I went to the door and looked out at the gray, angry sky. It was not cold, but chill. The wind howled and shivered among the leafless branches: everything promised a storm.

I was not at all sorry to see Mr. and Mrs. Moore drive up in their light buggy, with their two high-stepping, little brown horses. Mrs. Moore had in her arms a bundle in a long blue embroidered cloak--a baby, in short. She and her husband firmly believed this infant to be the most beautiful, most intelligent and altogether most charming creature which the world had ever seen. They had been married three years, and little Carry was their first child.

Mr. and Mrs. Moore were by no means ordinary people. Mrs. Moore--born Minny or Hermione Adams--was a very small woman, exceedingly pretty, with light brown curly hair, dark blue eyes and a complexion like an apple blossom.

Mr. Moore was the son of a Seneca mother and Cherokee father, with not a drop of white blood in his veins. So he thought, at least, but I never could quite believe it, because he could and did work, and never so much as touched even a glass of wine. His parents had died when he was very young, and he had been brought up and educated by a missionary, a gentle, scholarly old Presbyterian minister, whose memory his adopted son held in loving reverence.

The story of our acquaintance with Richard Moore is too long to be told here. Four years before he had come with us from the Pawnee country. He had married Minny Adams with the full consent of her parents and the opposition of all her other friends. Contrary to all prophecies, and with that inartistic disregard of the probable which events often show, they had been very happy together.

Mr. Moore--otherwise Wyanota--was a civil engineer, and stood high in his profession.

"Look here, mamma," he said as he drove up. "Will you take in the wife and the small child for to-night? I must go away."

"Certainly," said I, overjoyed. "But where are you going, to be caught in a storm?"

"Oh, they have got into a fuss with the hands over on the railroad, and have sent for me. I might have known Robinson wouldn't manage when I left him?"

"Why not?"

"English!" said Wyn, most expressively. "No one can stand the airs he puts on."

Now, such airs as Mr. Moore possessed--and they were neither few nor far between--were not put on, but were perfectly natural to him.

"Can't you come in and get your tea?" I asked as he handed me the baby and helped his wife down.

"No: I must go over directly and compose matters. Good-bye, little woman: by-bye, baby! Do you know, we think she's beginning to say 'papa?'" said Wyn, proudly; and then he kissed his wife and child and drove away.

I carried the infant phenomenon into the house and took off its wrappings. She was my namesake, and I loved the little creature, but I can't say she was a pretty baby. She was a soft, brown thing, with her father's beautiful southern eyes and her mother's mouth, but otherwise she certainly was not handsome. She was ten months old, but she had a look of experience and wisdom in her wee face that would have made her seem old at twenty years. She sat on my lap and watched me in a meditative way, as though she were reviewing her former estimate of my character, and considering whether her opinions on that subject were well founded. There was something quite weird and awful in her dignity and gravity.

"Isn't she a wise-looking little thing?" said Minny. "She makes me think sometimes of the fairy changeling that was a hundred and fifty years old, and never saw soap made in an egg-shell."

"This baby never would have made such a confession of ignorance, you may depend. She would not have acknowledged that anything lay out of the range of her experience. Take your chicken till I get tea, for I am my own girl to-night."

We had a very merry time over the tea-table and in washing up the dishes. Until the boys went to bed we were in something of a frolic with them and the baby, and it was not till the little one was asleep in her crib and Ed and Charley were quiet in bed that we noticed how wild the weather was getting.

The rain, which had at first fallen in pattering drops, was now driving in sheets before a mighty wind, which roared through the woods back of the house with a noise like thunder. The branches of the huge oaks in the front yard creaked and groaned as only oak boughs can. The house shook, the rain lashed the roof, and the wind clawed and rattled the blinds like some wild creature trying to get in.

"I hope Wyn is safe under shelter," said Mrs. Moore.

"He will have reached the end of his journey long before this. I hope he will have no trouble with the men, but he is not apt to. I pity poor Mr. Robinson. When Wyn chooses, his extreme politeness is something quite awful."

"I will say for my husband," observed Mrs. Moore, "that when he sets himself to work to be disagreeable, he can, without doing one uncourteous thing, be more aggravating than any one I ever saw in my life."

"It is perfectly evident that he never tries his airs on you, or you would not speak so. Hear the wind blow!"

"It is no use listening to the weather. The house will stand, I suppose. Have you got your work? Then let me read to you. It will seem like old times, before I was married."

Minny Moore was in some respects a very remarkable woman. Though little Carry was her first baby, she *could* talk on other subjects. She did not expect you to listen with rapture to the tenth account of how baby had said "Da-da," or thrill with agony over the tale of an attack of wind. She had been her husband's friend and companion before the baby was born: she did not entirely throw him over now that it had come. She had always been fond of reading, and she continued to keep up her interest in the world outside of her nursery. She thought that as her daughter grew up her mother would be as valuable as a guide and friend if she did not wholly sink the educated woman in the nurse-maid and seamstress. These habits may have been "unfeminine," but they certainly made Mrs. Moore much more agreeable as a companion than if she had been able to talk of nothing but the baby's clothes, teeth and ailments.

I took out my work, and Minny began to read **Locksley Hall**, which was then a new poem on this side the water. I had never heard it before, and I must confess I was much affected--more than I should be now. Mrs. Moore, however, chose to say that she thought Amy had made a most fortunate escape, that she had no doubt but the hero would have been a most intolerable person to live with, and that their marriage, had it come to pass, would have ended in Amy's taking in sewing to support both herself and her husband. As for the Squire, why we had no word for his character but his disappointed rival's, and his drinking might be all a slander. As to his snoring, why poets might snore as well as other people. If he loved his wife "somewhat better than his dog, a little dearer than his horse," "Why what more," said Mrs. Moore, "could any woman ask of a man given to horses and hunting? If Calvin Bruce ever cares more for a woman than he does for his brown pointer and his fast trotter, she may think herself happy indeed."

At that instant a sudden and furious blast rushed out of the woods, and tore and shook at the four corners of the house as if to wrench it from its foundations.

"It's quite awful to hear the wind scream like that," said Minny. "It is like the banshee. Hark! is not that some one knocking at the back door?"

I listened, and amid the rattling and shaking of blinds and timbers I heard what sounded like a hurried, impatient knock at the side door. "Who can it be on such a wild night?" I said, and took the candle and went to open the door. I set the light in the hall, for I knew the wind would blow it out. In spite of this precaution, however, the flame was extinguished, for as I drew back the bolt and lifted the latch the blast threw the door violently back on its hinges, and rushed into the hall as though exulting in having finally made an entrance.

"Pretty bad weather, mamma," said some one in the softest, sweetest voice, like a courteous flute, and there entered my old friend the Black Panther.

This gentleman measured seven feet in his moccasins, and as he stood in our little entry he looked gigantic indeed. He closed the door with some difficulty, and I relit the candle.

"You are quite wet through," I said, for the water dripped from his blanket and woolen hunting-frock. He carried his rifle in his hand, and I thought the old man looked very tired and sad, and even anxious.

"You all well?" he asked, earnestly.

"Certainly. The captain has gone away, and Minny and the baby are here for the night. My dear friend, where have you been in this weather? There is a good fire in the kitchen. Come and get dry there, and let me make you a cup of hot coffee and get you something to eat."

Here Minny came out into the hall and held up her hands in sunrise.

"Oh, uncle," she said, calling him by the name she had used toward him since her childhood, "how could you come out in all this rain, and bring on your rheumatism? How do you think any one is ever going to find dry clothes for such a big creature as you?"

The Panther gave a little grunt and a smile. He was used to Minny's lectures, and he followed us both into the kitchen, where she made him sit down by the fire and took off his wet blanket, waiting on him like a daughter, and scolding him gently meanwhile. The old gentleman had of late years been subject to rheumatism, and it was too likely that this exposure would bring on another attack. The Panther patted her two little hands between his own. Like most of his race, he had beautiful hands, soft and rounded even in his old age, with long taper fingers that had, I dare say, taken more than one scalp in their time.

"Pooh!" said he, lightly. "You think old Ingin melt like maple sugar? You well?" he asked, anxiously.

"Quite so."

"And little one?"

"As well as a little pig, fast asleep in the other room."

"Where your husband?"

"Gone over to the railroad on business."

"And yours?" he asked, turning to me.

"Gone to Carysville. Do you know anything about him? is anything the matter?" I asked, a little alarmed at his persistent questioning and an indefinite something in the old man's tone and manner.

"Oh no," said he, earnestly. "I come right over from our place."

"Walked from the reservation in this storm!" said I. "What could have made you do such a thing?"

"Nothing--just to see you. Not very strange come see two nice women," said the old gentleman, with a little complimentary bow.

The Panther was somewhat vain of his knowledge of what he called "white manners," but I never saw a white man who could be so gently dignified, so courteous, so altogether charming in manner, as the old chief when he chose. He hardly knew one letter from another, but he had had sixty-five years of experience in war and council. Many a man "got up regardless of expense" in college and society might have taken lessons in deportment from this old Pottawatomie. He had known Minny from her childhood. Her father's farm had been the first clearing in all that part of the country. Deacon Adams had always been on excellent terms with the Indians, and his little daughter had found her earliest playmates among their children. The Panther had carried Minny in his arms when she was a baby; and as his own family of boys and girls died one after another, he clung closer to the child who had been their pet as well as his own.

The Panther was one of those big, soft, easy men who seem made to be ruled by one woman or another. He was greatly respected in his tribe, and had much influence. When they had been a nation he had been one of their most distinguished warriors, and his word had been law. He had always maintained toward the "young men" a somewhat imperious manner. He had conducted himself with dignity and decision in all his visits to Washington, where he had been a great lion, and in all his dealings with the United States he had shown much wisdom and ability. But report said that when once within the domestic circle and before his squaw, the diplomatist and warrior was exceedingly meek. He bore his wife's death with resignation, but he had never married again. He loved Minny Adams better than anything on earth, and the girl had great influence over him. She, in her turn, was very fond of him. From her earliest years he had been her friend, confidant and admirer. He looked so fierce and dangerous, and was so kind and simple, that the alliance between the girl and himself was very much like that between a little child and a big mastiff--the child protected and leader, the dog protector and led.

Minny made flannel shirts for him, and he wore them: she trimmed his moccasins, and the dainty cambric ruffles which he wore when in grand costume were got up by her hands. The Panther, however, did not often appear in full dress. She tried to teach him to read, and she did get him through the alphabet, but he greatly preferred hearing stories read to learning to do it for himself, and was especially fond of the *Arabian Nights*, which he quite believed. She even coaxed him to go to church with her, and might have made a convert of him but for the interference of an exceedingly silly young clergyman. The Panther rather liked to hear the Bible, but I fear he was more attracted by the sound than the sense: his favorite chapter was the story of David and Goliah. He used to say that "Ingin religion was good for Ingin, and white religion was good for white man." However, he never offered the least opposition to the missionary who had settled among his people: indeed, he rather patronized that gentleman.

He and Wyanota were excellent friends. It was good to see the deference and respect with which the younger man treated the elder. I always said that it was the Panther who made the match between Minny and Mr. Moore. Their house was one of his homes, and he was a frequent guest at our own. He petted and spoiled my two children: he was very soft and kind to me, whom he called "Mamma," after Wyn's example, and he considered that my husband "understood good manners"--a compliment which he did not pay to every one.

A dear little daughter whom we had lost had been very fond of him: the child had died in his arms. I was alone at the time, and the old man's sympathy was such a comfort to me in my trouble that for his own sake, as well as for our little girl's, he had become very dear to us.

For an Indian, the Panther might be called almost a sober character. He was seldom drunk more than four or five times a year, and when he was, he always was very careful to keep out of the way of his white friends until he was sober, when he would lecture the young men on the evils of intemperance in most impressive fashion. He was a good deal of an orator, possessing a voice of great sweetness and power; and though he was such an immense creature, all his movements were light and graceful as those of a kitten. He could speak perfectly good, even elegant, English when he chose, but he did not always choose, and generally omitted the pronouns; but his voice, manner and gestures in speaking were perfectly charming when he was in a good temper. When he was not, he was somewhat awful, but it was only under great provocation that he became savage. In general, he was an amiable, kind, lazy creature, whom it was very easy to love.

I could not but wonder that night, as I set out the table and made the coffee, what had brought the Panther so far in such wild weather. He did not seem like himself. He was usually very conversable, and would chat away by the hour together, in a fashion half shrewd, half simple, often very interesting; but now he was silent and *distrait*.

"Carry," said Mrs. Moore, "are there not some of Wyn's things here yet in that old trunk in your lumber-room?"

"Yes. Perhaps you can find something the chief can put on, and bring down a pair of the captain's socks and slippers."

"Oh, never mind, never mind," said the damp giant.

"But I will mind," said the little woman; and she went out and soon returned with the things, which she insisted he should go and put on.

"Well, always one woman or another," said the Panther in a tone of resignation: "always squaw git her own way. You see that little girl, mamma? Could squeeze her up just like a rabbit. Always she order me round since she so high, and I just big fool enough let her;" and he went into the next room, and presently came out arrayed in dry garments, as to his upper man at least. I set the table with the best I had in the house, and Minny and I sat down to get a cup of coffee with our guest.

At any other time the old gentleman would have purred and talked over this little feast like an amiable old cat, but now he was rather silent; and I noticed that in the pauses of the wind he would stop as though listening for some expected sound. I began to think he was concealing from me some misfortune or danger, and the same thought was evidently in Minny's mind, for she watched him anxiously.

When we went back into the parlor the Panther walked to the baby's crib, and stood for a moment looking at the sleeping child with a tenderness which softened his whole aspect. Then he asked for the little boys.

"They are fast asleep in the next room," I said. "Go and look at them, and you will be sure."

The Panther smiled, but he went into my room, which opened from the parlor, and bending down softly kissed the two little faces resting on the same pillow.

I drew a large chair to the fire for him, and Minny filled his pipe, for I had "followed the drum" too long to object to smoking. The giant stretched his length of limb before the fire, but he did not seem quite at ease, even under the influence of the tobacco. He looked a little troubled and anxious, and lifted his head once or twice with a sudden motion, like a dog who has misgivings that something is wrong out-doors.

The baby stirred in her sleep, and the chief began gently to rock the cradle. "'Spose she order me about too, by and by," he said, "like her mother."

"Oh, you like to make that out," said Minny, "because you are such a great big, strong man. If you were a little bit of a creature, you would always be standing on your dignity to make yourself look tall. The last time Wyn and I were at Detroit we went to church, and I heard the very smallest man I ever saw preach a tremendous sermon about the man being the head of the woman, insisting mightily on the respect we all owe to the other sex. When we came out I asked Wyn what he thought, and he said he thought it was exactly such a sermon as such a very tiny man might be expected to preach."

"Ah! and he heard you both, my dear," said I; "and he says Mr. Moore has no element of reverence in his character!"

Here the Panther dropped his pipe, and starting from his chair looked like his namesake just ready for a spring, as the sharp, quick bark of a little dog was heard from the nearest house.

"Only dog," he said in a tone of relief, and resumed his smoking.

"Uncle," said Minny, "I do wish you would tell me what the matter is, or what you are listening for. You make me think there is something wrong."

I looked up and seconded Minny's request.

"'Spose I tell you, you think it all Ingin nonsense," he said, looking a little embarrassed.

"Even if I did, sir, I should feel more comfortable," I said.

"Yes, do tell us, please," said Minny, earnestly.

"Well, then," said the old man, speaking with an effort, "last night went out after a coon--up in the woods right back of here--"

"Yes: well?"

"And went up on that little hill over your pasture, and then," said the old man lowering his voice and speaking with great earnestness, "hear *red fox bark*--one, two, three times out loud, and then again farther off. There, now!"

I was greatly relieved at finding that I was threatened by nothing worse than the oracle of the red fox. I knew the Indian superstition that if this animal is heard to bark anywhere near a dwelling, he foretells death within twenty-four hours to some one beneath its roof.

"But," said I, "the red fox is only a sign for Indians. He does not bark for white people, and you were not under a roof at the time, so it cannot apply to you."

"Don't know!" said the Panther, shaking his head. "Never know that sign fail. Then here this little woman and this baby--all the same as Ingin now."

Minny looked a little troubled. In spite of his reading, his college education and mathematics, Wyanota had sundry queer notions and superstitions, about which he very seldom spoke, but which nevertheless had some weight with him, and it is possible that he had in some degree communicated his ideas to his wife.

"I don't believe in signs," said Minny, but nevertheless she looked annoyed.

"So I thought," said the chief with a little smile. "Know mamma here think it all nonsense, or else come over this morning to tell her. Then think she not believe it and not mind, and so keep quiet. Then storm come up and wind blow, and couldn't stand it; so set out and walk over here to take care of her; and she--maybe she laugh at me?"

"No indeed, sir," said I, greatly touched by the anxious affection which had brought the old man so far in such weather. "How good you are to me! You mean to stay here to-night of course, and in the morning you will see that the red fox was simply barking for his own amusement; but I am sorry he drove you to take such a toilsome walk, though we are glad to have you here."

"My business take care of you when your men gone. Got no one my own blood," he said, rather sadly: "boys dead, girl dead, squaw dead--no one but you two care much for old man."

Minny went and kissed him softly. "You know I belong to you," she said, "and baby has no grandfather but you."

"Ah! your father!" said the Panther, rocking the cradle. "He and I always good friends. 'Member when you come, your mother she got no milk for you, poor little starved thing! My squaw she lose her baby--nice little boy too," said the old man, with a sigh--"she tell your mother she nurse you; so she did. You git fat and rosy right off. You all the same one of us after that. No spoil your pretty white skin, though," said the Panther, patting Minny's cheek with his brown fingers. "Seem just like that happen yesterday: now you got baby yourself. Ah! your father--mighty well pleased he be 'spose he see that little one."

"How often I wish he could!" said "Minny with a sigh, for both her father and mother were dead.

"You 'pend upon it, he comfortable somewhere," said the chief, consolingly. "Deacon Adams, he real good man. Look here, mamma! Like to ask you question. You say when we die white man go to one place, Indian go to another--"

"I don't say so, sir. I don't pretend to know all this world by heart, much less the other."

"Well, that what Indian say, any way. Now 'spose that so, what come of half-breed, eh?"

"What do you think?" I asked, for neither Minny nor I could venture an opinion on this abstruse point.

"Don't know," said the old man. "Saw young Cherokee in Washington: he marry pretty little schoolmistress go down there to teach, and their little boy die. Then that young man feel bad, and he fret good deal 'bout where that baby gone to, and he ask me, and I no able tell him. Guess me find out when get there: no use to trouble till then, You make these?" he asked, changing the subject, and looking with admiration at the captain's embroidered slippers which I had lent him.

"Yes. They were pretty when they were new. I'll make you a pair just like them, if you wish. Shall I?"

The old gentleman looked greatly delighted, for he was as fond of finery as any girl, and took no small pride in adorning his still handsome person.

I brought out all my embroidery-patterns, and the giant took as much pleasure as a child in the pretty painted pictures and gay-colored wools and silks. I made all the conversation I could over the slippers, willing to divert him from the melancholy which seemed to have taken possession of his mind. Over my work-basket he brightened a little, and chatted away quite like himself, and listened with pleasure to Minny's singing. We did not rise to go to bed till eleven o'clock, which was a very late hour for Maysville. When the Panther spent the night at our house, as was frequently the case, he never would go regularly to bed, but would take his blanket and lie down before the kitchen fire. With great politeness he insisted on getting the wood ready for morning, a thing he never would have dreamed of doing for a woman of his own race.

As he came back into the kitchen from the shed he took up his rifle, which he had set down by the door. As he did so an angry look came over his face. "Look here," he said: "somebody been spoil my rifle!"

I looked at the piece in surprise, for the lock was broken. "It cannot have been done since you came," I said. "There is no one in the house but ourselves."

"Of course not, of course not!" said the Panther, eager to show that he had no suspicion of his friends.

"Did you stop anywhere on your way?"

"Yes," said he with some slight embarrassment. "Stop at Ryan's," mentioning a low tavern on the borders of the reservation, which was a terrible thorn in the side of all the missionary's efforts. "Stop a minute light my pipe, but no drink one drop," he added with great earnestness; "but they ask me good deal."

"Did you put your gun down?"

"Guess so," he said after a moment's reflection. "Yes, know did put it down a minute or two."

"Then that was when the mischief was done, you may be sure. This lock was never broken by accident. It must have been a mere piece of spite because you would not stay. I wonder you did not notice it when you came out."

"In a hurry, and kept the buckskin over it, not to git it wet. Wish knew who did that," said he, with a look not good to see. "Guess not do it again."

"I am very sorry, but it can easily be mended."

I spread out on the floor for him the comfortable and blankets I had brought for his use, and hung up his woolen hunting-frock, now quite dry.

As I took it into my hand, I felt something very heavy in the pocket.

"I hope you have nothing here that will be spoiled with wet?" I said.

"Oh, nothing but money," said the chief, carelessly. "Mean to tell Minny to take some of it and buy clothes for me."

He took out as he spoke a handful of loose change--copper, silver and two or three gold-pieces--and a roll of bills a good deal damp, and put it all into my apron. I counted the money and found there were seventy-five dollars. Strong indeed must have been the attraction which had brought the old man away from the tavern-fire in his sober senses with such a sum of money in his pocket.

"Just got that," he said. "Part from Washington, part sell deer-skins."

There was no need to tell me that it had not been long in his possession. Money in the Panther's hands was like water in a sieve.

"You give me five dollars, give the rest to Minny," he said; and as this was by much the wisest arrangement for him, I did as he wished.

"You got captain's gun?" he asked me. "Never like to go to sleep without something to catch up: hit somebody 'spose somebody come."

"I am sorry to say the captain has his rifle with him, and I lent the shotgun to Jim Brewster this afternoon."

He looked annoyed, but he went out into the woodshed and returned with the axe, which was new and sharp. "Have something, anyway," he said, doggedly.

"Why, what do you think can possibly happen?"

"Don't know. Always like to have something to catch up. Good-night, mamma. You go to sleep."

I went to bed and fell asleep almost on the minute, but I could not have slept long when I was wakened by the noise of the wind against the shutters. The rain had ceased, but the blast was still roaring without. Minny and her child were in a room which opened out of the parlor opposite my own. The lamp which was burning there threw a dim light into my chamber, and showed me each familiar object and my little boys asleep beside me.

Some one says that between the hours of one and four in the morning the human mind is not itself. I fully believe it. In those hours you do not "fix your mind" on melancholy subjects--they fix themselves upon you. If you turn back into the past, there comes up before you every occasion on which you made a fool of yourself, every lost opportunity, every slight injury you ever experienced. If you look at the future, you see nothing but coming failure and disappointment. The present moment connects itself with every tale you ever heard or read of ghosts, murder, vampires or robbers.

That night, either because of the wind or because I had taken too strong coffee, I fell into "the fidgets," as this state of mind is sometimes called, and selected for immediate cause of discomfort the Panther's presentiment about the red fox. Who could explain the mysterious way in which animals are warned of approaching danger? Perhaps the old science of divination was not so entirely a delusion; and then I remembered all the old stories in Roman history of people who had come to grief by neglecting the oracles. The old idea that whatever incident is considered as an omen will be such in reality, seemed to me at that hour of the night not wholly an unreasonable theory.

I had known, to be sure, some fifty presentiments which came to nothing, but then I had known as many as three which had been verified: perhaps the present case might be one of the exceptions to the rule. Then I remembered all the stories in Scott's **Demonology**, which I had lately read, and quite forgot all the arguments intended to disprove them.

I thought of the broken gun-lock: I thought it not improbable that the Panther had, when at Ryan's, mentioned that he was coming to our house, and that it was very likely he had let it appear that he carried his money with him. Ryan's was one of the worst places in all the State. I remembered that the money was in the house, and I began to wish, like the Panther, that I had something to "catch up." Then there were so many noises about! I heard footsteps, which you will always hear if you listen for them on a windy night. When our petted old cat jumped from his place on the parlor sofa to lie down before the fire, I started up in bed in a sudden fright.

I must have been in this uncomfortable state of mind and body for the best part of an hour before I remembered that in a drawer in the front parlor lay two little old-fashioned pistols, unloaded but in good order.

I had grown so excited and uneasy that I felt as if I could not rest unless I got up, found those pistols and loaded them, though nobody had ever heard of a burglary in Maysville, and half the time the doors were left unlocked at night. Rather despising myself for my nervousness, but yielding to it nevertheless, I rose, put on my dressing-gown and slippers, lit my candle and went to find the two little pistols. I stepped very softly, not to disturb Minny, for I should have been quite ashamed then to have her know my cowardice. I looked in at the door as I passed. She was sound asleep, with her baby on her arm. The baby, however, was broad awake, but lying perfectly still, with her little finger in her mouth. Her eyes shone in the lamplight as she turned them on me--not startled like another child, but simply questioning. The little creature looked so unnaturally wise and self-possessed that I was reminded perforce of a wild tale Wyanota had once told me about a remote ancestress of his who had married some sort of a wood-demon. The legend ran that Wyanota's family was descended from the offspring of this marriage, and I think Wyn more than half believed the story.

I passed on, and going into the next room found the pistols, carried them back to my own chamber, and loaded them carefully. I was quite accustomed to the use of firearms. There had been times in my life when I never sat down to my work or went to rest without having rifle or pistol within easy reach of my hand. When I had loaded the weapons, I put them on the table by my bed and lay down again. My excitement seemed to have subsided, and I was just falling asleep when I heard a door in the kitchen violently burst open. I thought the wind had done it, and waited a moment to hear if the Panther would rise and shut it.

The next instant there was a shot, a wild cry as of mingled pain and fury, the sound of a heavy fall and a struggle. Before I had well realized that the noise was in the house, I found myself at the kitchen door with my pistols in my hand. I was greatly startled, but my one idea was to help my old friend. The miserable door resisted me for a moment. Seconds passed that seemed hours. When at last I tore it open, I saw a man in his shirt sleeves lying dead on the floor, his head shattered apparently by a blow from the axe: another, a large, powerful Irishman, was kneeling on the Panther's breast, with his hands at the old man's throat.

I sprang forward, but something swifter than I darted past me with a savage cry, and, tearing and biting with claws and teeth, flung itself full at the ruffian's face and naked throat. It was our big old brindle cat, Tom, roused from his place before the fire. The unexpected fierceness of Tom's assault took the man quite by surprise. Before he could tear the creature away I had the pistol at his head.

"If you move," I said, "I'll kill you;" for, as I saw that my old friend was hurt, wrath took the place of fear.

He gave in directly. Indeed the cat, a large, powerful animal, had almost scratched his eyes out. In the most abject tones the fellow implored me to let him go.

"Don't you do it, mamma," said the Panther, faintly.

"I don't mean to," I said.

Under the kitchen stairs was a dark closet with a strong outside bolt. I ordered the man into this place. He obeyed, and I drew the bolt upon him. His face and throat were streaming with blood from Tom's teeth and claws.

All this passed in much less time than it takes to tell it. Roused by the noise, the children, and Minny with the baby in her arms, were already in the kitchen.

"Oh, my dear, my poor darling!" said Minny, kneeling by the old man's side, "you are hurt!"

"Yes," he said, quietly, "pretty considerable bad. Charley, you fasten that door;" for the door into the shed, which had been secured only by a button, was wide open. "You get the hammer and two, three big nails, and drive 'em in," he continued. "Maybe more them darn scamps round."

Charley obeyed directions in a way which did him credit. Little Ned, with wide, surprised eyes, clung to me in silence; little Carry, seeing her mother in tears, put up a piteous lip and sobbed in her unbaby-like, sorrowful fashion; the old cat, in great excitement, went purring and talking from one to another.

"Tell me where you are hurt," I said, holding the chief's hand.

He had been shot through the stomach with a great, old-fashioned smooth-bore musket, which lay on the floor--a gun not carrying less than twenty-five to the pound. I had seen gunshot wounds before, and I knew that this was serious. It did not bleed much externally, but the edges of the wound were torn and discolored.

"That fellow dead?" asked the Panther.

"Yes indeed!" for the man's head was split like a walnut.

The old warrior looked gratified. "Mamma," he said, touching his hunting-knife, "you take that fellow's scalp."

"Don't think of such a thing," I said, not so much shocked as I might have been had I not lived on the Indian frontier. "Do you know who they are?"

"See them to Ryan's. Guess they some folks that mizzable railroad bring into this country. 'Spect they follow me. Mamma," said the Panther, looking up into my face, "tell you, red fox not bark for nothing. Better be old man than you."

"Oh, my dear old friend, if you had only not come to us to-night! It was all your love for us that has done this, but I pray God you may get well. Charley, do you think you can go for Doctor Beach?"

"Yes, mamma," said the boy, though he turned pale.

"No, no," said the Panther. "You no send that little fellow out in the dark. Besides, no good. You go wrap yourselves up. You two, you git bad cold."

At that moment we heard the sound of wheels and horses' feet.

"Go, Charley," said Minny. "Stop whoever it is, and tell them what has happened."

Charley ran out, and soon returned with Dr. Beach, who, happily for us, had been out on one of those errands which are always rousing doctors from their beds.

Dr. Beach was a burly, rough-mannered sort of man, but he could be very kind and tender in the exercise of his profession. He wasted no time in questions, but looked grave when he saw how the old man was hurt.

"Needn't tell me," said the Panther, quietly. "Know it's the end. Kill one of 'em, anyhow!" he concluded in a tone of calm satisfaction.

"And I wish with all my heart you had killed the other," said the doctor, bitterly. "He got off, I suppose."

The Panther showed his white teeth in a laugh. "No," he said, pointing to me: "she got him--she and the cat. Pretty well for one little squaw and pussy-cat. Mamma, you keep that kitty always."

"Where is the scoundrel?" asked the doctor.

"Shut up in that closet."

Here the man within cried out that he was "kilt" already, and should be hung if we did not let him go.

"I hope you will, with all my heart," said the doctor.

With some difficulty we helped the Panther into the parlor and laid him on the sofa.

He told us the story in a few words. He had been asleep when the door was burst open. The man whom he had killed had fired the shot. He had kept his feet to strike one blow with the axe, and the other man had sprung upon him as he fell.

The doctor did what little he could to ease his patient, and then went away, but soon returned with some men from the village, who were quite ready to lynch the criminal when they heard what he had done. They took the man away, however, and I am happy to say he afterward received the heaviest sentence the law would allow. He confessed that, knowing the chief had a large sum in his possession, himself and his companion had broken the lock of the rifle, intending to waylay the old man and shoot him in the woods. They had not, however, been able to overtake him till he reached the clearing, and then, fearing to encounter him, they had followed him at a distance and watched him enter our house. Knowing that the captain was gone, they had waited until all was quiet, and then made their entrance as described.

The Panther asked that some one might go to the reservation and send over three of his friends, whom he named. He was very anxious to see Wyanota, and Calvin Bruce, who had come with the doctor, instantly volunteered to take his trotting mare and do both errands. The chestnut did her work gallantly, though unhappily in vain, for the old man did not live to see his friends.

"Don't you fret, you two," he said, softly, as Minny and I watched over him. "Great deal the best way for old Ingin. Die like a man now: not cough myself to death, like an old dog. Minny, little girl, you tell your husband be good to our people, well as he can. Not much of our nation left now--not good for much, either," he added; "but you tell him and the captain stand their friends, won't you?"

"Indeed, indeed they will," said Minny in tears.

A Methodist clergyman of some kind, who preached in Maysville at that time, hearing what had happened, came in to offer his services and to pray with the dying man. The Panther thanked him courteously, but he clung to the simple creed of his fathers and his belief that "Ingin religion was good for Ingin;" and Mr. Lawrence had the sense and feeling not to disturb him by argument.

"Want your Charley to have my rifle," he said to me. "Nobody left of our people but my cousin's son, and he most a mizzable Ingin. You 'member that, please," he said to Mr. Lawrence, who sat quietly at the head of the sofa. "Do you think," he asked wistfully of the clergyman, "that I ever see these two again where I go?" The minister--Heaven bless him!--answered stoutly that he had not a doubt of it. "All right, then," said the Panther, quietly. "Now, mamma, you see red fox know, after all."

Minny brought her baby for him to kiss. Little Carry's dark eyes were full of tears, for, like most babies, she felt the influence of sorrow she could not understand. She did not scream, as another child would, but hid her face on her mother's bosom and sobbed quietly, like a grown-up woman. My two little boys, understanding all at once that their old friend was going away, burst out crying.

"Hush! hush!" he said, gently. "You be good boys to your mother. Say 'good-bye.'"

We kissed him, keeping back the lamentations which we knew would trouble him.

"Good-bye," he said, softly, and then he spoke some few words in his own tongue, as Minny told me afterward, about going to his lost children. Then a smile came over his face, a look of sweet relief and comfort softened the stern features, the hand that had held mine so close slowly relaxed; and with a sigh he was gone.

The old minister gently closed his eyes. "My dear," said Mr. Lawrence to Minny, who was in an agony of grief, "God knows, but it was His Son who said, 'Greater love hath no man than this--that a man lay down his life for his friends!'"

When we buried the old chief we wrote those words on the stone we placed over his grave.

Since then the New Year's Eve brings back to me very vividly the memory of the augury that so strangely accomplished its own fulfillment.

CLARA F. GUERNSEY.

Louie.

The great river was flowing peacefully down to the sea, opening its blue tides at the silver fretting of the bar into a shallow expanse some miles in width, a part of which on either side overlay stretches where the submerged eel-grass lent a tint of chrysoprase to the sheathing flow, and into which one gazed, half expecting to see so ideal a depth peopled by something other than the long ribbons of the weed streaming out on the slow current--the only cool sight, albeit, beneath the withering heat of the day across all that shining extent. Far down the shores, on the right, a line of low sand-hills rose, protecting the placid harbor from sea and storm with the bulwark of their dunes, whose yellow drifts were ranged by the winds in all fantastic shapes, and bound together by ropes of the wild poison-ivy and long tangles of beach-grass and the blossoming purple pea, and which to-day cast back the rays of the sun as though they were of beaten brass. Above these hills the white lighthouse loomed, the heated air trembling around it, and giving it so vague and misty a guise that, being by itself a thing of night and storm and darkness, it looked now as unreal as a ghost by daylight. On the other side of the harbor lay the marshes, threaded by steaming creeks, up which here and there the pointed sails of the hidden hay-barges crept, the sunshine turning them to white flames: farther off stood a screen of woods, and from brim to brim between swelled the broad, smooth sheet of the river, coming from the great mountains that gave it birth, washing clean a score of towns on its way, and loitering just here by the pleasant old fishing-town, whose wharves, once doing a mighty business with the Antilles and the farther Indies, now, in the absence of their half dozen foreign-going craft, lay at the mercy of any sand-droger that chose to fling her cable round their capstans. A few idle masts swayed there, belonging to small fishers and fruiters, a solid dew of pitch oozing from their sides in the sun, but not a sail set: a lonely watchman went the rounds among them, a ragged urchin bobbed for flounders in the dock, but otherwise wharves and craft were alike forsaken, and the sun glared down on them as though his rays had made them a desert. The harbor-water lay like glass: now and then the tide stirred it, and all the brown and golden reflections of masts and spars with it, into the likeness of a rippled agate. Not one of the boats that were ordinarily to be seen darting hither and yon, like so many water-bugs, were in motion now; none of the white sails of the gay sea-parties were running up and swelling with the breeze; none of the usual naked and natatory cherubs were diving off the wharves into that deep, warm water; the windows on the seaward side of the town were closed; the countless children, that were wont to infest the lower streets as if they grew with no more cost or trouble than the grass between the bricks, had disappeared in the mysterious way in which swarms of flies will disappear, as if an east wind had blown them; but no east wind was blowing here. In all the scene there was hardly any other sign of life than the fervent sunbeams shedding their cruel lustre overhead: the river flowed silent and lonely from shore to shore; the whole hot summer sky stretched just as silent and lonely from horizon to horizon; only the old ferryman, edging along the bank till he was far up stream, crossed the narrower tide and drifted down effortless on the other side; only an old black brig lay at anchor, with furled sail and silent deck, in the middle channel down below the piers, and from her festering and blistering hull it was that all the heat and loneliness and silence of the scene seemed to exude--for it was the fever-ship.

It was a different picture on the bright river when that brig entered the harbor on the return of her last voyage, to receive how different a welcome! But pestilence raged abroad in the country now, and the people of the port, who had so far escaped the evil, were loth to let it enter among them at last, and had not yet recovered from the recoil of their first shock and shiver at thought of it in their waters--waters than which none could have fostered it more kindly, full as they were in their shallow breadth of rotting weeds and the slime of sewers. Perhaps the owner of some pale face looked through the pane and thought of brother or father, or, it may be, of lover, and grew paler with pity, and longed to do kind offices for those who suffered; but the greater part of all the people hived upon the shores would have scouted the thought of going out with aid to those hot pillows rocking there upon the tide, and of bringing back infection to the town, as much as though the act had been piracy on the high seas. And they stayed at home, and watched their vanes and longed for an east wind--an east wind whose wings would shake out healing, whose breath would lay the destroying fever low; but the east wind refused to seek their shores, and chose rather to keep up its wild salt play far out on the bosom of its mid-sea billows.

Yes, on that return of the last voyage of the brig the stream had swarmed with boats, flags had fluttered from housetops and staffs, piers and quays had been lined with cheering people, all flocking forth to see the broken, battered little craft; for the brig had been spoken by a tug, and word had been brought to the wharves, and had spread like wild-fire through the town, that, wrecked in a tempest and deserted by the panic-stricken crew, the steadfast master and a boy who stood by him had remained with her, had refitted her as best they might when the storm abated, and had brought her into port at last through fortunate days of fair weather and slow sailing. The town was ringing with the exploit, with praise of the noble faithfulness of master and boy; and now the river rang again, and no conquering galley of naval hero ever moved through a gladder, gayer welcome than that through which the little black brig lumbered on her clumsy way to her moorings.

But though all the rest of the populace of the seaport had turned out with their greetings that day, there was one little body there who, so far from hurrying down to shore or sea-wall with a waving handkerchief, ran crying into a corner; and it was there that Andrew Traverse, the person of only secondary importance in the river scene, rated as a boy on the brig's books, but grown into a man since the long voyage began,--it was there he found her when the crowd had let him alone and left him free to follow his own devices.

"It's the best part of all the welcome, I declare it is!" said he, standing in the doorway and enjoying the sight before him a moment.

"Oh, Andrew," cried the little body with a sob, but crouching farther away into the corner, "it was so splendid of you!"

"What was so splendid of me?" said he, still in the doorway, tall and erect in the sunshine that lay around him, and that glanced along his red shirt and his bronzed cheek to light a flame in the black eyes that surveyed her.

"Standing by him so," she sobbed--"standing by the captain when the others left--bringing home the ship!"

"It's not a ship--it's a brig," said Andrew, possibly too conscious of his merit to listen to the praise of it. "Well, is this all? Ain't you going to shake hands with me? Ain't you glad to see me?"

"Oh, Andrew! So glad!" and she turned and let him see the blushing, rosy face one moment, the large, dark, liquid eyes, the tangled, tawny curls; and then over-come once more, as a sudden shower overcomes the landscape, the lips quivered again, the long-lashed eyelids fell, and the face was hidden in another storm of tears. And then, perhaps because he was a sailor, and perhaps because he was a man, his arms were round her and he was kissing off those tears, and the little happy body was clinging to him and trembling with excitement and with joy like a leaf in the wind.

Certainly no two happier, prouder beings walked along the sea-wall that night, greeted with hearty hands at every step, followed by all eyes till the shelter of deepening dusk obscured them, and with impish urchins, awe-struck for once, cry-ing mysteriously under their breath to each other, "That's him! That's the feller saved the Sabrina! That's him and her!" How proud the little body was! how her heart beat with pleasure at thought of the way in which all men were ready to do him honor! how timidly she turned her eyes upon him and saw the tint deepen on his cheek, the shadow flash into light in his eye, the smile kindle on his lips, as he looked down on her--glad with her pride and pleasure, strong, confident, content himself--till step by step they had left the town behind, wandering down the sandy island road, through the wayside hedge of blossoming wild roses and rustling young birches, till they leaned upon the parapet of the old island bridge and heard the wa-ter lap and saw the stars come out, and only felt each other and their love in all the wide, sweet summer universe.

Poor Louie! She had always been as shy and wary as any little brown bird of the woods. It was Andrew's sudden and glorious coming that had surprised her into such expression of a feeling that had grown up with her until it was a part of every thought and memory. And as for Andrew--certainly he had not known that he cared for her so much until she turned that tearful, rosy face upon him in welcome; but now it seemed to him that she had been his and he hers since time began: he could neither imagine nor remember any other state than this: he said to himself, and then repeated it to her, that he had loved her always, that it was thought of her that had kept him firm and faithful to his duty, that she had been the lodestar toward which he steered on that slow homeward way; and he thanked Heaven, no doubt devoutly enough, that had saved him from such distress and brought him back to such bliss. And Louie listened and clung closer, more joyful and more blest with every pulse of her bounding heart.

After all, sudden as the slipping into so divine a dream had been, it had need to be full as intense and deep, for it was only for a little while it lasted. A week's rapt walking in these mid-heavens, where earth and care and each to-morrow was forgotten, and there broke in upon them the voice of the Sabrina's owner seeking for Andrew Traverse.

Of course such conduct as that of one who preferred to do his utmost to save a sinking ship rather than seek safety with her flying crew, was something too un-usual to go unrewarded: it must be signalized into such a shining light that all other mariners must needs follow it. And if the sky had fallen, Andrew declared, he could have been no more surprised than he was when he found himself invited with great ceremony to a stately tea-drinking at the house of the owner of the Sabrina. "Now we shall catch larks," said he; and dressed in a new suit, whose gray tint set off the smoothness of his tanned cheek with the color sometimes mantling through the brown, he entered the house with all the composure of a gentleman used to nothing but high days and holidays. Not that either the state or ceremony at Mr. Maurice's required great effort to encounter with composure--trivial enough at its best, won-derful though it was to the townsfolk, unused to anything beyond. But Andrew had seen the world in foreign parts, and neither Mr. Maurice's mansion-house and gardens, nor his gay upholstery, nor his silver tea-service, nor his condescending manners, struck the least spark of surprise from Andrew's eyes, or gave them the least shadow of awe.

"This is some mistake," said the owner graciously, after preliminary compli-ment had been duly observed. "How is it that you are rated on the books as a boy--you as much a man as you will ever be?"

"A long voyage, sir, slow sailing and delays over so many disasters as befell us, three years out in the stead of a year and a half--all that brings one to man's estate before his reckoning."

"But the last part of the time you must have done able seaman's service?"

"The captain and I together," said Andrew with his bright laugh. "We were officers and crew and passengers, cox'n and cook, as they say."

"A hard experience," said Mr. Maurice.

"Oh, not at all, but worth its weight in gold--to me, at least. Why, sir, it taught me how to handle a ship as six years before the mast couldn't have done."

"Good! We shall see to what purpose one of these days. And you have had your share of schooling, they tell me?"

"All that the academy had to give, sir."

"And that's enough for any one who has the world to tussel with. How should you like to have gone through such hard lines, Frarnie?" turning to his daughter, a pale, moon-faced girl, her father's darling.

"Were you never afraid?" she asked in her pretty simpering way.

"Not to say afraid," answered Andrew, deferentially. "We knew our danger--two men alone in the leaky, broken brig--but then we could be no worse off than we were before; and as for the others--"

"They got their deserts," said Mr. Maurice.

"The poor fellows left us in such a hurry that they took hardly any water or biscuit; and at the worst our fate could not be so bad as theirs, under the hot sun in those salt seas."

"Well, well!" said Mr. Maurice, who loved his own ease too much to like to hear of others' dis-ease. And to turn the conversation from the possible horrors into which it might lapse, he invited his guest out into his gardens, among his grape-houses, his poultry and his dogs. It was a long hour's ramble that they took there, well improved on both sides, for Andrew of course knew it to be for his interest to please the brig's owner; and Mr. Maurice, who prided himself on having a singularly keen insight into character, studied the young man's every word and gesture, for it was not often that he came across such material as this out of which to make his captains; and to what farther effect in this instance he pursued his studies might have been told, by any one keener than himself, through the tone of satisfaction with which, on re-entering the parlor, he bade his daughter take Andrew down the rooms and tell him the histories of the surprising pictures there. For Mr. Maurice, one of the great fortunes of the seaport, being possessed by a mania of belief that every youth who cast tender eyes upon his daughter cast them not on her, but on her future havings and holdings, had long since determined to select a husband for her himself--one who evinced no servile reverence for wealth, one whom he could trust to make her happy. "And here," he said, "I am not sure but that I have him."

When Andrew went in to see Louie a moment on his way home that night, he was in great spirits over the success of his visit, and, dark as it was, made her blush the color of the rose over the low doorway where they stood when he asked how she would like to go captain's wife next voyage. And then he told her of Mr. Maurice's scrutiny and questioning, and the half hint of a ship of his own to sail some day, and of the pale-faced Miss Frarnie's interest, and of the long stroll down the parlors among the pictures, the original of one of which he had seen somewhere in the Mediterranean, when he and a parcel of sailors went ashore and rambled through the port, and looked in at a church, where, in the midst of music and incense and a kneeling crowd, they were shearing the golden locks off of young girls and making nuns of them. And Andrew forgot to tell of the way in which Miss Frarnie listened to him and hung upon his words: indeed, how could he? Perhaps he did not notice it himself; but if he had had a trifle more personal vanity, and had seen how this pale young girl--forbidden by a suspicious father much companionship with gallants--had forgotten all difference of station and purse, and had looked upon him, nobly made, handsome, gay, knowing far more than she did, much as upon a young god just alighted by her side a moment,--if Andrew had been aware of this, and had found any words in which to repeat it, then Louie might have had something to startle her out of her blessedness, and pain might have come to her all the sooner. But since the pain would have been as sharp then as at any future time, it was a pitying, pleasant Fate that let her have her happiness as long as might be. For Louie's love was a different thing from the selfish passion that any clown may feel: she had been happy enough in her little round of commonplace satisfactions and tasks before Andrew came and shed over her this great cloud of delight--happy then just in the enjoyment of that secret love of hers that went out and sought him every night sailing over foreign sunlit waters, and hovered like a blessing round his head; and now that he had come and folded her about and about with such warm devotion, it was not for the new happiness he gave her that she loved him, but in order to make his own happiness a perfect thing; and if her heart's blood had been needed for that, it would have been poured out like water. The pale-faced Frarnie--if question could be of her--might never know such love as that: love with her could be a sentiment, a lover one who added to her pleasure, but a sacrifice on her part for that lover would have been something to tell and sing for ever, if indeed it were possible that such a thing should be made at all.

So day by day the spell deepened with Louie, and for another week there was delightful loneliness with this lover of hers--strolls down through the swampy woods hunting for moss to frame the prints he had brought home uninjured, and which were to be part of the furnishing of their future home; others across the salt meadows for the little red samphire stems to pickle; sails in the float down river and in the creeks, where the tall thatch parted by the prow rustled almost overhead, and the gulls came flying and piping around them: here and there, they two alone, pouring out thought and soul to each other, and every now and then glancing shyly at those days, that did not seem so very far away, when they should be sailing together through foreign parts; for Louie's father, the old fisherman, was all her household, and a maiden aunt, who earned her livelihood in nursing the sick and attending the dead, would be glad to come any day and take Louie's place in the cottage.

At the end of the week, Mr. Maurice sent for Andrew to his counting-room; and after that, on one device or another, he had him there the greater part of every day, employing him in a score of pleasant ways--asking his advice as to the repairs of the Sabrina, taking him with him in his chaise jogging through the shipyard, where a new barque was getting ready for her launching, examining him the while carefully from time to time after his wont; at last taking him casually home to dinner with him one day, keeping him to tea the next, and finally, fully satisfied with the result of his studies in that edition of human nature, giving him the freedom of the family as much as if he had been the son of the house.

"I've some plans ahead for you, my boy," said he one day with a knowing shake of the head; and Andrew's innocent brain began to swim straightway between the new barque and the Sabrina.

"Look at him!" said Mr. Maurice to his wife one evening as Andrew walked in the garden with Miss Frarnie. "My mind's made up about him. He's the stuff for a sea-captain, afraid neither of wind nor weather nor the face of clay--can sail a ship and choose her cargo. He's none of your coxcombs that go courting across the way:

he's a man into the core of his heart, and as well bred as any gentleman that walks; though Goodness knows how he came by it."

"These sea-coast people," said his wife, reflectively (she was inland-born herself), "see the world and learn."

"Well, what do you say to it? I don't find the flaw in him. If Heaven had given me a son, I'd have had him be like this one; and since it didn't, why here's my way to circumvent Heaven."

"Oh, my dear," said the wife, "I can't hear you talk so. And besides--"

"Well? Besides what?"

"I think it is always best to let such things take their own course. We did."

"Of course we did," laughed Mr. Maurice. "But how about our fathers and mothers?"

"I mean," said Mrs. Maurice, "not to force things."

"And who intends to force them? It's plain enough the young fellow took a fancy to our Frarnie the first time he laid eyes on her, isn't it?"

"I mean," said Mrs. Maurice again, "that if Frarnie should have the same fancy for him, I don't know that there'd be any objection. He is quite uncommon--quite uncommon when you consider all things--but I don't know why you want to lead her to like any one in particular, when she has such a nice home and is all we have."

"Girls will marry, Mrs. Maurice. If it isn't one, it will be another. So I had rather it should, be one, and that one of my own choosing--one who, will use her well, and not make ducks and drakes of her money as soon as we are gone where there's no returning, and without a 'thank you' for your pains. Look at them now! Should you imagine they thought there was any one else on earth but each other at this moment? They're fond of each other, that's plain. They'd be a remarkable-looking couple. What do you think of it?"

"Frarnie might have that India shawl that I never undid, to appear out in," said Mrs. Maurice, pensively, continuing her own reflections rather than directly replying. "And I suppose we needn't lose her really, for she could make her home with us."

And so the conspiracy advanced, its simple victims undreaming of its approach--Louie sighing faintly to think she saw so little of Andrew now, but content, since

she was sure it was for his best interest to make the friendship of the Sabrina's owner; Andrew fretting to see how all this necessary submission to superiors kept him
from Louie, but more than half compensated with the dazzling visions that danced
before his eyes of the Sabrina in her new rig--of the barque coming down for her
masts and sails from her launching.

The Sabrina had been so badly injured by her disasters that it took much more
time to repair her than had at first been thought. "I'm going to stand by the old
brig," said Andrew to some one--by accident it was in Mr. Maurice's hearing. "But
if I'd known it was going to take so long to have her whole again, I should have
made a penny in taking a run down the bay, for I had an offer to go second mate on
the Tartar."

"I'll go one better than that," said Mr. Maurice then. "Here's the Frarnie, nearly
ready to clear for New Orleans and Liverpool, with your old captain. You shall
go mate of her. That'll show if you can handle a ship. The Sabrina won't be at the
wharf till the round voyage is over and the Frarnie coming up the stream again.
What say you?"

Of course what Andrew said was modest thanks--what he felt was a rhapsody
of delight; and when he told Louie that night, what she said was a sob, and what she
felt was a blank of fright and foreboding. Oh what should she do? cried the selfish
little thing--what should she do in the long, long, weary days with Andrew gone?
But then in a moment she remembered that this was the first step toward going
master of that craft in which her bridal voyage was to be taken. "And what a long
step it is, Andrew!" she cried. "Was the like of it ever known before? What a long,
long step it would be but for that bitter apprenticeship when you and the captain
brought the wreck home!"

"Ay," said Andrew, proudly: "I served my time before the mast then, if ever
any did."

"And I suppose with the next step you will be master of the Sabrina? Oh, I
should so like it!"

"I don't know," said Andrew, more doubtfully than he had used to speak. "I'm
afraid the owners will think this is enough. This is a great lift. I'll do my best to
satisfy them, though; for I'd rather sail master of the Sabrina than of the biggest
man-of-war afloat."

"We used to play round her when we were children," said Louie, encouraging-ly. "Don't you remember leading me down once to admire the lady on her stern?--like a water-witch just gilded in the rays of some sunrise she had come up to see, you said."

"Yes; and we used to climb her shrouds, we boys, and get through the lubber-hole, before we could spell her name out. She's made of heart of oak: she'll float still when the Frarnie is nothing but sawdust. We used to watch for her in the newspapers--we used to know just as much about her goings and comings as the owner did. Somehow--I don't know why--I've always felt as if my fate and fortune hung upon her. It used to be the top of my ambition to go master of her. It is now. I couldn't make up my mind to leave her when the others did that cruel morning after the wreck; and when the captain said he should stay by her, my heart sprang up as if she had been a living thing, and I stayed too. And I'd rather sail her than a European steamer to-day--that I would, by George!"

"Oh, of course you will," said the sympathizing voice beside him.

"I don't know," said Andrew again, more slowly and reflectively. "I've the idea--and I can't say how I got it--that there's some condition or other attached to my promotion--that there's something Mr. Maurice means that I shall do, and if I don't do it I don't get my lift. It can't be anything about wages: I don't know what it is!"

"Perhaps," said Louie, innocently, and without a glimpse of the train her thoughtless words fired--"perhaps he means for you to marry Frarnie!" laughing a little laugh at the absurd impossibility.

And Andrew started as if a bee had stung him, and saw it all. But in a moment he only drew Louie closer, and kissed her more passionately, and sat there caressing her the more tenderly while they listened to a thrush that had built in the garden thicket, mistaking it for the wood, so near the town's edge was it, and so still and sunny was the garden all day long with its odors of southernwood and mint and balm; and he delayed there longer, holding her as if now at least she was his own, whatever she might be thereafter.

As he walked home that night, and went and sat upon the wharf and watched the starlit tide come in, he saw it all again, but with thoughts like a procession of phantoms, as if they had no part even in the possible things of life, and were indeed nothing to him. How could they have any meaning to him--to him, Louie's lover?

What would the whole world be to him, what the sailing of the Sabrina, without Louie? And then a shiver ran across him: what would Louie be to him without the sailing of the Sabrina! for that, indeed, as he had said, was the top of his ambition, and that being his ambition, perhaps ambition, was as strong with him as love.

But with this new discovery on Andrew's part of Mr. Maurice's desires, Andrew could only recall circumstances, words, looks, hints: he could not shape to himself any line of duty or its consequences: enough to see that Mr. Maurice fancied his simple and thoughtless attentions to Frarnie to be lover-like, and, approving him, looked kindly on them and made his plans accordingly; enough to see that if he should reject this tacit proffer of the daughter's hand, then the Sabrina was scarcely likely to be his; and that in spite of such probability, the first and requisite thing in honor for him to do was to tell Mr. Maurice of his marriage engagement with Louie, and then, if the man had neither gratitude nor sense enough to reward him for his assistance in saving the brig, to trust to fortune and to time, that at last makes all things even. As he sat there listening to the lapping of the water and idly watching the reflected stars peer up and shatter in a hundred splinters with every wash of the dark tide, he could not so instantaneously decide as to whether he should make this confession or not. "What business is it of Maurice's?" he said to himself. "Does he think every one that looks at his scarecrow of a daughter--" But there he had need to acknowledge to himself his injustice to Miss Frarnie, a modest maiden who had more cause to complain of him than he of her, since he had done his best to please her, and her only fault lay in being pleased so easily. She was pleased with him: he understood that now, though his endeavors to enlist her had been for a very different manifestation of interest. Perhaps it flattered him a little: he paused long enough to consider what sort of a lot it would be if he really had been plighted to Frarnie instead of Louie. Love and all that nonsense, he had heard say, changed presently into a quiet sort of contentment; and if that were so, it would be all the same at the end of a few years which one he took. He felt that Frarnie was not very sympathetic, that her large white face seldom sparkled with much intelligence, that she would make but a dull companion; but, for all that, she would be, he knew, an excellent housewife: she would bring a house with her too; and when a man is married, and has half a dozen children tumbling round him, there is entertainment enough for him, and it is another bond between him and the wife he did not love too well at first; and if she were his, his would be the Sabrina also, and when the Sabrina's days were over perhaps a great East Indiaman, and with that the respect and deference of all his townsmen: court would be paid to him, his words would be words of weight, he would have a voice in the selection of town-officers, he would roll up money in the bank, and some day he should be master of the great Maurice mansion and the gardens and grapehouses. It was a brilliant picture to him, doubtless, but in some way the recollection of two barelegged little children digging clams down on the flats when the tide was out, with the great white lighthouse watching them across the deserted stretches of the long bent eel-grass, rose suddenly and wiped the other picture out, and he saw the wind blowing in Louie's brown and silken hair and kissing the color on her cheeks; he saw the shy sparkle of her downcast eyes, lovely and brown then as they were now; and as he stood erect at last, snapping his fingers defiantly, he felt that he had bidden Mr. Maurice's ships and stocks and houses and daughter go hang, and had made his choice rather to walk with Louie on his arm than as master of the Sabrina.

It was a good resolution; and if he had but sealed it by speaking next day to Mr. Maurice of his engagement, there would not have been a word to say. But, though he valiantly meant to do it, it was not so easy, after all, as he had thought, and so he put it off for a more convenient season, and the season did not come, and the day of sailing did. And the outfit that went on board the Frarnie was made and packed by the hands of Mrs. Maurice and her daughter--such an outfit as he had never dreamed of; such warm woolens for the storms, such soft linens for the heats, such finery for port, such dainties and delicacies as only the first mate of the Frarnie could think to have. And as for Louie, it was no outfit, no costly gift of gold or trouble either, that she could give him: she had nothing for him but a long, fine chain woven of her own hair, and she hung it round his neck with tears and embraces and words that could not be uttered and sighs that changed to sobs, and then came lingering delay upon delay, and passionate parting at the last. But when the crew had weighed anchor and the sails were swelling and the waves beyond the bar crying out for them, Miss Frarnie and her mother could still be seen waving their handkerchiefs from an upper window; and half blind with the sorrow and the pain he choked away from sight, and mad with shame to think he had found no way but to accept their favors, Andrew felt that their signal must be answered, and sullenly waved his own in reply; and then the pilot was leaving the barque, and presently the shore and all its complications, and Louie crying herself sick, were forgotten in the excitement of the moment and its new duties.

"Didn't say a word of love to Frarnie, eh?" remarked Mr. Maurice in answer to his wife's communications that evening. "A noble lad, then! I like him all the better for it. He shall have her all the sooner. He won't abuse our confidence: that's it. He'll wait till he's bridged over the gap between them. The first mate of a successful voyage is a better match for my daughter than the boy who stayed by the Sabrina, brave as he was. He's fond of her? Don't you think so? There's no doubt about that? None at all! All in good time--all in good time. I'll speak to him myself. They're going to write to each other? I thought so."

Short as the trip was that the Frarnie made in that favorable season, it seemed to Louie an interminable period; but from the cheerful, hopeful smile upon her lips no one would ever have known how her heart was longing for her lover as she went about her work; for the little housekeeper had quite too much to do in keeping the cottage clean, the garden weedless, the nets mended, to be able to neglect one duty for any love-sick fancies it might be pleasant to indulge. From morning till night her days were full in bringing happiness to others: there was her father to make comfortable; there were the sick old women, of whom her aunt brought word, to concoct some delicacy for--a cup of custard, to wit, a dish of the water-jelly she had learned how to make from the sea-moss she gathered on the beach, a broiled and buttered mushroom from the garden; there were the canaries and the cat to be cared for, and the dog that Andrew left with her to feed and shower caresses on; and there was the parrot's toilet to be made and her lesson to be taught, and the single jars of preserves and pickles and ketchups to be put up for winter, and the herbs to be dried: there were not, you may see, many minutes to be wasted out of that busy little life in castle-building or in crying. One day there came a letter with Victoria's head and the Liverpool stamp upon it: she knew it by heart presently, and wore it next her heart by night and day; and even if she had known that Miss Frarnie Maurice received one in the same handwriting by the same mail, it would hardly have made much difference to her; and one day the Sabrina, all freshly coppered and painted and repaired, with new masts and sails, and so much else that it was not easy to say what part of her now represented the old brig, came round to her old wharf and began to take in cargo. Louie ran down one evening with her father, and went all over her from stem to stern, only one old sailor being aboard; and she could have told you then every rope from clew to ear-ring; and, as if it were all the realization of a dream, a thousand happy, daring thoughts of herself and Andrew then filled her fancy like birds in a nest; and so swiftly after that did one day flow into another for Louie that the Frarnie lay in the mid-stream once more before she had more than begun to count the days to that on which her Liverpool letter had promised that she should see its writer come walking into her father's cottage again.

But she never did see him come walking into her father's cottage again. That promised day passed and the night, and another--a long, long day that seemed as if it would never quench its flame in sunset, and a night that seemed as if it would never know the dawning; but the threshold of the fisherman's cottage Andrew Traverse crossed no more.

For Mr. Maurice, on his notable errand of circumventing Heaven, had been ahead of Fate, and had gone down on the pilot-boat to meet the Frarnie--with no settled designs of course, but in his own impatient pleasure; and, delighted with the shipmaster's report and with the financial promise of the voyage, the cargo, the freights, and ventures and all, had greeted Andrew with a large-hearted warmth and after a manner that no churl could withstand; and unwilling to listen to any refusal, had taken Andrew up to the mansion-house with him the moment the ship had touched the wharf.

"You don't ask after her?" said Mr. Maurice when they were alone in the chaise together. And knowing well enough what he meant, Andrew blushed through all his bronze--knowing well enough, for had he not gone below in a mighty hurry and tricked himself out in his best toggery so soon as he understood there was no escape from the visit? Louie would have been glad enough to see him in his red shirt and tarpaulin!

"Oh, you scamp!" said Mr. Maurice, quickly then detecting the blush. "Don't say a word! I've been there myself: I know how you're longing to see her; and she's been at the window looking through the glass every half hour, the puss!"

"Mr. Maurice," began Andrew, half trembling, but wholly resolved, he thought--although it must be confessed that with time, and distance, and Frarnie's effusive letters and flattering prospects on the other hand, Louie's image was not so bright at that moment as it had been at others, and for that very reason Andrew was taking great credit to himself for his upright intentions--credit enough to tide him over a good deal of baseness if need were,--"Mr. Maurice--" he began; and there he paused to frame his sentence more suitably, for it was no easy thing to tell a man that he was throwing his child at one who did not care for her, and that man the disposer of his fortunes.

But Mr. Maurice saved him any such trouble. "I know all you're going to say," he exclaimed. "I understand your hesitation, and I honor you for it. But I'm no fool, and there's no need to have you tell me that you want my Frarnie, for I've known that long ago."

"Mr. Maurice!"

"Yes, I have," answered the impulsive gentleman. "Mrs. Maurice and I talked it over as soon as we saw which way the wind lay; but of course we decided to say nothing till we were sure, quite sure, that it was Frarnie and not her prospects--"

"Oh, sir, you--"

"Tush, tush! I know all about it now. But it becomes a father to be wary," continued the other, taking the words from Andrew's lips in spite of himself, and quite wary enough not to mention that in Frarnie's easily-excited favor a young scapegrace was very likely to supplant Mr. Andrew if things were not brought to a point at once. "It was my duty to look at all sides," he said, without stopping for breath. "Now I know you, and I see you'd rather give the girl the go-by for ever than have her think you wanted her because she was her father's daughter, and not some poor fisherman's."

"Indeed, indeed--" began Andrew again, leaning forward, his cheeks crimson, his very hands shaking.

"Of course, my boy," interrupted his companion as before--"of course. Don't say a word: you're welcome to her at last. I never thought I'd surrender her to any one so freely; but if I were choosing from all the world, Andrew, I don't know any one I'd choose sooner for my son. She's a sensible girl, my Frarnie is, at bottom. We know her heart: it's a good heart--only the froth of all young girls' fancies to be blown off. And the Sabrina always was a pet of mine, and, though I've said nothing of it, I've meant her for Frarnie's husband this many a day." And before Andrew, in his flurry and embarrassment and bewilderment, could enunciate any distinct denial of anything or avowal of anything else, the chaise was at the door, and Mrs. Maurice was waiting for him with extended hands, and Frarnie was standing and smiling behind, half turned to run away. And Mr. Maurice cried out: "Captain Traverse of the Sabrina, my dear! Here, Frarnie, Frarnie! none of your airs and graces! Come and give your sweetheart an honest kiss!" And Andrew, doubting if the minister were not behind the door and he should not find himself married out of hand, irresolute, cowardly, too weak to give up the Sabrina and that sweet new title just ringing in his ears, was pushed along by Mr. Maurice's foolish, hearty hand till he found himself bending over Frarnie with his arm around her waist, his lips upon her cheek, and without, as it seemed to him, either choice or volition on his part. But as he looked up and saw the portraits of the girl's grandfathers, where they appeared to be looking down at him stern and questioning, a guilty shame over the wrong he was doing their child smote him sorely: he saw that he had allowed the one instant of choice to slip away; the sense came over him that he had sealed his own doom, while a vision of Louie's face, full of desolation and horror, was scorching in upon his soul; and there, in the moment of betrothal, his punishment began. He stole down to the Sabrina's wharf that evening, after the moon had set, and looking round to see that it was quite forsaken at that hour, he took from his neck a long, slender hair-chain to drop over into the deep water there; but as he held the thing it seemed suddenly to coil round his hand with a caress, as if it were still a part of Louie's self. He stamped his foot and ground his heel into the earth there with a cry and an oath, and put the chain back again whence he had taken it, and swore he would wear it till they laid his bones under ground. And he looked up at the dark lines of the brig looming like the black skeleton of an evil thing against the darkness of the night, and he cursed himself for a traitor to both women--for a hypocrite, a craven, a man sold to the highest bidder. Well, well, Captain Traverse, there are curses that cling! And Louie sat in the gloom at the window of the fisherman's cottage down below the town, and sighed and wondered and longed and waited, but Captain Traverse went back to the Maurices' mansion.

*   *   *   *   *

It is one of the enigmas of this existence how women forgive the wrong of such hours as came to Louie now--hours of suspense and suffering--hours of a misery worse than the worm's misery in blindness and pain before it finds its wings.

At first she expected her lover, and speculated as to his delay, and fretted to think anything might detain him from her; and now she was amazed, and now vexed, and now she was forgiving the neglect, accusing herself and making countless excuses for him; and now imagining a thousand dire mishaps. But as the third day came and he was still away--he who had been always wont to seek her as soon as the craft was made fast to wharf--then she felt her worst forebodings taking bodily shape: he was ill, he had fallen overboard, he had left the vessel at Liverpool and shipped upon another, and a letter would come directly to say so; or else he had been waylaid and robbed and made away with: not once did she dream that he was false to her--to her, a portion of his own life!

How it was with him there were numberless ways in which she might have discovered, for every soul of her acquaintance knew Andrew, and must be aware of the fact if he were missing or ailing, or if any other ill chance had befallen him. But as often as she tried to address one or another passing by the window, her voice failed her and her heart, and she asked no questions, and only waited on. A life of suspense, exclaims some one, a life of a spider! And when we are in suspense, says another, all our aids are in suspense with us. Day after day she stayed continually in the house, looking for him to come, never stirring out even into the garden, lest coming she might miss him. Night after night she sat alone at her window till the distant town-clocks struck midnight--now picturing to herself the glad minute of his coming, the quick explaining words, the bursting tears of relief, the joy of that warm embrace, the touch of those strong arms--now convinced that he would never come, and her heart sinking into a bitter loneliness of despair.

It grew worse with her when she knew that he was really in the town, alive and well; for, from the scuttle in the roof, by the aid of her father's glass, she could see the Sabrina, and one day she was sure that a form whose familiar outlines made her pulses leap was Andrew himself giving orders on the deck there; and after that she tortured herself with conjectures till her brain was wild--chained hand and foot, unable to write him or to seek him in any maidenly modesty, heart and soul in a ferment. Still she waited in that shuddering suspense, with every nerve so tightly strung, that voice or footfall vibrated on them into pain. If Andrew, in the midst of the gayeties by which he found himself accepted of the Maurices' friends, was never haunted by any thought of all this, his heart had grown stouter in one year's time than twenty years had found and left it previously.

But Louie's suspense was of no long duration, as time goes, though to her it was a lifetime. A week covered it--a week full of stings and fevered restlessness--when her father came in one day and said bitterly, thinking it best to make an end of all at once: "So I hear that a friend of ours has been paid off at last. Captain Andrew Traverse of the Sabrina is going to marry his owner's daughter Frarnie. Luck will take passage on that brig!" And when Louie rose from the bed on which she lay down that night, the Sabrina had been a fortnight gone on her long voyage--a voyage where the captain had sailed alone, postponing the evil day perhaps, and at any rate pleading too much inexperience, for all his dazzling promotion, to be trusted with so precious thing as a wife on board during the first trip. He had not felt that hesitation once when portraying the possibilities of the voyage to another.

It was not a long illness, Louie's, though it had been severe enough to destroy for her consciousness both of pain and pleasure. Her aunt had left other work and had nursed her through it; but when, strong and well once more, she went about her old duties, it seemed to her that that consciousness had never returned: she took up life with utter listlessness and indifference, and she fancied that her love for Andrew was as dead as all the rest. The poor little thing, laying this flattering unction to heart, did not call much reason to her aid, or she would have known that there was some meaning in it when she cried all day on coming across an old daguerreotype of Andrew. "It isn't for love of him," she sobbed. "It's for the loss of all that love out of my life that was heaven to me. Oh no, no! I love him no longer: I can't, I can't love him: he is all the same as another woman's husband." But, despite this stout assertion, she could not bring herself to part with that picture: he was not in reality quite the husband of another woman, and till he was indeed she meant to keep it. "He is only promised to her yet, and he was promised first to me," she said for salve to conscience; and meanwhile the picture grew so blurred with conscious tears, and perhaps with unconscious kisses, that it might have been his or another's: Miss Frarnie herself, had she seen it, could not have told whose it was.

Notwithstanding all the elasticity of youth, life became an inexpressibly dull thing to Louie as the year wore into the next--dull, with neither aim nor object, the past a pain to remember, the future a blank to consider. She could live only from day to day, one day like another, till they grew so wearisome she wondered her hair was not gray--the pretty hair that, shorn from her head in her illness, had grown again in a short fleece of silky curls--for it seemed to her that she had lived a hundred years. And because troubles never come alone, and one perhaps makes the other seem lighter and better to be borne, in the thick of a long winter's storm they brought home her father, the old fisherman, drowned and dead.

Captain Traverse knew of the old fisherman's death through the newspapers that found him in his foreign ports--not through Miss Frarnie's letters, for she knew almost nothing of the existence or non-existence of such low people; and therefore, conjecture as he needs must concerning Louie's means of livelihood now, there was no intelligence to relieve any anxiety he might have felt, or to inform him of the sale of the cottage to pay the debt of the mortgage under which it was bought, or of the support that Louie earned in helping her aunt watch with the sick and lay out the dead: he could only be pricked with knowledge of the fact that he had no right to his anxiety, or to the mention of her name even in his prayers--if he said them.

Poor little Louie! A sad end to such a joyous youth as hers had been, you would have said; but, in truth, her new work was soothing to her: her heart was simply in harmony with suffering, with death and desolation, and by degrees she found that comfort from her double sorrows in doing her best to bring comfort to others which it may be she could never have found had she been the pampered darling of some wealthy house. Often, when she forgot what she was doing, Louie made surmises concerning Frarnie Maurice, wondering if she were the noble thing that Andrew needed to ennoble him--if she were really so strong and beautiful that the mere sight of her had killed all thought or memory of an older love; trying to believe her all that his guardian angel might wish his wife to be, and to acknowledge that she herself was so low and small and ignorant that she could only have injured him--to be convinced that it was neither weakness, nor covetousness, nor perjury in Andrew, having met the sun, to forget the shadows; wondering then if Frarnie cared for him as she herself had done, and crying out aloud that that could never be, until the sound of her own sobs woke her from her forbidden dream. But at other times a calm came to Louie that was more pathetic than her wildest grief: it was the acquiescence in what Providence had chosen for Andrew, cost herself what it might--it was the submission of the atom beneath the wheels of the great engine.

It is true that as, late in the night, when all the town was asleep and only silence and she abroad, she walked home by herself from some deathbed whose occupant she had composed decently for the last sleep, she used to wish it were herself lying there on that moveless pillow, and soon to be sheltered from the cruel light by the bosom of the kindly earth. For now, as she passed the birches softly rustling in the night wind, and hurried by, she remembered other times when she had passed them, and had stopped to listen, cared for, protected, with Andrew's arm about her; and now, as the clocks, one after another, remotely chimed the hour, the sound smote her with a familiar sweetness full of pain; and now, as she came along the sea-wall and saw the dark river glimmering widely and ever the same, while its mysterious tide flowed to meet the far-off spark of the lighthouse lantern, she recalled a hundred happy hours when she and Andrew in the boat together had rocked there in soft summer nights, with sunset melting in the stream and wrapping them about with rosy twilight; or those when whispers of the September gales swelled the sail, and the boat flew like a gull from crest to crest of the bar; or those when misty sea-turns crept up stream and folded them, and drowned the sparkle of the lighthouse and the emerald and ruby ray of the channel lights, and left them shut away from the world, alone with each other on the great gray current silently sweeping to the sea--times when she knew no fear, trusting in the strong arm and stout heart beside her, before the river had brought death to her door; when the whole of life seemed radiant and rich--times that made this solitary night walk trodden now seem colder and drearier and darker than the grave--that made her wish it ended in a grave.

And so at length the year slipped by, and spring had come again, and the sap had leaped up the bough and burst into blossom there, and the blood had bubbled freshly in the veins of youth, and hope had once more gladdened all the world but Louie. With her only a dull patience stayed that tried to call itself content, until she heard it rumored among the harbor-people that the Sabrina was nearly due again, and with that her heart beat so turbulently that she had to crush it down again with the thought that, though Andrew every day drew nearer, came up the happy climates of southern latitudes and spread his sails on favoring gales for home, he only hastened to his wedding-day. And one day, at last, she rose to see a craft anchored in the middle channel down below the piers, unpainted and uncleaned by any crew eager to show their best to shore--a black and blistered brig, with furled sails and silent deck; and some men called it the fever-ship, and some men called it the Sabrina.

As the news of the brig's return and of her terrible companion spread through the town, a panic followed it, and the feeling with which she was regarded all along the shore during that day and the next would hardly be believed by any but those who have once been in the neighborhood of a pestilence themselves. Exaggerated accounts of a swift, strange illness, by many believed to be the ancient plague revived again and cast loose through the land from Asiatic ships had reached the old port; and aware that they were peculiarly exposed by reason of their trade, small as it was, the people there had already died a thousand deaths through expectation of the present coming of the fever already raging in other parts. Hitherto, the health-officers, boarding everything that appeared, had found no occasion to give anything but clean papers, and the town had breathed again. But now, when at last it spread from lip to lip that the fever lay at anchor in mid-channel, knees shook and cheeks grew white, and health-officer and port-physician, in spite of the almost instantaneous brevity of their visit to the infected vessel, were avoided as though they were the pestilence themselves, and not a soul in all the town was found to carry a cup of cold water to the gasping, burning men cared for only by those in less desperate strait than themselves, and who, having buried two-thirds of their number in deep-sea soundings, were likely to be denied as much as a grave on shore themselves; while to Mr. Maurice, half wild with perplexity and foreboding and amazement at Miss Frarnie's yet wilder terror,--to him the red lantern hung out by the brig at nightfall magnified itself in the mist into a crimson cloud where with wide wings lurked the very demon of Fever himself.

Not a soul to carry the cup of cold water, did I say? Yes, one timid little soul there was, waiting in a fever of longing herself--waiting that those who had a right to go might do so if they would--waiting till assured that neither Frarnie Maurice nor her parents had the first intention of going, though affianced husband and chosen son lay dying there--waiting in agony of impatience, since every delay might possibly mean death,--one little brave and timid soul there was who ventured forth on her errand of mercy alone. The fisherman's old boat still lay rocking in the cove, and the oars stood in the shed: Louie knew how to use them well, and making her preparations by daylight, and leaving the rest till nightfall, lest she should be hindered by the authorities, she found means to impress the little cow-boy into her service; and after dark a keg of sweet water was trundled down and stored amidships of the boat, with an enormous block of ice rolled in an old blanket; a basket of lemons and oranges was added, a roll of fresh bed-linen, a little box of such medicines as her last year's practice had taught her might be of use; and extorting a promise from the boy that he would leave another block of ice on the bank every night after dark for her to come and fetch, Louie quickly stepped into the boat, lifted the oars, and slipt away into the darkness of the great and quiet river.

When, three days afterward, Captain Traverse unclosed his eyes from a dream of Gehenna and the place the smoke of whose torment goes up for ever, a strange confusion crept like a haze across his mind, tired out and tortured with delirium, and he dropped the aching lids and fell away into slumber again; for he had thought himself vexed with the creak of cordage and noise of feet, stived in his dark and narrow cabin, on a filthy bed in a foul air, if any air at all were in that noisome place, reeking with heat and the ferment of bilge-water and fever-smell; and here, unless a new delirium chained him, a mattress lay upon the deck with the awning of an old sail stretched above it and making soft shadow out of searching sun, a gentle wind was blowing over him, a land-breeze full of sweet scents from the gardens on the shore, from the meadows and the marshes. Silence broken only by a soft wash of water surrounded him; a flake of ice lay between his lips, that had lately been parched and withering, and delicious coolness swathed his head, that had seemed to be a ball of burning fire. The last that he remembered had been a hot, dry, aching agony, and this was bliss: the sleep into which he fell when waking from the stupor that had benumbed his power of suffering--a power that had rioted till no more could be suffered--lasted during all the spell of that fervid noon sun that hung above the harbor and the town like the unbroken seal of the expected pestilence. A strange still town, fear and heat keeping its streets deserted, its people longing for an east wind that should kill the fever, yet dreading lest it should blow the fever in on them; a strange still harbor, its great peaceful river darkened only by that blot where the sun-soaked craft swung at her anchor; a strange still craft, where nothing stirred but one slender form, one little being that went about laying wet cloths upon this rude sailor's head, broken ice between the lips of that one, moistening dry palms, measuring out cooling draughts, and only resting now and then to watch one sleeper sleep, to hang and hear if in that deep dream there were any breathing and it were not the last sleep of all. And in Louie's heart there was something just as strange and still as in all other things throughout that wearing, blinding day; but with her the calm was not of fear, only of unspeakable joy; for if Andrew lived it was she that had saved him, and though he died, his delirium had told her that his heart was hers. "If he dies, he is mine!" she cried triumphantly, forgetting all the long struggle of scruple and doubt, "and if he lives, he shall never be hers!" she cried softly and with that inner voice that no one hears.

And so the heat slipped down with the sun to other horizons, coolness crept in upon the running river's breast with the dusk, dew gathered and lay darkly glittering on rail and spar and shroud as star by star stole out to sparkle in it; and Andrew raised his eyes at length, and they rested long and unwaveringly on the little figure sitting not far away with hands crossed about the knees and eyes looking out into the last light--the tranquil, happy face from which a white handkerchief kept back the flying hair while giving it the likeness of a nun's. Was it a dream? Was it Louie? Or was it only some one of the tormenting phantoms that for so many burning days had haunted him? He tried in vain to ask: his tongue clove to the roof of his mouth; he seemed to be in the power of one of those fierce nightmares where life depends on a word and the word is not to be spoken. Only a vision, then: he closed his lids thinking it would be gone when he lifted them, but he did not want it to be gone, and looked again to find it as before. And by and by it seemed to him that long since, in a far-off dream, he had gathered strength and uttered the one thought of his fever, "Louie, what do you do now?" and she had answered him, as though she thought aloud, "I stroke the dead;" and he had cried out, "Then presently me too, me too! And let the shroud be shotted heavily to bury me out of your sight!" And he was crying it out again, but while he spoke a mouth was laid on his--a warm, sweet mouth that seemed to breathe fresh spirit through his frame--his head was lifted and pillowed on a breast where he could hear the heart beneath flutter like a happy bird, and he was wrapped once more in slumber, but this time slumber sweet as it was deep.

Morning was dawning over the vessel's side, a dream of rosy lustre sifting through the purple and pearly mist, behind which the stars grew large and lost while it moved away to the west in one great cloud, and out of which the river gleamed as if just newly rolled from its everlasting fountains,--morning was dawning with the sweet freshness of its fragrant airs stealing from warm low fields, when Andrew once more lifted his eyes only to find that tranquil face above him still, that happy heart still beating beneath his pillowed head. "Oh, Louie," he sighed, "speak to me--say--have I died?--am I forgiven?--is this heaven?"

"To me, dear--oh to me!" answered she with the old radiant smile that used to make his pulse quicken, and that, ill as he yet was, reassured him as to his earthly latitude and longitude.

"And it was all a dream, then?" he murmured. "And I have not lost you?" He raised his wasted hand and drew from his breast the little hair chain that he had hidden there so long ago. "It was a fetter I could not break," he whispered. "I wrote her all about it long ago. I wrote her father that he should have his vessel back again--and I would take my freedom--and not a dollar's wages for the voyage would I ever draw of him. But I should never have dared see you--for--oh, Louie--how can you ever--"

"Hush, hush, dear!" she breathed. "What odds is all that now? We have our life before us."

"Only just help me live it, Louie."

"God will help us," she answered. And as she spoke a sudden rainbow leaped into the western heaven as if to seal her promise, and as it slowly faded there came a wild salt smell, an air that tingled like a tonic through the veins: the east wind was singing in from sea, bringing the music of breaker and shore, and the fever was blasted by its breath throughout the little Sabrina.

HARRIET PRESCOTT SPOFFORD.

Old Sadler's Resurrection:
A Yarn of the Mexican Gulf.

Talking about ghosts," said the captain, "listen while I spin you a bit of a yarn which dates back some twenty-five years ago, when, but a wee bit of a midshipman, I was the youngster of the starboard steerage mess on board the old frigate Macedonian, then flag-ship of the West India squadron, and bearing the broad pennant of Commodore Jesse Wilkinson.

"It would hardly interest you to tell what a clever set of lieutenants and ward-room officers we had, and how the twenty-three reefers in the two steerage messes kept up a racket and a row all the time, in spite of the taut rein which the first lieutenant, Mr. Bispham, kept over us. He wore gold-rimmed spectacles; and I can see him now, with the flat eagle-and-anchor buttons shining on his blue coat, as he would pace the quarter-deck, eyeing us young gentlemen of the watch, as demurely we planked up and down the lee side, tired enough, and waiting for eight bells to strike to rush below and call our relief. He was an austere man, and, unlike the brave old commodore, made no allowance for our pranks and skylarking.

"Among our crew, made up of some really splendid fellows, but with an odd mixture of 'Mahonese,' 'Dagos,' 'Rock-Scorpions,' and other countrymen, there was an old man-of-war's man named Sadler--a little, dried-up old chap of some sixty years, who had fought under Nelson at Trafalgar, so he said, and had been up and down, all around and criss-cross the world so often that he had actually forgotten where he had been, and so had all his geography lessons, learned by cruising experience, sadly mixed up in his head; which, although small, with a little old, weazened frontispiece, was full of odds and ends of yarns, with which he used to delight us young aspirants for naval honors, as he would spin them to us on the booms on moonlight nights, after the hammocks had been piped down. How well do I remember the old fellow's appearance!--his neat white frock and trowsers, his low-quarter purser's shoes, with a bit of a ribbon for a bow; no socks, save the natural, flesh-tinted ones, a blue star, done in India ink, gleaming on his instep; his broad blue collar, decorated with stars and two rows of white tape, falling gracefully from a neck which, as we youngsters asserted, had received its odd-looking twist from hanging too long by a grape vine, with which the Isle of Pines' pirates had strung him up when he was chasing them under old Commodore Kearney's command. Anyhow, old, sharp-faced, wrinkled and tanned to the color of a sole-leather trunk, the whole cut of his jib told you at once that he was a regular man-of-war's man-one of a class whose faults I can hardly recall while remembering their sense of duty, their utter disregard of danger, and the reliance with which you can lead them on to attack anything, from a hornet's nest to an iron-clad.

"Well, it so happened, one hot day, while cruising in the Gulf of Mexico, that the news came to us that old Sadler was dead; and sure enough it was so, for the old fellow had quietly slipped his moorings, and, as we all hoped, had at last gone to where the sweet little cherub sits up aloft who looks out for the soul of poor Jack. Then, after the doctors had had a shy at him, to see why he had cleared out so suddenly, his remains were taken in charge by his messmates, who rigged the old man out in his muster clothes, sewed him up in his clean white hammock, with an eighteen pound shot at his feet, and reported to the officer of the deck that the body was ready for burial. So, about six bells in the afternoon watch, the weather being very hot, and not a breath of air to ripple the glassy surface of the water, the lieutenant of the watch directed one of the young gentlemen to tell the boatswain to call 'All hands to bury the dead;' and soon fore and aft the shrill whistles were heard, followed by that saddest of all calls to a sailor at sea--'All hands bury the dead!'

"Our good old boatswain, Wilmuth, seemed to linger on the words with a feeling akin to grief at parting with an old shipmate, and as the last man reached the deck, he touched his hat and in a sad sort of way reported, 'All up, sir,' to the first lieutenant, who in his turn reported, 'Officers and men all on deck, sir,' to the commodore, who thereupon gave an order to the chaplain to go on with the services.

"The courses were hauled up, main-topsail to the mast, band on the quarter-deck, colors half-mast, and all hands, officers and men, stood uncovered, looking silently and sadly upon the body as it lay upon the gang-boards in its white hammock, ready for the last rites. Solemnly and most impressively were the services read, and at the words, 'We commit his body to the deep,' a heavy splash was heard, and poor old Sadler had gone to his long home for ever. Some of us youngsters ran up in the lee main rigging to see him go down, and as we watched him go glimmering and glimmering down to a mere speck, we wondered where he was bound, and how long it would take him to fetch Davy Jones' locker on that tack.

"'Pipe down, sir,' says the commodore to Mr. Bispham; 'Pipe down, sir,' says Mr. Bispham to Mr. Alphabetical Gray, who was officer of the deck; 'Pipe down, sir,' says Mr. Gray to the gentleman of the watch; 'Pipe down, sir,' says this youngster to the boatswain; and then *such* a twitter of pipes followed this order, and all hands were piped down, while poor old Sadler was still off soundings, and going down as fast as the eighteen-pound shot would take him.

"Now, you know that people coming from a funeral on shore always have a gay sort of air, suppressed it may be, but still cropping out; and just so is it with sailors at sea; for, Sadler's body committed to the deep, all hands felt better: the fore and main tacks were hauled aboard, the main yard was filled away, and the jib sheet hauled aft, and we all settled down into every-day life, which, after all, is not half so monotonous on board a man-of-war as you might suppose.

"Well, as I have said, the weather was very hot, the surface of the water was as smooth as a mill-pond, the wind was all up and down the mast, and so the old ship was boxing the compass all to herself, and not making a foot of headway.

"At one bell in the first dog watch, Boyle, the ship's cook, reported the tea-water ready, and after this came the inevitable evening-quarters--and some old man-of-war's men would think the country was going to 'Jemmy Square-toes' stern first if they didn't have quarters--then down hammocks for the night at six bells, and after that just as much of fun, frolic, dance, song and yarn spinning as all hands wanted until eight bells, when the watch was called.

"John Moffitt, the sailing master, the best fellow in the ward-room mess, and a great favorite with the youngsters, was officer of the deck from six to eight o'clock; and my messmate, Perry Buckner, of Scott county, Kentucky, the most dare-devil midshipman of us all, was master's mate of the forecastle; Hammond, Marshall, Smith and I were the gentlemen of the Watch; Rodney Barlow was quartermaster at the 'con;' the lookouts had just been stationed; the men were singing, dancing, spinning yarns and otherwise amusing themselves about the decks, while the old ship was turning lazily around in the splendid moonlight as if admiring herself.

"Discipline, you know, is the very life of a man-of-war, and this must account for what now took place. Tom Edwards, a young foretopman, had the lee lookout, and as seven bells struck he sang out, 'Lee cat-head;' but the last syllable died away on his lips as his eyes rested upon an object--a white object--standing bolt upright in the water before him, about a hundred yards distant and broad off on the lee bow. Suppressing a strong desire to shriek, and recovering himself, he touched his hat and said, 'Mr. Buckner, will you step up here, sir, if you please?'

"'What is she, Edwards?' said Buckner, as he quickly mounted the hammock-rail.

"One look, a dip down, a shiver, and, O Lord! what did he see but ***old Sadler standing straight as a ramrod, and heading right for the ship!***

"It took Buck a full minute to recover himself, and then, with one eye on the lee bow and the other on the quarter-deck, he walked aft and deliberately touching his cap, reported to Moffitt, 'Old Sadler broad off on the lee bow, sir.'

"'The d---- he is!' exclaimed Moffitt; but, checking himself, he said, 'Mr. Hammond, report Sadler's arrival to the commodore; and you, Mr. M----, report it to the first lieutenant, sir.'

"My eyes were as big as saucers as I rushed down the steerage ladder and into the ward-room, where I found the first lieutenant quietly seated reading over the black list; and when, with my heart in my throat, I said, 'Mr. Bispham, old Sadler is on the lee bow, sir,' he serenely replied, 'Very well, Mr. M---- I'll be on deck directly.'

"'O Lord!' said I to myself--'to take a ghost as easily as all that!' Bolting up the ladder on my way back to the deck, and trembling lest I should see the ghost popping his head in through one of the gun-deck ports, I ran into Hammond, who dodged me like a shot.

"When I got on deck the news was all out, for Tom Edwards couldn't stand it any longer, but had just yelled out, 'Ghost ho! ghost ho! Look out! stand from under! here he comes!' and bolted aft, scared out of his wits.

"In ten seconds all hands were on deck--ship's cook, yeoman, 'Jemmy Legs,' 'Jemmy Ducks,' 'Bungs,' Loblolly boy,' captain of the hold, and, by this time, all the officers too, with the midshipmen scuttling up the ladders as fast as their legs and hands could carry them.

"Moffitt had hauled up the courses and squared the main yard, as much to make a diversion as anything else, although the men thought it was to keep old Sadler from boarding us; and as they rushed up on deck they filled the booms; lee rigging, hammock--netting and every available spot from which a sight of the old fellow could be had.

"Very soon they saw that he was not approaching the ship: the old sinner was just turning and turning around in the water, like a fishing-cork, dancing away all to himself, while the moonlight, first on one side, and then on the other, in light and shadow, gave a queer sort of look to his features, sometimes sad and sometimes funny.

"After watching him for a few minutes, Bill Ellis, the second captain of the foretop, hailed him thus: 'Sadler, ahoy! What do you want?'

"No answer being received, one of the mizzentop boys suggested that the old man had come back for his bag and hammock, and that they ought to be thrown overboard to him; but all this was cut short by the appearance of the commodore on the quarter-deck, and upon him all eyes were turned as he stepped upon the port horseblock, where a good view could be had.

"Now, old Jess was as brave an old fellow as ever sailed a ship, but he did not fancy ghosts, and the knowledge that all hands were looking at him to see how he took it made him feel a little nervous; but with a firm voice he called for his night-glass, and when the quartermaster, with a touch of his hat, handed it to him, he quietly arranged the focus, and, as we all supposed, was about to point it at Sadler, who was still dancing away for dear life all to himself. But old Jess was too smart for that: he quietly directed his glass to another quarter, to gain a little time, and, gradually sweeping the horizon, brought it at last, with a tremor of mortal dread, to bear dead upon the ghost. Bless my soul! how the old gentleman shook! But recovering himself, with a big gulp in his throat he turned to the chaplain and said, 'Did you read the *full* service over him to-day, Mr. T----?'

"'I did, sir, as well as I can remember,' replied Mr. T.

"'Then, sir,' said the commodore, turning to Mr. Bispham and speaking in an authoritative tone, 'we must send a boat and bring him on board.'

"'O Lord! O Lord!--bring a ghost on board!' groaned the men.

"'Silence, fore and aft!' said Mr. Bispham, 'and call away the second cutter.'

"'Away there, you second cutters, away!' sung out the boatswain's mate. But they didn't 'away' one step, and we youngsters could hear the men growling out, 'What does the commodore want with old Sadler? This isn't his place: let the old man rip: he is dead and buried all right. We didn't ship to go cruising after ghosts: we shipped to reef topsails and work the big guns; and if old Jess wants old Sadler on board, he had better go after him himself.' Some said he had come back after his bag and hammock, and the best way was to let him have them, and then he would top his boom and clear out. Others said the purser had not squared off his account; and one of the afterguard was seen to tickle the mainmast and whistle for a breeze, to give the old fellow a wide berth. But it wouldn't do: discipline is discipline; and after a free use of the colt and a good deal of hazing, the boat's crew came aft, the cutter was lowered, and the men, with their oars up and eyes upon the ghost, were waiting the order to shove off, the bow oarsman having provided himself with a boarding-pike to 'fend off,' as he said, if the old man should fight.

"We youngsters knew that *somebody* else was needed in that boat, and that *somebody* was a midshipman with his side-arms; but not a boy of us said a word about it, and we were afraid even to catch the first lieutenant's eye, lest he should be reminded that no young officer had, as usual, been ordered to go; but the order came at last. When Moffitt asked the first lieutenant, 'What officer, sir, shall I send in that boat?' we scattered like a flock of birds, but all too late; for Mr. Bispham referred the matter to the commodore, who, with a twinkle in his eye, said, 'Who discovered the ghost, sir?'

"'Midshipman Buckner reported him, sir,' was the reply.

"'Then,' said the commodore, 'by priority of discovery he belongs to Mr. Buckner, who will take charge of the cutter and bring him on board.'

"I heard all this from my place behind the mizzen mast, and you may guess how glad I was not to have been selected; but a groan, a chattering of the teeth, a trembling and shaking of bones close by my side, caused me to look around, and there was poor Buck, with his priority honors thick upon him.

"'Get your side-arms, sir,' said Moffitt: 'take charge of the cutter and carry out the commodore's order.'

"'Ay, ay, sir!' said Buck, but oh with what a change in his voice! As he buckled on his sword I could see what a struggle he was making to feel brave. As he went over the gangway to get into the boat I caught his eye, and if you could have seen that forlorn look you would have pitied him; for there was old Sadler turning and turning in the water, looking first this way, and then the other, and, as Buck thought, just ready to hook on to him and carry him down among the dead men.

"It is no light matter to go up to a ghost, front face, full face, and look him in the eye; but what must it be when you have to go up to him *backward*, as that cutter's crew had to do while pulling their oars, leaving only Buck and the cox-swain to face him? They just couldn't do it, and at every stroke they would suddenly slew around on their thwarts and look at the old fellow, who seemed to them as big as an elephant, and just ready to clap on to them, boat and all, as soon as they turned to give another stroke. Poor fellows! they made but little headway, and what with catching crabs, fouling their oars, blasting old Sadler's eyes, and denouncing him generally (one fellow fairly yelled outright when the bow oarsman accidentally touched him), they had a hard pull of it; but still they made some progress, and when Buck sang out, 'Way enough,' every oar flew inboard, every man faced suddenly around, and with this the cutter keeled over, and, her bow touching old Sadler on his shoulder, ducked him out of sight for a second, at which all hands shouted, thinking that he had gone for ever; but in a moment more up he popped, fresh as a lark, higher than ever before, and this time right abreast of the stern-sheets, where he bobbed and bowed to Buck, at which, with a yell of terror, all hands went overboard, and, floundering in the water, begged for mercy. The cutter had some little headway, and this of course brought Sadler astern on the other quarter, and then there was a wild rush to get back into the boat, for fear the old fellow was doubling on them to make a grab.

"The commodore, hearing the row and fearing disaster, ordered another boat to the rescue, but ere it reached the spot, Buck had, in some manner, quieted his men, who, seeing the ghost still standing bolt upright in the water and dancing away as if nothing had happened to scare *him*, manned their oars again and pulled cautiously toward him; while he, with that changeable moonlight grin on his face, was bobbing up and down to the boat's crew, as if Buck were the commodore himself coming to pay him a visit.

"'Stand by, there in the bow, to hook on to him,' sang out Buck.

"'Ay, ay, sir! I'll fix him;' and with that, and a heavy expletive in regard to the old fellow's eyes, the bow oarsman slammed his boarding-pike right into the ghost, just abaft his left leg, and as the sharp steel touched the body, a whizzing sound, like the escape of steam, was heard, and without a word old Sadler vanished from sight for ever."

"But, captain, tell us what really brought the old gentleman back," said one of the auditors.

"Well, just think of that tight white hammock, the light weight of the shot, and the very hot weather--think, too, how easily a fishing-cork is balanced in the water by a very small sinker, and lastly how confined air will buoy up anything--and you have the whole secret of his coming back. Let that air suddenly escape, and you have the secret of his disappearance.

"Buck used to say that 'priority of discovery' was a good thing in the days of Columbus, but if it was to be continued in force in the United States navy, hang him if he should ever report another ghost, even if he should see him walking the quarter-deck with the speaking-trumpet under his arm."

R. D. MINOR.

www.bookjungle.com *email: sales@bookjungle.com fax: 630-214-0564 mail: Book Jungle PO Box 2226 Champaign, IL 61825*

The Codes Of Hammurabi And Moses
W. W. Davies

QTY

The discovery of the Hammurabi Code is one of the greatest achievements of archaeology, and is of paramount interest, not only to the student of the Bible, but also to all those interested in ancient history...

Religion   ISBN: *1-59462-338-4*   **Pages:132**
MSRP $12.95

The Theory of Moral Sentiments
Adam Smith

QTY

This work from 1749. contains original theories of conscience amd moral judgment and it is the foundation for systemof morals.

Philosophy ISBN: *1-59462-777-0*   **Pages:536**
MSRP $19.95

Jessica's First Prayer
Hesba Stretton

QTY

In a screened and secluded corner of one of the many railway-bridges which span the streets of London there could be seen a few years ago, from five o'clock every morning until half past eight, a tidily set-out coffee-stall, consisting of a trestle and board, upon which stood two large tin cans, with a small fire of charcoal burning under each so as to keep the coffee boiling during the early hours of the morning when the work-people were thronging into the city on their way to their daily toil...

Pages:84

Childrens   ISBN: *1-59462-373-2*   *MSRP $9.95*

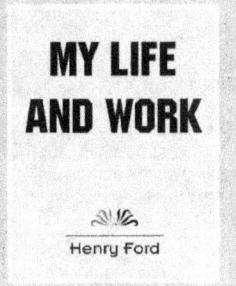

My Life and Work
Henry Ford

QTY

Henry Ford revolutionized the world with his implementation of mass production for the Model T automobile. Gain valuable business insight into his life and work with his own auto-biography... "We have only started on our development of our country we have not as yet, with all our talk of wonderful progress, done more than scratch the surface. The progress has been wonderful enough but..."

Pages:300

Biographies/   ISBN: *1-59462-198-5*   *MSRP $21.95*

The Art of Cross-Examination
Francis Wellman

QTY

I presume it is the experience of every author, after his first book is published upon an important subject, to be almost overwhelmed with a wealth of ideas and illustrations which could readily have been included in his book, and which to his own mind, at least, seem to make a second edition inevitable. Such certainly was the case with me; and when the first edition had reached its sixth impression in five months, I rejoiced to learn that it seemed to my publishers that the book had met with a sufficiently favorable reception to justify a second and considerably enlarged edition. ..

Pages:412

Reference   **ISBN:** *1-59462-647-2*   *MSRP $19.95*

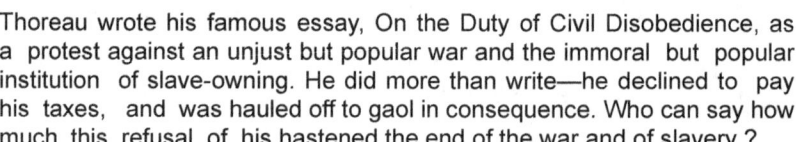

On the Duty of Civil Disobedience
Henry David Thoreau

QTY

Thoreau wrote his famous essay, On the Duty of Civil Disobedience, as a protest against an unjust but popular war and the immoral but popular institution of slave-owning. He did more than write—he declined to pay his taxes, and was hauled off to gaol in consequence. Who can say how much this refusal of his hastened the end of the war and of slavery ?

Law   **ISBN:** *1-59462-747-9*   **Pages:48**

MSRP $7.45

Dream Psychology Psychoanalysis for Beginners
Sigmund Freud

QTY

Sigmund Freud, born Sigismund Schlomo Freud (May 6, 1856 - September 23, 1939), was a Jewish-Austrian neurologist and psychiatrist who co-founded the psychoanalytic school of psychology. Freud is best known for his theories of the unconscious mind, especially involving the mechanism of repression; his redefinition of sexual desire as mobile and directed towards a wide variety of objects; and his therapeutic techniques, especially his understanding of transference in the therapeutic relationship and the presumed value of dreams as sources of insight into unconscious desires.

Pages:196

Psychology   **ISBN:** *1-59462-905-6*   *MSRP $15.45*

The Miracle of Right Thought
Orison Swett Marden

QTY

Believe with all of your heart that you will do what you were made to do. When the mind has once formed the habit of holding cheerful, happy, prosperous pictures, it will not be easy to form the opposite habit. It does not matter how improbable or how far away this realization may see, or how dark the prospects may be, if we visualize them as best we can, as vividly as possible, hold tenaciously to them and vigorously struggle to attain them, they will gradually become actualized, realized in the life. But a desire, a longing without endeavor, a yearning abandoned or held indifferently will vanish without realization.

Pages:360

Self Help   **ISBN:** *1-59462-644-8*   *MSRP $25.45*

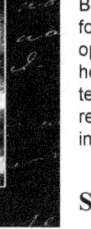

The Rosicrucian Cosmo-Conception Mystic Christianity *by Max Heindel*   ISBN: *1-59462-188-8* **$38.95**
The Rosicrucian Cosmo-conception is not dogmatic, neither does it appeal to any other authority than the reason of the student. It is: not controversial, but is: sent forth in the, hope that it may help to clear...   New Age/Religion Pages 646

Abandonment To Divine Providence *by Jean-Pierre de Caussade*   ISBN: *1-59462-228-0* **$25.95**
"The Rev. Jean Pierre de Caussade was one of the most remarkable spiritual writers of the Society of Jesus in France in the 18th Century. His death took place at Toulouse in 1751. His works have gone through many editions and have been republished...   Inspirational/Religion Pages 400

Mental Chemistry *by Charles Haanel*   ISBN: *1-59462-192-6* **$23.95**
Mental Chemistry allows the change of material conditions by combining and appropriately utilizing the power of the mind. Much like applied chemistry creates something new and unique out of careful combinations of chemicals the mastery of mental chemistry...   New Age Pages 354

The Letters of Robert Browning and Elizabeth Barret Barrett 1845-1846 vol II   ISBN: *1-59462-193-4* **$35.95**
by Robert Browning and Elizabeth Barrett   Biographies Pages 596

Gleanings In Genesis (volume I) *by Arthur W. Pink*   ISBN: *1-59462-130-6* **$27.45**
Appropriately has Genesis been termed "the seed plot of the Bible" for in it we have, in germ form, almost all of the great doctrines which are afterwards fully developed in the books of Scripture which follow...   Religion/Inspirational Pages 420

The Master Key *by L. W. de Laurence*   ISBN: *1-59462-001-6* **$30.95**
In no branch of human knowledge has there been a more lively increase of the spirit of research during the past few years than in the study of Psychology, Concentration and Mental Discipline. The requests for authentic lessons in Thought Control, Mental Discipline and...   New Age/Business Pages 422

The Lesser Key Of Solomon Goetia *by L. W. de Laurence*   ISBN: *1-59462-092-X* **$9.95**
This translation of the first book of the "Lemegton" which is now for the first time made accessible to students of Talismanic Magic was done, after careful collation and edition, from numerous Ancient Manuscripts in Hebrew, Latin, and French...   New Age/Occult Pages 92

Rubaiyat Of Omar Khayyam *by Edward Fitzgerald*   ISBN:*1-59462-332-5* **$13.95**
Edward Fitzgerald, whom the world has already learned, in spite of his own efforts to remain within the shadow of anonymity, to look upon as one of the rarest poets of the century, was born at Bredfield, in Suffolk, on the 31st of March, 1809. He was the third son of John Purcell...   Music Pages 172

Ancient Law *by Henry Maine*   ISBN: *1-59462-128-4* **$29.95**
The chief object of the following pages is to indicate some of the earliest ideas of mankind, as they are reflected in Ancient Law, and to point out the relation of those ideas to modern thought.   Religiom/History Pages 452

Far-Away Stories *by William J. Locke*   ISBN: *1-59462-129-2* **$19.45**
"Good wine needs no bush, but a collection of mixed vintages does. And this book is just such a collection. Some of the stories I do not want to remain buried for ever in the museum files of dead magazine-numbers an author's not unpardonable vanity..."   Fiction Pages 272

Life of David Crockett *by David Crockett*   ISBN: *1-59462-250-7* **$27.45**
"Colonel David Crockett was one of the most remarkable men of the times in which he lived. Born in humble life, but gifted with a strong will, an indomitable courage, and unremitting perseverance...   Biographies/New Age Pages 424

Lip-Reading *by Edward Nitchie*   ISBN: *1-59462-206-X* **$25.95**
Edward B. Nitchie, founder of the New York School for the Hard of Hearing, now the Nitchie School of Lip-Reading, Inc, wrote "LIP-READING Principles and Practice". The development and perfecting of this meritorious work on lip-reading was an undertaking...   How-to Pages 400

A Handbook of Suggestive Therapeutics, Applied Hypnotism, Psychic Science   ISBN: *1-59462-214-0* **$24.95**
by Henry Munro   Health/New Age/Health/Self-help Pages 376

A Doll's House: and Two Other Plays *by Henrik Ibsen*   ISBN: *1-59462-112-8* **$19.95**
Henrik Ibsen created this classic when in revolutionary 1848 Rome. Introducing some striking concepts in playwriting for the realist genre, this play has been studied the world over.   Fiction/Classics/Plays 308

The Light of Asia *by sir Edwin Arnold*   ISBN: *1-59462-204-3* **$13.95**
In this poetic masterpiece, Edwin Arnold describes the life and teachings of Buddha. The man who was to become known as Buddha to the world was born as Prince Gautama of India but he rejected the worldly riches and abandoned the reigns of power when...   Religion/History/Biographies Pages 170

The Complete Works of Guy de Maupassant *by Guy de Maupassant*   ISBN: *1-59462-157-8* **$16.95**
"For days and days, nights and nights, I had dreamed of that first kiss which was to consecrate our engagement, and I knew not on what spot I should put my lips..."   Fiction/Classics Pages 240

The Art of Cross-Examination *by Francis L. Wellman*   ISBN: *1-59462-309-0* **$26.95**
Written by a renowned trial lawyer, Wellman imparts his experience and uses case studies to explain how to use psychology to extract desired information through questioning.   How-to/Science/Reference Pages 408

Answered or Unanswered? *by Louisa Vaughan*   ISBN: *1-59462-248-5* **$10.95**
Miracles of Faith in China   Religion Pages 112

The Edinburgh Lectures on Mental Science (1909) *by Thomas*   ISBN: *1-59462-008-3* **$11.95**
This book contains the substance of a course of lectures recently given by the writer in the Queen Street Hail, Edinburgh. Its purpose is to indicate the Natural Principles governing the relation between Mental Action and Material Conditions...   New Age/Psychology Pages 148

Ayesha *by H. Rider Haggard*   ISBN: *1-59462-301-5* **$24.95**
Verily and indeed it is the unexpected that happens! Probably if there was one person upon the earth from whom the Editor of this, and of a certain previous history, did not expect to hear again...   Classics Pages 380

Ayala's Angel *by Anthony Trollope*   ISBN: *1-59462-352-X* **$29.95**
The two girls were both pretty, but Lucy who was twenty-one who supposed to be simple and comparatively unattractive, whereas Ayala was credited, as her Bombwhat romantic name might show, with poetic charm and a taste for romance. Ayala when her father died was nineteen...   Fiction Pages 484

The American Commonwealth *by James Bryce*   ISBN: *1-59462-286-8* **$34.45**
An interpretation of American democratic political theory. It examines political mechanics and society from the perspective of Scotsman James Bryce   Politics Pages 572

Stories of the Pilgrims *by Margaret P. Pumphrey*   ISBN: *1-59462-116-0* **$17.95**
This book explores pilgrims religious oppression in England as well as their escape to Holland and eventual crossing to America on the Mayflower, and their early days in New England...   History Pages 268

QTY

The Fasting Cure *by Sinclair Upton*   ISBN: *1-59462-222-1* **$13.95**
In the Cosmopolitan Magazine for May, 1910, and in the Contemporary Review (London) for April, 1910, I published an article dealing with my experiences in fasting. I have written a great many magazine articles, but never one which attracted so much attention... New Age/Self Help/Health Pages 164

Hebrew Astrology *by Sepharial*   ISBN: *1-59462-308-2* **$13.45**
In these days of advanced thinking it is a matter of common observation that we have left many of the old landmarks behind and that we are now pressing forward to greater heights and to a wider horizon than that which represented the mind-content of our progenitors... Astrology Pages 144

Thought Vibration or The Law of Attraction in the Thought World   ISBN: *1-59462-127-6* **$12.95**

by William Walker Atkinson   Psychology/Religion Pages 144

Optimism *by Helen Keller*   ISBN: *1-59462-108-X* **$15.95**
Helen Keller was blind, deaf, and mute since 19 months old, yet famously learned how to overcome these handicaps, communicate with the world, and spread her lectures promoting optimism. An inspiring read for everyone... Biographies/Inspirational Pages 84

Sara Crewe *by Frances Burnett*   ISBN: *1-59462-360-0*   **$9.45**
In the first place, Miss Minchin lived in London. Her home was a large, dull, tall one, in a large, dull square, where all the houses were alike, and all the sparrows were alike, and where all the door-knockers made the same heavy sound... Childrens/Classic Pages 88

The Autobiography of Benjamin Franklin *by Benjamin Franklin*   ISBN: *1-59462-135-7* **$24.95**
The Autobiography of Benjamin Franklin has probably been more extensively read than any other American historical work, and no other book of its kind has had such ups and downs of fortune. Franklin lived for many years in England, where he was agent... Biographies/History Pages 332

Name	
Email	
Telephone	
Address	
City, State ZIP	

☐ **Credit Card**   ☐ **Check / Money Order**

Credit Card Number	
Expiration Date	
Signature	

Please Mail to: Book Jungle
                              PO Box 2226
                              Champaign, IL 61825
      or Fax to: 630-214-0564

ORDERING INFORMATION

web: *www.bookjungle.com*
email: *sales@bookjungle.com*
fax: *630-214-0564*
mail: *Book Jungle PO Box 2226 Champaign, IL 61825*
or PayPal *to sales@bookjungle.com*

Please contact us for bulk discounts

DIRECT-ORDER TERMS

**20% Discount if You Order
Two or More Books**
Free Domestic Shipping!
Accepted: Master Card, Visa,
Discover, American Express